POWERS OF GOOD AND EVIL

Powers of Good and Evil

Moralities, Commodities and Popular Belief

Edited by Paul Clough and Jon. P Mitchell

Berghahn Books
New York • Oxford

First published in 2001 by **Berghahn Books**

www.berghahnbooks.com

© 2001 Paul Clough and Jon P. Mitchell

Library of Congress Cataloging-in-Publication Data

Powers of good and evil : social transformation and popular belief /
edited by Paul Clough and Jon P. Mitchell.
    p. cm.
   Includes bibliographical references and index.
   ISBN 1-57181-992-4 (hbk. : alk. paper) ISBN 1-57181-313-6
(pbk. : alk. paper)
    1. Ethnophilosophy. 2. Philosophical anthropology. 3. Belief and
doubt. 4. Good and evil. 5. Social change. I. Clough, Paul. II.
Mitchell, Jon P.

GN468 .P68 2000
306.4–dc21   00-049347

British Library Cataloguing in Publication Data
A catalogue record for this book is available from the British
Library.

Printed in the United States on acid-free paper

ISBN 1-57181-992-4 (hardback)
ISBN 1-57181-313-6 (paperback)

Contents

v

List of Illustrations

Contributors

Isabelle Borg
Mediterranean Institute, University of Malta

Paul Clough
Anthropology Programme, University of Malta

Peter Geschiere
Department of Cultural Anthropology, University of Leiden, Netherlands

Birgit Meyer
Research Centre Religion and Society, University of Amsterdam, Netherlands

Hildi J. Mitchell
School of Social Sciences, University of Sussex

Jon P. Mitchell
School of Cultural and Community Studies, University of Sussex

Nadia Theuma
MedCampus, University of Malta

Bonno Thoden van Velzen
Department of Anthropology, University of Amsterdam

Jojada Verrips
Department of Anthropology, University of Amsterdam

Wilhelmina van Wetering
Department of Anthropology, University of Amsterdam

Introduction

Jon P. Mitchell

University of Sussex

In the early 1990s, it was custom and practice for all Social Anthropology graduate students at the University of Edinburgh to present an annual seminar to the whole department. In 1994, I had just returned from two years' fieldwork in Malta and did my duty, embarking on a rather tortuous meditation on the nature of belief. During the discussion, we began to talk about holy places – churches, chapels and other *foci* for popular devotion. If these were places of goodness, I was asked, where was evil – where was Hell? It was a leading question, for although the church is a holy place, it is also a site, above all else, for the depiction of evil and its consequences.

This observation presents an apparent paradox, that in creating or representing moral good, religious systems also inevitably create evil. Indeed it is through representations of evil that morality itself becomes manifest (Parkin 1985: 6). Morality sets boundaries or limits that define acceptable behaviour. But in setting these boundaries, morality also invokes transgression. To set a boundary is always to be aware of what lies beyond it. Demarcating moral acceptability therefore involves elaborating transgression. Similarly, elaborating transgression involves the demarcation of a moral boundary. This dynamic of mutual constitution of boundary and transgression, acceptability and unacceptability, good and evil is central to the concerns of this volume.

This book is about fear of excess. Using examples from a variety

1

of different contexts, it demonstrates the extent to which social and economic change – or more importantly, *perception* of social and economic change – leads to a kind of moralising against excess that establishes a boundary within which people are censured to remain, but in turn creates a proliferation of images of transgression, and of the consequences of transgression.

Taussig (1995: 370) has argued that it was above all Georges Bataille who gave us an understanding of the relationship between morality and economics, defining it as 'entwining excess with transgression so as to create a radically different history and science of political economy, capitalism and communism'.

For Taussig, Bataille's argument that excess lies at the centre of world political economy, helps us to understand the prominence of luxury and excess in the demonology of South American peasants (see also Taussig 1980). Using examples from both the Bolivian tin mines and the Colombian sugar plantations, Taussig had previously shown how Devil imagery and the invocation of Devil pacts were a means by which peasants both resisted and came to terms with the implications of the new economy – and particularly commodity fetishism. Among the plantation growers affluence, luxury, excess were seen as a direct consequence of pacts with the Devil in which a planter would trade his soul for success. The pacts were not without their downside, however. Their long term consequence was infertility and eventual ruin.

This focus on the evils of such Devilish pacts evokes a classic theme in the anthropology of malignancy. In accounts informed by the functional orientation of much anthropological thinking, the invocation of excess and its association with evil serves as a kind of levelling mechanism to ensure that peasant society maintains a happy – if poor – equilibrium (see Ardener 1970, Marwick 1970). Accusing somebody who appears to be over-accumulating – and is therefore guilty of excess – of entering into Devil pacts, or of being a witch, is seen as a way of ensuring an equal distribution of resources and discouraging economic inequality. Yet as persuasive as this argument might be, it does not fully explain the enduring fascination with excess, even in situations where it is deeply morally problematic. Indeed, one might equally argue that such accusations represent a positive acknowledgement of the power entailed in accumulation. Taussig invokes Bataille to help explain this paradox. Just as moral boundaries and their transgression are mutually constitutive, so for Bataille expenditure and excess 'mobilises prohibitions and transgressions in a ceaseless, twofold, instantaneous movement' (Taussig 1995: 389). Hence, in identifying a limit to the accumulation of wealth – a boundary beyond which it is immoral to progress – the transgression of that limit is also implicated.

This two-way, one might say dialectical, process involving both sanction and censure, transgression and prohibition, signals an inherent ambivalence in people's engagement with social and economic transformations. Just as good produces evil, so people's views of the good life produce images of malignancy that both limit and encourage transgression and excess. Seen in this light, rather than rejecting or resisting economic transformations, this kind of moralising against excess simply seeks to rein them in. Socio-economic changes are placed in an ambivalent light, in which they are both fascinating and abhorrent; luxury is both desirable and dangerous; excess both thrilling and terrifying. The fear is of *excessive* change, rather than change *per se*, and therefore constitutes a significant mode of controlling and understanding the social and economic processes that people feel subject to.

Representations of Evil

Fear of excess is represented via the complex and often horrific imagery of evil. Excess is a material thing, but the subject of this book is the various ways in which this material process – or material profligacy – is represented in the immaterial, or the supernatural. This linkage of materiality and immateriality – sometimes expressed as a *reduction* of the immaterial to the material – has been a central theme in the social science of religion and religious phenomena. In their different ways, the so-called 'founding fathers' of the social sciences – Marx, Durkheim and Weber – were concerned with this relationship.

Marx, in his anti-idealist critique of history, sees religion as an element of society's superstructure which is not only at a remove from the base realities of material existence, but contributes to the misrepresentation of those realities. Thus, in that oft-quoted phrase, religion is seen as 'the *opium* of the people. The abolition of religion as the *illusory* happiness of the people is required for their *real* happiness' (Marx & Engels, cited in Pals 1996: 141, italics in the original). The representation of the material in the immaterial, then, provides for a mystification or concealment of 'real' material relations.

The material and the immaterial come together, in Marx's work, in his theory of commodity fetishism (1920), which is a characteristic feature of capitalist culture and society. Although material objects appear neutral, argues Marx, they are in fact imbued with the relationships entailed in their production and exchange. These 'metaphysical and mythological niceties' (41) are misrecognised as properties of the object itself, which in turn assumes a kind of magical quality. To understand capitalist attitudes towards the commodity, we must 'have recourse to the mist-enveloped regions of the religious world' (43) but remember that those regions are simply a representation of a more substantive material force.

For Durkheim (1966: 22), religion is also seen as a representation of reality, but rather than concealing the verities of social existence, it makes them manifest, and indeed consolidates them:

> religion is something eminently social. Religious representations are collective representations which express collective realities; the rites are a manner of acting which take rise in the midst of assembled groups and which are destined to excite, maintain or recreate certain mental states in these groups.

Weber, for his part, saw religion – and particularly the changes entailed in the Protestant Reformation – as a social reality that could contribute to the development of economic reality. For him, Protestantism enabled the development of capitalism, in an argument that turned the tables on Marx's theory of superstructural reflection (Weber 1930). In these three different theories we see, therefore, a continuum or spectrum of ideas: from religion concealing social reality to religion being a social reality to religion contributing to social reality. In the most coherent and categorical statement on religion since these early ventures we find Geertz (1973a) turning away from the deterministic – even reductionist – tendencies of Marx and Durkheim, towards the Weberian emphasis on the autonomy of the immaterial from the material. Explicitly drawing on Weber's *verstehen* sociology (1973b), Geertz launched a social science based on meaning and symbol, which saw the investigation of religion as a task which looked initially for the coherent pattern of religious meanings, and then tried to see what effect that might have on social or economic reality, rather than vice versa (1973a: 125).

The focus on systems of meaning, seen as relatively autonomous causal factors in the development of history, was increasingly criticised in the 1970s. With the growing popularity of 'practice' theories that emphasise not only meaning *per se* but also how meaning is constructed, negotiated and legitimated, a broadly Marxian focus was reintroduced, that emphasised the importance of power and political economy in relation to religious meaning (Asad 1983, Ortner 1984). Once more, the immaterial was being seen in relation to the material.

Taussig's (1980) work was emblematic of this new focus on 'culture and political economy' (Schneider & Schneider 1976). Alongside him, the Comaroffs, Dirks, Werbner and others developed an oeuvre that focused specifically on the relationship between the immaterial and the material, the religious and the economic in the context of rapid social change, and particularly that experienced in colonial and postcolonial situations (Comaroff 1985, Comaroff & Comaroff 1992, Dirks 1992, Werbner 1989, Werbner & Ranger 1996). In this context, the proliferation of images of excess and evil is seen as part of a resistance to or accommodation of the economic processes introduced by colonialism – capitalism, market economics, money, new forms of accumulation. All these become the objects of a resistive or responsive (re)enchantment of people's life-worlds that runs counter to received wisdom concerning the rationalising disenchantment brought about by capitalism. In a certain teleology, 'modernity' and all that goes with it should make obsolete the speculation of South American peasants on the demonic and devilish origins of accumulation and luxury. That it does not has preoccupied a generation of scholars who seek to explore the reasons why.

This book takes the argument a step further by examining the (re)enchantment of the world in both the postcolonial and the metropolitan contexts. In doing so, it demonstrates that the processes involved in representing excess as malevolence are not necessarily the product of autonomous, 'indigenous' – for which in many contexts read 'primitive' – cultural movements struggling to oppose the forces of change. Despite the apparent demonisation of 'modernity' in the images of evil, to read this as an unequivocal rejection of 'modernity' is an over-simplification. An ambivalence prevails, which encompasses a simultaneous fascination with and desire to be 'modern', and deep anxiety about where society is heading. The demonic, in this understanding, is not a barrier or resistance to change, but part of it. Images of evil do not result from modernity's subjects drawing on a pre-existent stock of 'authentic' cultural forms, to oppose or resist the rapid social change that the introduction of a capitalist economy can precipitate. Rather, the proliferation of images of excess or evil might actually be seen as part and parcel of that 'modernity' (Englund 1996, Kahn 1997).

The prevailing ambivalence inherent in this 'modernity' is born out in the attitudes toward the demonic contained in this volume. The demons that haunt the subjects of this book are often as equally fascinated by their horrors as repulsed by them. This signals a moral indeterminacy or ambivalence that rails against the prevailing dualistic assumptions that have characterised the study of morality.

Moral Ambivalence

Parkin (1985: 9) suggests there has been a prevalent distinction, in the analysis of moral systems, between monistic and manichean moralities. These are seen respectively to unite and divide good from evil. Thus in the monistic tradition, evil is seen alongside good, as a balancing force or property of a single cosmological force. In Manichean traditions, on the other hand, there is a separation made between an essentially pure and unsullied goodness, and an unequivocal evil. The monistic and the Manichean, he argues, can be seen as opposite poles on a continuum between which lie Christianity, orthodox Islam and Judaism, conceived as 'semi-dualist' religions: 'the three Semitic religions are semi-dualist, each with beliefs in Satan, who appears to act independently of God at times, but whom God has in the past already vanquished, and whom ordinary mortals should now conquer with God's help'.

The tension between an autonomous power of evil, and one that is an inexorable part of a single supernatural power, is born out in the examples dealt with in this volume. Good and evil can be seen as properties of the same power or the same process – neither the demonic representations nor the socio-economic processes they are associated with are unequivocal. They are both fascinating and abhorrent; desirable and terrifying. This kind of ambivalence is observed both cross-culturally and in different historical contexts – from contemporary Cameroon to early modern Malta, contemporary Netherlands to seventeenth-century America. Although these contexts are different, and in each case the arguments, anxieties, manifestations and concerns are different, they share a number of common features, which form the significant themes of this book.

The Themes

First and foremost, the examples addressed in this volume come from societies or social groups that could be described as politically and economically peripheral, or, more importantly, social groups that perceive themselves as peripheral. This peripherality contributes to a fear of externality, or fear of external excess, that both feeds from and contributes to a tendency to moral panic. As the societies in question become embroiled in processes of social change, the agents of that change become classified as external, and demonised.

The metaphor of peripherality as it relates to issues of rapid social change, and particularly the accommodation of or resistance to capitalism, derives from work in political economy, and particularly 'world systems theory' (Wallerstein 1974, 1980). This approach focuses on the relationship between 'core' and 'periphery' economic zones and particularly the extent to which the former produced the latter as dependent and subordinate. Through an unequal exchange of capital-intensive goods produced in core zones and labour-intensive goods produced in the peripheries, the core expanded at the expense of the periphery. Such a theory was criticised in anthropological circles for overlooking the historical and cultural variations within both core and periphery – subsuming the particularity of specific situations under a grand theoretical scheme (Thomas 1996: 566). It has also, consequently, been criticised for an overly materialist account of peripherality – a kind of economic determinism in which the condition of peripherality is related only to the division of labour between core and periphery. The contributions to this volume maintain the focus on the specificity of different peripheral contexts, and propose that the various representations of evil and excess that can be found in them are at least (semi)autonomous (Nugent 1988: 90) from brute material forces. In doing so they locate peripherality not necessarily in objective conditions but in people's own conceptions of who they are and how they got there. Peripherality, then, is a condition of people's experiences of the world, and a way in which they think about their relationship to it. It is an ethnographic rather than a socio-economic fact.

Identifying peripherality as a condition of existence rather than a product of material forces has the effect of disarticulating core–periphery from particular geographical zones. If peripherality is as much a state of mind – or culture – as a state of economy,

7

then it can exist as strongly in the areas that a more materialist reading might characterise as core, as in the geographical periphery. Hence Anglo-American Mormons (chapter 6) are just as peripheral as Suriname Maroons (chapter 1), because despite their integration into and enthusiasm for capitalism, they nevertheless consider themselves as separate from its mainstream. This separation from and anxiety about the mainstream manifests itself in the complex demonology explained here by Hildi Mitchell. Similar processes are at work in Malta (chapters 3, 5 and 8), West Africa (chapters 2 and 4) and Netherlands (chapter 7), where peripherality is couched in terms of a distance from the centres of production for global popular culture, and anxiety is manifest in paranoia about the erosive and destructive effects of horror movies.

Such fears and anxieties are controlled and contextualised in the process of representation. If the moral evaluations surrounding rapid social change are ambivalent ones, then fixing them in an imagery of evil serves to demonstrate its controllability and containment (Parkin 1985: 18). The representation of evil, which in many of the cases dealt with here involves a personification in the form of the Devil, makes tangible an unthinkable and dangerously ambiguous force. Thus, the examples in this volume demonstrate the extent to which representations of rapid social change set up images of evil precisely in order to shoot them down. Creating the Devil, as a power of evil, serves to demonstrate that the powers of good can control him. This is no more clearly demonstrated than in Ghana (chapter 4), where the Pentecostalist churches propagate images of the Devil in order to demonstrate the strength of the good powers over evil. A simple injunction, 'You devil go away from me!' serves as a motif for the struggle against a constant malevolent threat. Elsewhere such representations also demonstrate evil's controllability. Artistic representations of St Michael's battle against the Devil (see chapter 8) show the ultimate conquest of good over evil, and thereby simultaneously fix and counteract a dangerously ambivalent force.

The representations produced through this process are demonstrably corporeal. The chapters in this volume describe fears of being eaten, stolen, sold, disfigured, possessed. This focus on immediate bodily threat contrasts in important ways with the more classical anthropological accounts of the threat of witchcraft. In Evans-Pritchard's (1976) celebrated account of Zande witchcraft, for example, although witchcraft is a corporeal presence, located in the substance *mangu* – a black swelling or bag attached to the liver

(2) – its bodily threat is not a matter of preoccupation. The Azande are relatively uninterested in whether people have the substance. Rather it is on particular witchcraft events that they focus (56). Similarly, the threat of a witch's power is not conceived as an immediate, frightening one (19): 'When misfortunes occur [a Zande] does not become awe-struck at the play of supernatural forces. He is not terrified at the presence of an occult enemy. He is, on the other hand, extremely annoyed.'

The subjects of this volume, by contrast, are frightened by the presence of these powers of evil. More than causing mere annoyance, these powers are scary because they can literally take over and control the body. They are immediate, felt threats. As demonstrated in the Maltese context (chapters 3 and 5), anxieties about contemporary social transformations emerge as anxieties about possession and threat to the body.

The contrast with the Zande material might be seen as one between a 'traditional' form of malignancy – witchcraft – that is informed by a corporate social orientation to the world, as opposed to a 'modern' form that focuses on the individual person as powerfully symbolised by the body. Indeed, an increased significance of the body has been identified as one of the consequences of – particularly late – modernity (Giddens 1990). In both Cameroon and Malta (chapters 2 and 3) the representations or fantasies of evil appear to be demonstrably new – even modern – phenomena. As Peter Geschiere points out (chapter 2), Cameroonian witchcraft fears and fantasies should not be seen as a kind of traditional relict, but as part and parcel of contemporary responses to a contemporary situation.

That such images of evil also proliferate in early modern Malta (chapter 8) and seventeenth-century America and Sweden (chapter 1) raises questions, though, about the association of such bodily threats with late modernity. Rather than distinguishing 'modern' threats to the body from 'traditional' non-corporeality such as Zande witchcraft, it might make more sense to distinguish situations characterised by rapid social change combined with a sense of peripherality, from situations in which these factors are absent. In the former situation, which includes both contemporary Malta and Cameroon, and seventeenth-century America and Sweden, new images of evil emerge as direct and frightening threats not only to the body social, but also to people's actual bodies. That all four cases involve people coming to terms with the consequences of the introduction of capitalism confirms that although located at

different times and in different places, there are nevertheless com-
monalities in the consequences of 'modernity'.

Common also is the central importance of excess in the provo-
cation of fear. Doing too much, even of a good thing, is dangerous,
problematic and even frightening. Hence in both Mormon and Maltese contexts, capital accumulation is morally acceptable within
certain limits. Excess is evil (chapters 3 and 6). This tension or
moral ambivalence runs through the contributions to the volume,
demonstrating the inter-dependence of the powers of good and
evil.

The Chapters

In the first chapter, Bonno Thoden van Velzen and Ineke van
Wetering examine occult discourses, and the emplotment of evil
fantasies among Suriname Maroons, seventeenth-century Swedes,
and in the classic Salem witch hunt. Using metaphors from Freud,
they demonstrate how the fantasies of demons or witchcraft in
these circumstances involve a kind of dramatisation or 'stage-managing' of anxieties. The stories condense a variety of concerns into
single, manageable narratives that achieve the effect of displacing
financial or material worries into the realm of the immaterial. In all
three cases, the lure of new prosperity, coupled with anxiety over
whether it will be attainable, feeds the proliferation of evil imagery.

In Suriname, the terror focuses on a succession of different
threats: from the fear of having one's soul tied down by a witch, to
the pernicious 'Demon Masters' who make a pact with the Devil
that enables them to hire evil spirits as workers, to female demon
mediums who channel the malevolent spirits to their own benefit.
The significance of gender is alluded to here and in the discourses
surrounding witch persecutions in both seventeenth-century Sweden and America. In both cases, the witch panics surround the
accusations and confessions of young women who assume centre
stage in the prosecution and execution of witches. As themselves
frequently marginal to or 'muted' within social life (Ardener 1977,
Davis 1995), such women would seem doubly suited to manage
the proliferation of evil imagery. They were peripheral to what
were already peripheral contexts. Suriname, during the time
described by van Velzen and van Wetering, encountered a
boom–bust cycle of gold-prospecting prosperity and trading collapse resulting in widespread migration and a general sense of

crisis. This sense of peripherality also feeds the development of occult discourses in Sweden and America, where the centres of most anxiety were peripheral to nearby affluence and prosperity.

In the second chapter, Peter Geschiere develops the theme of moral ambivalence in Cameroonian witchcraft discourses. In a comparative survey of the different trajectories of interaction between witchcraft discourses and socio-economic changes, he demonstrates that rather than being either a 'levelling' or an 'accumulative' force, witchcraft encompasses both tendencies. Similarly, the powers associated with witchcraft or sorcery are not unequivocally evil. Rather, the powers – *liemba* among the Bakweri, *djambe* among the Maka, *famla* or *kupe* among the Bamileke and the Bamenda – are relatively free from definitive moral connotations. They can be good or bad, depending on context.

Geschiere's comparative project stresses the novelty of these various witchcraft discourses, arguing that although there are similarities in their provenance, responses to them differ markedly. There is no one model of malignancy and no one pattern for dissipating its influence. The differences relate to structural considerations in the societies he examines – particularly contrasts in the organisation of kinship and authority, which inform a national politics of ethnicity that in turn informs attitudes towards and struggles over the state.

The third chapter moves us from West Africa to the central Mediterranean. In the first of three chapters on Malta, Jon Mitchell examines discourses surrounding the apparent proliferation of Satanic practices in early-1990s Malta, contrasting this escalation with the concurrent diminution of another type of evil – the evil eye. The increase in Satanism and decline in the evil eye are linked to an inherent ambivalence towards 'tradition' and 'modernity' – the latter particularly standing for the over-bearing presence and influence of the European Union. Discourses of Satanic practice, which emphasise profligate sexuality, material greed and drug abuse, feed a kind of moral panic about the erosive influence of Europe on traditional Maltese Catholic values.

If the rise of Satanism stresses the positive aspects of 'tradition', then the decline of the evil eye signals its negative side, stressing 'modernity' as a positive force. The evil eye in early-1990s Malta was said to be a thing of the past, associated with a 'traditional' superstitiousness that ill befits a modern nation state. The tranformations in evil, therefore, are linked to a profound Maltese ambivalence towards 'modernity' and 'tradition', but also to differences in the ways the two powers are understood. Whilst the power of Satan is a felt power, argues Mitchell, that of the evil eye is not. In a situation which saw the increased legitimacy of bodily experience in religion, Satan triumphs as an immediate, bodily threat.

Chapter four also stresses Satan's threat to the body, in an examination of Pentecostalist Christianity in south-eastern Ghana. Birgit Meyer traces the processes whereby – like the evil eye in Malta – witchcraft is superseded by concern for the power of the Devil as the Ewe people convert to Christianity and accommodate new attitudes to 'modernity'. Such attitudes encompass a fascination with and desire for European goods, but a fear of their supernatural powers. Again, sexuality is linked to material goods and material excess. Material fantasy implicates sexual fantasy.

Central in these Ghanaian discourses are *Mami Water* spirits – mermaids and mermen that entice humans into marriage, promising unsurpassed riches in return for reproductive infertility. Their goods are regularly found in Ghanaian markets, and the unwary consumer can become embroiled in their powers by making an injudicious purchase. The Pentecostalist churches offer a safe way to consume. Not opposed to materialism, their message is one of constraint. Thus, although embedded in a materialist, 'modernist' morality, they nevertheless propagate a fear of excess.

The fifth chapter also focuses on Pentecostalist Christianity, this time the Catholic Charismatic Renewal Movement in Malta, which has expanded considerably over the past twenty-five years. Nadia Theuma focuses particularly on the history and structure of the movement, stressing the contradictions between an egalitarian ethos and a hierarchical structure. She also examines the motivations for joining the movement, and accounts of the transformations people experience when they do. The emphasis on personal engagement with the Holy Spirit, particularly salient in accounts of *glossolalia* or speaking in tongues, emphasises a modernist concern with individual experience at the expense of 'traditional' authority. That the 'traditional' structure of authority is replaced by another serves to emphasise the contradiction.

Joining the movement is expressed in terms of a kind of deliverance from the stresses of everyday material life. Theuma's informants contrast life inside the movement with one dominated by politics, drinking, playing cards. But, as for the Ghanaian Pentecostalists, conversion does not constitute a renunciation of worldly desires. Rather, it encompasses an appeal for restraint. For Charismatics, materiality is not evil *per se*, but profligacy is.

A similar theme emerges in chapter six, in which Hildi Mitchell explores the importance, indeed the centrality, of materiality – in the form of capitalism – to Mormonism. Focusing on Mormon doctrine and practice in Britain and the USA she argues that money, far from being the root of all evil, is positively valued, provided it is accumulated in the right kinds of contexts and put to use in an approved fashion. This materiality is central to Mormon cosmology, which rejects the Cartesian mind-body split to see spirits and even God as a material being. It also informs their demonology. Good and evil spirits can be discerned by their respective embodiment and disembodiment. Because they have no bodies, evil spirits are a constant threat to the human body, which they try to enter and take over as their surrogates. Once more, the fear of evil is the fear of bodily incursions.

Chapter seven discusses the apparent threat of evil inherent in horror films, together with responses towards them by the state in the UK and the Netherlands. Jojada Verrips argues that rather than being inherently corrupting, such films should be seen as moral tales about the dangers of contemporary society, and their watching as '*rites de passage*'. Successive attempts to censor or even ban these films crucially miss this important role, focusing instead on the 'external' threat to 'traditional' religious moralities. Verrips identifies a contradiction, or double standard, in anti-horror pressure groups. Based as they often are on notions of religious morality or good taste, their arguments seem to ignore the fact that the religious representation of good is often replete with images of evil. Similarly, they ignore the points at which 'high art' manifests its own bloodthirsty prurience. Just as such morally approved media produce goodness through the depiction of evil, so it should be understood that horror films play an important role in demarcating the acceptable boundaries of moral action. Without them, he suggests, contemporary society would be morally bankrupt.

The final chapter explores representations of evil in Maltese art from the fifteenth century to the present. Tracing various themes in the iconography of evil, from the serpent or dragon motif to the temptress Salome to the sexually and aesthetically ambivalent Devil, Isabelle Borg argues that these representations have developed alongside Maltese society. In the early modern context, dominated by a patron-client sensibility, icons of evil appear as foils to the heroic *foci* of popular faith. The Devil is shown being vanquished by St Michael and *ex-voto tabelle* represent the power of the Madonna over the powers of evil. The latter, commissioned and donated in thanks for Our Lady's intercession, reproduce the Saint's patronage. More recently, however, depictions of evil become increasingly ambivalent. The Devil emerges as an androgynous trickster figure, and even a beautiful youth, seductive yet threatening. The change of representations constitutes a change of sensibilities, from one in which evil is already conquered, the paintings giving reassurance, to one in which it is dangerously present. The latter offers not only a degree of ambivalence but also an injunction to viewers to take their own responsibility for recognising evil. In the former, the Devil is set up to knock down, in the latter we are invited to do the vanquishing ourselves.

Paul Clough's conclusions recapitulate some of the themes discussed here, situating the chapters in the context of developments in political economy and relations of power. He focuses on relations between economic and conceptual 'centre' and 'periphery' in order to speculate on the forces at play in the elaboration of particular moral cosmologies. In distinguishing between 'tight' and 'loose' accounts and representations of good and evil, he signals a contrast between situations in which these representations are relatively durable and those in which they are more vulnerable to (re)interpretation. He links this distinction to the development of power. In situations where ecclesiastical power is particularly well diffused, or in which industrial organisation has developed into a unified and materialist conceptual apparatus, he argues, the proliferation of images of good and evil is slower than when this process is absent or only partial. He thus derives from the variety of themes and contexts a pattern of general tendency – people who perceive a power gap or 'deficit' between themselves and a more powerful 'other' are particularly prolific in their representation of good and evil. For those who are subject to more totalising hegemonic or discursive regimes, however, this productivity is stifled. However, unlike the Colombian peasant who has sold his soul to the Devil, these infertile 'peripheries' are not barren. Rather, they may emerge as potent producers of moral evaluations and representations of the powers of good and evil.

Acknowledgements

This book began at the second annual Conference of the Anthropology Programme at the University of Malta in 1996. Entitled 'Devils, Witches and Healers' it drew together scholars from anthropology, history, folklore, theology and art history. Only some of those who presented papers and contributed to the lively discussions are directly represented here, although we are grateful to all of them for their enthusiastic participation. For their enthusiasm and encouragement we would like to thank Marion Berghahn, Jeremy Boissevain, Vicki Cremona, Sybil and Charlie Mizzi, Filippo Osella and David Zammit. As editors, we would like to thank the contributors for their patience, hard work and persistent faith in the worth of this venture, and particularly Hildi Mitchell, who has devoted time and effort beyond the call of duty. We alone are responsible for the comments in the Introduction and Conclusion, and hope that we have done justice to the industry and intellect contained in the pages between them.

References

Ardener, E., 1970, 'Witchcraft, Economics and the Continuity of Belief', in Douglas, M., ed., *Witchcraft Confessions and Accusations*. London: Tavistock: 141-60.

Ardener, E., 1977, 'Belief and the Problem of Women', in Ardener, E., ed., *Perceiving Women*. London: J. M. Dent & Sons: 1-17.

Asad, T., 1983, 'Anthropological Conceptions of Religion: Reflections on Geertz', *Man* n.s. 18 (2): 237-59.

Comaroff, J., 1985, *Body of Power, Spirit of Resistance*. Chicago: Chicago University Press.

Comaroff, J. and Comaroff, J., 1992, *Ethnography and the Historical Imagination*. Chicago: Chicago University Press.

Davis, N. Z., 1995, *Women on the Margins : Three Seventeenth-Century Lives*. Cambridge, Mass: Harvard University Press.

Dirks, N. B., 1992, *Colonialism and Culture*. Ann Arbor: University of Michigan Press.

Durkheim, E., 1966 [1915], *The Elementary Forms of the Religious Life*. Trans. Joseph Swain, New York: Free Press.

Englund, H., 1996, 'Witchcraft, Modernity and the Person: The Morality of Accumulation in Central Malawi', *Critique of Anthropology* 16 (3): 257-79.

Evans-Pritchard, E. E., 1976 [1937], *Witchcraft, Oracles and Magic Among the Azande*. Oxford: Oxford University Press, abridged ed.

Geertz, C., 1973a, 'Religion as a Cultural System', in Geertz, C., *The Interpretation of Cultures*. London: Fontana: 87-125.

Geertz, C., 1973b, 'Thick Description: Toward an Interpretive Theory of Culture', in Geertz, C., *The Interpretation of Cultures*. London: Fontana: 3-30.

Giddens, A., 1990, *The Consequences of Modernity*. Cambridge: Polity Press.

Kahn, J. S., 1997, 'Demons, Commodities and the History of Anthropology', in Carrier, J., ed., *Meanings of the Market*. Oxford: Berg: 69-98.

Marwick, M., ed., 1970, ed, *Witchcraft and Sorcery*. Harmondsworth: Penguin.

Marx, K., 1920 [1886], *Capital: A Critical Analysis of Capitalist Production*. Trans. Moore, S. and Aveling, E., ed. F. Engels. London: William Glaisher.

Nugent, S., 1988, 'The "Peripheral Situation"', *Annual Review of Anthropology,* 17: 79–98.

Ortner, S. B., 1984, 'Theory in Anthropology Since the Sixties', *Comparative Studies in Society and History,* 26: 126–66.

Pals, D., 1996, *Seven Theories of Religion.* Oxford: Oxford University Press.

Parkin, D., 1985, 'Introduction', in Parkin, D., ed., *The Anthropology of Evil.* Oxford: Basil Blackwell: 1–25.

Schneider, J. and Schneider, P., 1976, *Culture and Political Economy in Western Sicily.* New York: Academic Press.

Taussig, M., 1980, *The Devil and Commodity Fetishism in South America.* Chapel Hill: University of North Carolina Press.

Taussig, M., 1995, 'The Sun Gives Without Receiving: A Old Story', *Comparative Studies in Society and History,* 37 (2): 368–98.

Thomas, P., 1996, 'World System', in Barnard, A. and Spencer, J., eds., *Encyclopedia of Social and Cultural Anthropology.* London: Routledge: 566–67.

Wallerstein, I., 1974, 1980, *The Modern World System.* New York: Academic Press, 2 vols.

Weber, M., 1930 [1904–5] *The Protestant Ethic and the Spirit of Capitalism.* Trans. Talcott Parsons, London: Unwin.

Werbner, R., 1989, *Ritual Passage, Sacred Journey : The Process and Organization of Religious Movement.* Washington: Smithsonian Institute Press.

Werbner, R. and Ranger, T. O., 1996, eds., *Postcolonial Identities in Africa.* London: Zed Books.

1

Dangerous Creatures and the Enchantment of Modern Life

*Bonno Thoden van Velzen and
Imeka van Wetering*

University of Amsterdam

Introduction: Occult Discourses

The Devil does not restrict his visits to European countries; he is a regular guest at many a banquet on more remote shores. By concluding 'pacts' the Devil strikes deals that characteristically involve great profits and high risks. When the Devil puts in an appearance, witches and demons usually attend his parties as well. Economic growth rather than economic decline appears to give rise to Devil pacts, and to a flowering of demon cults and witch persecutions. A strong, obsessive interest in the evil triad is emblematic of societies undergoing rapid change, rather than of backward-looking and traditional communities.[1] It is the first type of society that is subjected to a drastic restructuring of its internal relations. New opportunities invariably give rise to new rivalries and foment anxieties. Temptations to sever kinship links or communal bonds foster beliefs in the proximity of evil. Hence rapid socio-economic changes breed confusion, moral uncertainty, unrest – in short, anxiety. These sentiments in their turn appear to activate Devil, witch and demon beliefs.

The subject of this paper is these occult discourses, how to interpret them and what their message is. Many decades ago anthropologists realised that accusations of witchcraft inform us about a society's strains and tensions. Marwick (1970: 280–95), for one, argues that witchcraft accusations and convictions can profitably be studied as indicators of social stress, as measuring rods that show us where a society's fault-lines run.

Such an approach, however valuable, cannot reveal the full richness of occult discourses. Critics, like Crick (1982: 344–45), were quick to point this out. The micro-sociological conceptions of anthropology lay bare some important processes, but undeniably have limitations. It would not do to suggest, he claims, that witchcraft is explained by misfortune. It is not clear, however, that Crick's suggestion to study underlying classificatory structures as an alternative, would bring us very far. We would, moreover, be very wrong in underestimating our predecessors. The same Manchester school anthropologists who pursued the repudiated lines of inquiry showed they were aware of the bounds to knowledge imposed by their approach. As Turner phrased it, 'If witch beliefs were solely the products of social tensions and conflicts, they would betray their origin by possessing a more markedly rational form and content' (1964: 315). In order to get a better grasp of that which escaped current paradigmata he turned to Freud's *The Interpretation of Dreams* (1962).[2]

It is one thing to understand the line of battle, and the primary issues people fight about, to capture the experiences and sentiments of the human agents is something else. Occult discourses are studied here as collective fantasies (Elias and Scotson 1965; Thoden van Velzen 1995), as sets of ideas that are not identical with ideologies, with 'unified schemes of configurations developed to underwrite or manifest power' (Wolf 1999: 4). They are different from Durkheim's collective representations (Durkheim 1925: 13–14) in the sense that they need not be sanctioned by society, or figure prominently in public debate, nor are they used for demarcating group boundaries. Collective fantasies are products of the imagination – they always are related to the realities of power, but in a loose and non-deterministic way. The collective fantasies we study are inferred from the clues that dangerous creatures leave, from the tell-tale signs that mark their trails. We suggest to add to our forerunners' proposals a study of iconography, of the images of Devil, demon and witch, and then to study this as a form of social hieroglyphics that could offer us a *via regia* to society's complexities and ambiguities.

A Devil's Contract

Taussig (1980) advocated such an approach in his well-known *The Devil and Commodity Fetishism in South America*. The author demonstrates that devil contracts, reputedly made by labourers on sugar plantations in Colombia, are reactions to economic pressures, often attempts to free oneself from an economically depressing situation. As in Goethe's *Faust*, the protégé on these sugar plantations sells his soul to the Devil in exchange for material benefits. In the long term, this reckless speculator has to pay dearly for the transaction. He gets all the wealth he asked for, but none of it will last; everything slips through his fingers. His fate is illness, despair, and an untimely, frightful death.[3]

Taussig's move has had liberating effects upon the anthropology of the occult. Notions about supernaturally induced evil no longer had to carry the stigma of the irrational. Quite the contrary: the images produced by popular fantasy counted as realistic, and an eloquent comment on the true nature of capitalism. The proposed link between economic vicissitudes and a defensive imagination freed a Marxist approach from the stalemate of 'the supernatural as opium for the people'. Also, the limitations of the ideology concept - implying that the world of ideas is a mere reflection of class interests - were overcome. The road to an exploration of the workings of consciousness and psyche, as a complement to, but based upon foreknowledge of material conditions, was now open.

Yet, some questions arise from this path-breaking venture. Are we to infer from Taussig's contribution that a prevalent belief in Devil's pacts will generally mean that capitalism is as unambiguously rejected as his material on a Colombian peasantry suggests? Our own fieldwork experience among Suriname's Ndyuka Maroons gives cause to doubt this. Cases from European history likewise fail to lend support to such a conclusion.

Also, the way fantasies are produced merits attention. Although the anxieties underlying the iconography and discourses of Evil often spring from processes in the economic centres, and therefore tend to be permeated with the idiom of rationality and modernity, the language of the emotions is bound to be written with archaic and even exotic signs. It springs from unrest resulting from an unfinished confrontation.

Taussig (1980: 123) argues that such products of the collective imagination should be understood as 'sacred texts'. The key question then becomes how to read these 'sacred texts'. In the Colombian case the theatrical format of the Devil's contract makes it relatively easy to understand. When Devil and protégé meet a plot unfolds that immediately reveals the emotions involved. The ultimate consequences of the Devil's contract point squarely to the morale of the story.

But anthropologists usually encounter more obstacles. It seldom happens that they can record such telling dramas. More often than not, they have to content themselves with fragments of sacred texts, with unrelated figments of the imagination. The deciphering of such fragments is far more problematic. Texts are enigmatic phenomena – they may and often have double and hidden meanings. Passionate feelings may hide behind the most harmless-looking images. Apart from a manifest aspect, often fantastic or absurd, there is a latent message that will not readily yield its secrets. It is for this reason that we wish to distinguish between the manifest and latent level: some statements are easily made, often in public, without much embarrassment, whereas other sentiments are clearly held back. In public discussions, beliefs in devils and witches are rarely connected in a straightforward manner with social and economic issues. The link is disguised. Yet, these beliefs can hardly be expected to lack such hidden dimensions. In decoding sacred texts we thus meet with at least two problem areas: the *fragmentary* nature of the text and the circumstance that the message enclosed is often *masked*.

The phenomena have been observed in the past and the contemporary world, in the modernising West and in so-called non-Western milieux. This underpins the oft-made assertion that a distinction between 'the west and the rest' is untenable. The issues have been dealt with from various angles: historians, sociologists and anthropologists have made contributions. This presents us with an ideal occasion to make comparisons and see what inferences can be made. Our main example is the demon beliefs in our area of fieldwork among the 20th century Ndyuka Maroons of Suriname's interior. The 'confessions' of the Mora witches (Sweden, 1668–70), and the Salem witch craze (New England, 1692) are mustered as comparative but secondary examples.

Evil spirits among the Maroons

An evil spirit among the Ndyuka Maroons of eastern Suriname[4] is, like elsewhere in the world, a crystallisation of fears. Some are inspired by strangers, often ephemeral and passing. Others are anchored at a deeper level in the human psyche. In particular, the dread of one's own asocial inclinations, of degradation and derailment, may take on a terrifying intensity. Such emotional stirrings often remain indefinable, and elude attempts to cast them in a concrete and clear form. Historical processes further compound the situation. In the course of history, Ndyuka have been confronted with a variety of economic opportunities, prohibitions and risks. These social and economic changes either directly or indirectly affect the participants' emotional system.

Two stages in economic involvement were the most turbulent: the days of the gold rushes (1885–1925), and the incorporation of Maroon communities into the modern nation state of Suriname (after 1960). Although the basic traits of demon-beliefs are constant, each phase adds its accents and additions.

River transport

Around 1885 great changes occurred in Suriname's interior. Since the beginning of the 1880s rich placers – sandy areas with gold deposits – were discovered on the upper courses of the rivers in Suriname and French Guyana. Transport to this El Dorado was only feasible by means of dugout canoes. Ndyuka and other Maroons enjoyed a virtual monopoly over river transport and could therefore demand high freight rates. The work was extremely taxing. It often meant paddling and punting a canoe carrying one or two tons of cargo against the full force of the river for two weeks or longer. In the rapids the boat had to be unloaded; this happened several times a day. The boatmen then carried their freight over slippery stones to a higher level of the river. When the rains were heavy, the night's rest might be lost. For hours Ndyuka baled water out of the canoes to keep them from sinking. The river transporters worked hard; many complained of backaches but often persevered until they collapsed. The relatives left behind in the villages had to fend for themselves. Women, children and old people suffered considerable hardships. For Maroons the golden years of river transport brought full participation of all adult men in the money economy, and a neglect of traditional obligations by boatmen.

The rise of the transport industry coincided with the birth of the *Gaan Tata* cult, a Maroon anti-witchcraft movement that erupted in the 1890s and dominated religious and political life in the interior for many decades (Thoden van Velzen and Van Wetering 1988).

The boatmen succeeded in securing the assistance of *Gaan Tata*'s priests against the witches. The persons so stigmatised were mostly older women. At *Gaan Tata*'s shrines the priests explained that envy and greed brought these women to commit their heinous crimes (van Wetering 1973).

But the evil beings could not be locked away in one social compartment for long. Soon witches began to be detected among the boat owners themselves. Our source on this second strand of demonology is the writings of Willem van Lier who collected this information mainly between 1910 and 1926.[5] Van Lier characterises a demon in the following way: 'Mostly he appears to the human eye in the form of a male dwarf with a large head, one half of him being of wood, the other half of flesh and bone' (1945:6).

That the iconography depicts the dwarf as male suggests that men are seen as the key actors in this second occult discourse. The creature was partly of wood which suggests a reduction of human qualities or simply humanness. As this wooden side was turned to any potential adversary to avert blows,[6] the image of callousness was evoked. An evil spirit was like a thing, without the human capacity to adapt to changing circumstances. The medium possessed by the spirit was reduced to the state of a robot who could only produce standard reactions. Aggressiveness and vaulting ambition had become normal, almost automatic responses.

In the heydays of river transport (1885–1925), the boatmen truly behaved like demons or machines with little compassion for their kith and kin – family obligations were grossly neglected. The pursuit of fortune, as the elderly today reminiscence, had turned the entrepreneurs into bullies, a menace to themselves and their dependants.

But the greatest threat was seen to be coming from men of their own kin group. That, and the 'degeneration into robots' theme betrayed inner fears. Van Lier (1945: 6) mentions numerous cases of insanity, attributed by Ndyuka to demon seizures. The author adds that a full recovery was a rare phenomenon. According to Van Lier the most terrifying demon was the *lauw bakroe* (the demon that brings madness). It is hard to dismiss the idea that the many mental disorders were linked to the rapacious gold industry and the demands it made on the river transporters, but overstrained expectations and the inevitable disappointments may have played an even bigger role.

An important element, and probably specific for this period, is the 'tying of the soul' (*tee akaa*). A specific form of witchcraft was involved here. Malevolent, perverted individuals – in short, witches – would tie the *akaa* (soul or vital force). Although no direct link was made with demon beliefs, the 'tied soul' was one of the terrors of the river transport era. Nowadays, Ndyuka hardly mention this danger, and presumably it no longer reflects contemporary concerns. However, the horrifying image sheds light on the fears people felt in those days. Van Lier comments (1945:8): 'Woe to the unfortunate whose soul has been caught and tied by a witch. If a witch truly hates his or her victim and wants his complete undoing, he or she will not only tie the soul, but nail it down, preferably unto a sacred tree, deep in the forest. Or even worse, the soul is tied to a stone and thrown into the river.'

Van Lier continues by pointing out that in all cases known to him the afflicted were men. The iconography outlined here suggests that the fear to be side-tracked is at the root of this angst – the fear of no longer being in the centre where 'things happen', or are supposed to happen. The image of being nailed down at a remote place deep in the backwoods indicates such a fear.

The nightmarish image of a soul weighed down by stones that sinks to the bottom of the river is equally related to male rivalry. The river is the 'locale' of success, where fortunes are made. To have one's soul sunk to the bottom and see other boatmen on the river surface on their way to customers is perhaps even a greater horror.

The migrants

Around 1920 the peak of prosperity was reached: the placers had been depleted and few new ones were discovered. In a few years' time a shortage in transport capacity changed into a surplus. The egalitarian character of Ndyuka culture could reassert itself. After 1965, however, the situation again changed drastically. For the first time in history, Suriname's policy-makers made a serious effort to open the interior for new economic ventures. Government agencies employed hundreds of Ndyuka boatmen for the exploration of the forested hinterland. The departure of tens of thousands of Surinamese citizens to the Netherlands created opportunities for Ndyuka entrepreneurs that had never existed before. In the coastal area and in the capital Paramaribo they could buy houses, taxis, trucks, and shops at bargain prices. During the 1970s, waves of prosperity started to reach the heartland of the Ndyuka Maroons, the villages along the Tapanahoni River in south-east Suriname.

For a second time in Ndyuka history, their society became subject to centrifugal forces. Not all Ndyuka migrants, not even a majority, had found paid employment or had managed to establish themselves as small-time entrepreneurs. In the interior the situation was worse – few people shared in the new affluence. In sum, looking at the Ndyuka Maroons during the preceding decades, we observe that differences in levels of income increased greatly. As we will presently see, demonology betrays the tensions that resulted from the widening gap between rich and poor.

In Ndyuka villages of the 1970s and 1980s, the prosperity of many migrants spawned envy and distrust among their less fortunate kinsmen. It was also quite obvious that possession by demons (*bakuu*) was on the rise. During the 1960s, demon mediums were exceptional cases. But twenty-five years later such forms of possession assumed epidemic proportions. People would now say, in response to our question: 'Instead of asking us who in this village is a demon medium, why don't you ask who is *not*, it will be easier to answer your question because the list is so short'.

Two demon dramas can be analytically distinguished. The first, the older one, is centred around a Faustian 'Devil contract'. The principal character here is an ambitious man, usually a successful entrepreneur who sells his soul for material gain; most of his victims are women. In the second drama females occupy centre stage. Although they constantly refer to a nefarious character who concluded that pernicious Devil's contract, women are no longer passive victims. Seized by demons they are now in command of the situation, clamouring for attention and material rewards, while assaulting suspects with impunity. [7]

A Devil's Contract

It is a fairly widespread notion that successful males are liable to buy demons for the elimination of rivals. Such 'Demon Masters' (*bakuu basi*) or 'Masters' as we will name them here, are usually believed to have economic objectives in mind. Many people openly speculate that migrants have truck with demons. A telling detail revealing the link with a booming but uncertain economic world is the representation of demons as 'money machines' or drudges. To hire an evil spirit as a 'money machine' is not without its risks. Sooner or later a demon will make unexpected demands on his Master. He may, for example, threaten to withhold his services unless he will receive a human life as an offering (Lenoir 1973:

140). After he has been granted the human sacrifice, problems grow as the evil creature is beginning to lose all its value as a 'money machine'. The same is true if a Master decides to turn a demon loose on his fellows. From that moment on the evil spirit is unfit for ordinary work. In other cases, a demon 'jumps' on a Master's kinsman, while the latter often has no prior knowledge of the demon contract. Only later, often much too late, he or she gets wind of it. The fate of Atyado, a Ndyuka migrant, and his relatives, is a case in point.

Atyado bought two demons in Paramaribo from a Hindustani man – a male and a female one. The two demons worked like dogs. Whatever job Atyado took, whether it was building a house or boat, or preparing a horticultural garden, he always succeeded in finishing it more quickly than anyone else. People opined that demons were responsible for Atyado's success. When Atyado was dying, he confided in his sister and explained that he would bequeath the two demons to her. She certainly had some use for the gift; she was a widow and had to fend for herself. The demons worked to her full satisfaction, but in the meantime they had propagated, giving birth to six male and six female young demons. Atyado's sister could not lodge all these creatures. She sent the young demons to her relatives. Within a short time cases of demonic possession occurred among most of her kin. On her deathbed Atyado's sister confessed that she had sent them. Her relatives were not too happy with these presents. Some argued that they had no work to do for demons, as they already had a breadwinner. Not being gainfully employed themselves, of what use could demons be?

It is clear that demon mediums belong to two classes: those who are believed to have purposely established a relationship with a demon, and those who became possessed by such an evil spirit without having had any wish to engage with these creatures. When people are denounced as belonging to the first category, that of the Masters, it is tantamount to an accusation of witchcraft. They are usually males and few in numbers. The 'victim category', people claiming to be possessed by a demon sent by someone else, encompasses many more people, most of them females. In the recent past, when demon possession was considered a rare occurrence, such malevolent spirits were immediately exorcised, and were never heard of later. Nowadays, exorcisms seldom take place, or prove efficacious. Although the 'victims' do not try to hide that they have been invaded by a demon, they appear to cherish their mediumship.

The link with city life appears to be much more complex than a simple reaction of repulsion against humans who sell their souls to money machines, which earlier used to be the set explanation.

Depending on the way the victims behave, the ethnography of the demon epidemic goes in two different directions. The reports based on field work conducted mainly in the 1970s[8] stress the ambivalence of victims toward the new wealth that became available in Ndyuka communities of the interior. In those studies Ndyukas show their fear for the new social relationships created by affluent migrants, as well as their own fascination and attraction by the glamour and opulence of city life. However, reports from anthropologists working a decade later strike a more gloomy note. Details of fascination with city life are not absent, but the demons are pictured first of all as killers rather than 'money machines'. We will present material on both periods.

A Sophisticated Demon

It is from the iconography and from the mise-en-scène or enplotment[9] of the demon drama that we learn what was at stake during the 1970s. Most of the icons one meets in the demon dramas of those years had never before been associated with such creatures. The language, for example, reeled off by the new demons is *Sranan Tongo*, a Creole spoken on the coast, mutually intelligible with the Creole of the Ndyuka Maroons, but clearly different. *Sranan Tongo* was the language of sophisticated city people, and had a higher prestige for the younger generation than the idiom spoken by the rustic folk back home. Pronunciation and intonation of the spirit language used by mediums were those of radio announcers (Vernon 1980: 21). Occasionally, demons had a grasp of Chinese, the language of the shopkeepers. Today the great majority of demon mediums are female. In the heydays of river transport the role of men was pivotal; males were then the main actors of the demon drama. But this aspect of the iconography has changed as well. Some mediums, who are willing to tell what their demon looks like, describe a light-coloured Creole child or a doll in pretty city clothes (Vernon 1980: 4). This new form of demonic possession is thus explicitly linked to the urban lifestyle, and the glamour that surrounds it in the eyes of the population of the hinterland. But the drama also strikes a note of caution: the demons' appetite for sweets is regarded as insatiable – they will eat great quantities of sugar, even a barrel-full (Lenoir 1973: 139–40).

The enplotment is even more revealing. Vernon (1980, 1985) offers telling examples from a Ndyuka village on the Tapanahoni River at the end of the 1970s. The drama started when a boat with returning migrants approached their home village in the interior. A female passenger changed her city dress for the traditional wrap-around skirt. At the boat landing, she suddenly jumped on the sandy beach, ran toward the village, and expressed her demon mediumship by violent gestures and language. Other females from the village, demon mediums themselves, joined her. Moments later, serious conflicts erupted. A young woman, who accompanied the newly-arrived medium on her tour through the village, disclosed in trance that she had been invaded by a demon sent by her uncle.

The man had lived in Paramaribo for many years before he returned to his village in old age. The woman, or rather her spirit, accused the old man of having killed seven persons with the assistance of a couple of demons bought in Paramaribo. The progeny of these evil spirits had been swarming out all over their kin group. Although the old man rejected the accusations, the village elders reprimanded him sternly. The situation threatened to get truly out of hand when the group of demon mediums assaulted the old man with sticks. A lynching was barely prevented by the elders and other bystanders. When barred from beating the suspect, the mediums continued their tour of the village, clamouring for soda pop, sweets, and other goods sold in village shops (Vernon 1980: 29). Small wonder that elders are wary of returning migrants. They used to give them a warm welcome, while at the same time warning people of the cargo the migrants' boats could bring. Demons, they claimed, could be hiding like cockroaches among the city goods (31).

These new forms of demonic possession had some characteristics in common. As most mediums are female, the demon drama gave women a central place. Although they had truck with demons themselves, these women pointed an accusing finger at males. Men, driven by greed, were responsible for the first, decisive purchases. Women were victims, properly speaking.

Also new is the assertiveness and even aggressiveness of females. Demon mediums often produced an endless stream of words and would not bear contradiction. Mediums demanded consumer goods from shops. In trance mediums dared to accuse others of witchcraft, which is one of this society's strongest taboos – it is not only improper, but even sinful, to charge living persons with such a crime. More than once Vernon had been witness to assaults by mediums on men and women suspected of witchcraft. One of the village headmen voiced his misgivings over the mediums as follows: '. . . little ladies who run around the village with *winti* (spirits) screaming in their heads trying to kill people' (1980: 29).

The relation between this type of possession and the urban milieu is clearly indicated. The first manifestations of demonic possession occur, as a rule, on setting foot in the native village, even before there has been a chance to change from urban attire to traditional dress. The realisation that there was nothing ahead but only a step back into the deprivation of a subsistence economy may have been a decisive motive. Vernon offers us the following reaction by a woman who was a demon medium: 'this thing they call money is a terrible thing. As soon as you see it, your whole body begins to tremble' (1985: 15).

Lastly, a significant element in the iconography is the fact that demons act collectively, in groups. In the stories about the demons of the past this element is lacking. A basis for proliferation of the evil spirits could have been there at the outset, with the first transaction in the city. This was true in Atyado's case, for instance. He bought a male and a female demon who soon started to propagate. Lenoir (1973: 139) reports the case of a Paramaka (one of the three Maroon tribes of eastern Suriname), who was suspected of having purchased demons in bulk. Ndyuka told Vernon (1980: 16) that they had observed a group of twelve demons sneaking between houses. A renowned shaman had to step in at last to knock them off the roof with a stick. Green's (1974: 254–56) case-study of a demon drama among the Matawai (a Maroon tribe of western Suriname) reveals the preference of demons for working in gangs. Years after the onset of the drama, six of the gang's first group of demons were still active. Although all histories start with a contract between a purchaser (Master) and one or two demons, their number often increases at high speed – it is like a malicious growth that rapidly forms secondary tumours within the social fabric.

It is not always clear how a particular representation of evil spirits is related to the pattern of social and economic change. Take, for instance, the last item – the quick reproduction of demons. Is this a comment on the social flux caused by migration and urbanisation, or an expression of the contagiousness of demonic possession? We cannot be sure, but there certainly is a link between rapid economic change and the rise of new, striking images of demons.

Demons as Killers

During the early 1990s the lure of city life was still clearly evident in the demon dramas. During a seance, Van Wetering (1992: 123) heard one particularly dangerous spirit disclose its name. He called himself 'Jemissie Whitewalk', a neat condensation of 'Johnnie Walker', 'White Horse', and maybe even of 'James Bond', a figure well-known from the video theatres that have sprung up in many a Ndyuka village. At any rate, the demon liked whiskey, the drink sophisticated people in the city were rumoured to be fond of.

But in daily life, the seductive aspects of city life seem to be losing to the dangers that lurk in new social relationships. Van Wetering, when writing about a Ndyuka settlement in the early 1990s, remarks on the 'demon epidemic' (1992: 118):

> Not only on more or less formal occasions, but also in daily conversations demons would crop up any time. When washing dishes at the riverside or preparing manioc in the cooking sheds, at all places where women would gather, it would not be long before someone would volunteer a hair-raising story about horrors that had stricken some people, somewhere. And almost invariably, *bakuu* [demons] were involved. Thus, the threat of demonic interference in normal life was kept vivid. Also, interpretations involving *bakuu* were given about the thing that happened here and now.

The author spoke with two sisters who were almost the only females among their relatives who had *not* succumbed to demon mediumship: they pointed to the disasters that had struck their kin group, which they had fled. She concludes (1992: 118):

> Most stories entail a sudden, unexpected death. It seems that cardiac failure, which appears to occur rather frequently, is interpreted in this matter. In these rumours, demons are systematically described as killers, not as the 'money machines' they reputedly are.

A demon drama, part of a corpus of continuously-reproduced myths, is told in a fantastic, archaic language. The narrative conveys a message that is masked, but intelligible to those willing to grasp its meaning. Translated into images, the story links cause and effect. According to Freud (1900), this is what the dream language does. Myths and dreams, products of 'primary process', and as such, undisciplined by rational thought, nevertheless represent or give form to ideas. Not privileging speech and words, Freud held that even the most abstract thought can be expressed in images (Laplanche and Pontalis 1988: 390). This is why the dream mechanisms, first of all the mechanism of 'dramatisation' ('Considerations of Representability'), are called upon to provide an analytic key. The Ndyuka accounts of demonic involvements rank as clear instances of dramatisation, enplotment or 'stage-managing' (Thoden van Velzen 1997). Taussig's Devil's contracts likewise seem cases in point. The case to be discussed next will show the applicability of the two other dream mechanisms, displacement and condensation.

The Devil's Garments

Between 1668 and 1677 Sweden[10] was the scene of extensive witch persecutions. Particularly, the witch trials held between 1668 and 1670 attracted a great deal of attention among contemporaries and later generations. Undoubtedly, Joseph Glanvill's *Saducismus Triumphatus* (1681) and Balthasar Bekker's *De Betoverde Weereld* (The Bewitched World) (1691–93) did much to draw Europe's attention to the events in Sweden. In the fourth volume Bekker included in detail the 'confessions' of the Swedish witches, drawing on a published excerpt (Anonymous 1670) from the report of the Swedish Royal Commission investigating the witch allegations.[11]

The witch troubles started around Whitsun of 1668 in Ålvdalen (Ankarloo 1971, 1983), in Dalarna, an area (now a county) in central Sweden. Gertrud Svensdaughter, a twelve-year-old girl, disclosed that she had visited Blåkulla, the devil's pasture. The place could only be reached by a trip through the air on the back of bewitched creatures. Often Blåkulla was the scene of a witches' sabbath. Peak events included the initiation of novices and baptism by the devil; a copious meal accompanied by harp playing concluded by a dance; and, finally, sexual intercourse with the Prince of Darkness. The newly-initiated could then start to function as assistants to the devil, the novices' first assignment being to lure children to Blåkulla.

Such notions had been current in Sweden for centuries (see Wall 1978). What was new were the great numbers of persons, mainly children, involved. For Gertrud confessed that she had not been alone during her nocturnal sojourn at Blåkulla. Under interrogation by her judges she named many others whom she had met in the devil's pasture. Another girl, seventeen years old, also from Ålvdalen, stepped forward to support Gertrud's statements. Subsequently, scores of people were interrogated; twenty-nine were found guilty, of whom twelve were condemned to death. In the meantime the witch craze spread to villages along the shores of Lake Siljan, a region to the south-east of Gertrud's village.

In December 1668, when a second court convened in Mora the suspects also hailed from villages in Dalarna. Six death sentences were passed. Women who refused to confess and showed no remorse were regarded as dangers to the spiritual well-being of others – they were supposed to have designs on young children in particular. People believed that they lured them to Blåkulla.[12] In 1669, in Oxberg, neighbouring on Ålvdalen, and in Mora parish, more children stepped forward with confessions.

The places touched by the first witch panic (1668–71) were situated along Dalarna's rivers and near the Siljan and Orsa lakes in the same area. In the seventeenth century this was a poor agricultural area[13] – rivers and lakes girded by huge areas covered by fir trees with, scattered here and there, some small farms. But at a distance of some fifty to a hundred kilometres to the south-east of the witch craze's epicentre the mining town of Falun attracted the attention of commercial Europe – in its giant mine copper was extracted in enormous quantities.[14] The Swedish war economy of the seventeenth century depended on the sale of copper, and Falun was the motor of that economy.[15] The town had about 5,000 inhabitants at the time, of whom 1,000 were employed in the mine. Foreign commercial banks and insurance firms were represented by agents in Falun. This urban centre must have been an odd element in this remote region of Sweden – a mining centre with international contacts in an economically marginal region.

The iconography strongly suggests that the unrest in central Sweden, and the ensuing witch hunts, were connected with the contrast between Falun and the surrounding area. Certainly, many aspects of the demonology were conventional images well-known in preceding centuries – the belief in a devil's meadow where witches and novices would gather, nocturnal journeys through the air, and the inversion of Christian rituals such as consecration and baptism. But some other conceptions were rather new. The witches from the villages around lake Siljan and lake Orsa presented their interrogators with the following information: 'The food they eat there is cabbage-soup with bacon, oatmeal porridge, butter, milk and cheese. Sometimes they tell that it tastes well and sometimes bad' [16] (Anonymous 1670 :10).

The food was brought by animals especially marked out for this task of preying and plundering. Cats and ravens were mentioned. Musical entertainment was also part of the attractions, to be followed by dancing and copulation. Bekker writes in an ironic vein (1693: 221):

> Those of Elfdalen [Älvdalen] have confessed (do these people realise what they are confessing?) that the devil plays the harp for them. After this he takes those he likes best to a room (a sign that some decency is left in the devil) and has sexual intercourse with them. They all confess to have had sex with him. This is never omitted; the devil must be very randy for old grannies, for these were the majority.

The anonymous writer mentioned the following events (Anonymous 1670: 7):

> After having called out: Antesser [one of the Devil's names], come, take us to Blokula, the prince of darkness will soon appear in many different garments, but most people saw him with a grey, dull smock, red trousers and blue stockings, having a red beard, a top hat with many flashy bands around it and long ribbons tied to the trousers.

In Glanvill it is rendered thus (1978: 316):

> Whereupon, immediately he [the Devil] used to appear, but in different Habits; but for the most part we saw him in a gray Coat, and red and blue Stockings: he had a red Beard, a high-crown'd Hat, with Linnen of divers colours wrapt about it, and long Garters upon his Stockings.

The image of the devil is puzzling. He donned a strange combination of clothes: the grey smock was the farmer's traditional garment, but his fashionable trousers, stockings, and his top hat did not match that sober jacket. Both hat and trousers were garishly adorned with coloured ribbons and other frills. We contend that the peasants, eking out a meagre existence along the rivers and lakes of central Sweden, felt both attracted and repulsed by the opulent life-style of Falun's mine management and merchants. Certainly, the confessions of the witches were procured after considerable psychological pressure by the interrogators.[17] But that does not explain their contents. Is it not plausible that a desire for a better and more glamorous life-style prompted the poor peasants, most of them single women, often widows, to fantasise a world where decent food was amply available, where the devil's sexual attentions did not stop with younger women, and where one could visit the houses of the rich by flying straight through their window panes, or descend through their chimneys? Such flights of fantasy would bring them into houses where coveted wealth was on display (Glanvill 1978 :317):

> Being asked how they could go with their Bodies through Chimneys and broken panes of Glass, they said, that the Devil did first remove all that might hinder them in their flight, and so they had room enough to go.

Does not the figure of the devil itself reveal the desire of the poor? He was wearing a farmer's smock, but the rest of clothes intimated the possibility of transmogrification. We suggest that the collective fantasies[18] matured under the pressure of a confrontation between the mine-town's prosperity with the frugality of life in the surrounding countryside. It seems likely that a growing differentiation within the agrarian communities themselves may have added to the brutal confrontation of the poor peasants with Falun's wealth. Some farmers must have profited from the sales potential offered by a market of 5,000 persons not employed in agriculture. But we have not investigated this matter any further. The situation could have led to intrapsychic conflicts, in which aversion and appeal vied for priority.

Again, Freud's *The Interpretation of Dreams* comes to mind. Of the three processes that structure the language of dreams, Freud considered 'condensation' and 'displacement' to be the two most important. 'Condensation' refers to the circumstance that one single representation can encompass several notions and divergent emotions.[19] The devil's apparel demonstrates the process of condensation at work: urban elegance and rural dullness. 'Displacement' refers to a process whereby relatively innocent images are taken to stand for matters that evoke violent emotions. The flying through window panes, an apparently meaningless detail, could hide a compelling desire to pass through invisible barriers and visit the houses of those who actually possess window panes – the rich.

Madame Bubble

New England's Salem is another example of a place where social-economic cleavages and demon beliefs appear clearly connected. Boyer and Nissenbaum (1974) argue that the witch-craze in Salem at the close of the seventeenth century was linked to speculations about growing urban prosperity. The epidemic of demonic possession and subsequent witch accusations started when stark discrepancies in the standards of living between town and country could no longer be ignored. Demos (1982: 385) has summarised these differences in a way that reminds us of the cleavage between Falun and the surrounding Swedish countryside.

For Salem was a place split down the middle – was, in fact, two places of markedly different spatial, economic and cultural orientations. On the one side (near the coast) stood Salem Town, a flourishing centre of commerce, cosmopolitan in outlook and urban in style, dominated by an increasingly affluent cadre of merchants and tradesmen. On the other side (in the interior) lay Salem Village, an agricultural hamlet of limited resources, provincial, homogeneous, wedded to traditional ways and values.

In Salem Village, an agrarian community where land had become a scarce commodity, people were painfully aware of much more promising developments in the commercial sector of neighbouring Salem Town. Although the merchants were devoted to the Puritan faith, in the eyes of the peasants they had succumbed to the temptations of Mammon. In their way of thinking, merchants had helped the Devil to build a bridgehead in Salem Town. The struggle between poor and wealthy branches of families was also pursued in the agrarian community.

The witch hunt started in the house of clergyman Parris, a one-time planter who, after setbacks in Barbados, moved to New England where he opened a business. After another failure he had recourse to the ministry. From the pulpit Parris denounced the merchants who, by their corrupt way of life, threatened and tempted the honest peasants. Boyer and Nissenbaum (1974: 162) convincingly argue that Parris was personally tormented and fascinated by Mammon's representatives. Tituba, a woman from Barbados who had accompanied Parris on his journey to New England, found a position in Parris's rectory. Elizabeth, Parris's nine-year-old daughter, and a number of her friends, frequently came to listen to Tituba's stories about black magic. Vicar Parris's vehement charges, West Indian demonology and a European witch belief that lingered on in New England, were the ingredients from which the 'witch bitches', as the children came to be known, fabricated their demonology. The Devil promised Salem's children money, pretty clothes, fashionable shoes and various other items imbued with the glamour of an urban life-style.

When appearing before children the Devil looked like a prosperous farmer or merchant. Boyer and Nissenbaum (1974: 209–16) draw attention to a similarity between these representations and the allegorical characters painted by Bunyan in *The Pilgrim's Progress*, such as 'Mr. Wordly Wiseman' and 'Mr. Money-Love'. In particular, the figure of Bunyan's 'Madame Bubble' was shown to be extremely treacherous – the author referred to her as 'a witch'. She wore beautiful clothes, loved 'banqueting and feasting', spoke 'smoothly with a smile at the end of each sentence'. Madame Bubble was continuously fingering the gold in her large purse and felt most at ease with those who were 'cunning to get money'. Well-off, worldly, refined, she promised the moon to the young who would follow her – truly a spectre for Puritan society.

A marked economic contrast engendered conflicts and spawned new phantasms. The children accused adults of corruption. But as in the Swedish case, ambivalence was transparent in the children's imaginings. The Devil could be abhorrent, but he also promised beautiful clothes and shoes. To all intents and purposes, he was Madame Bubble's male counterpart.

Conclusion

Let us once more look at Taussig's study of Devil's pacts in Columbia. What seems relevant here is the author's finding (1980: 17) that the people most likely to be suspected of concluding Devil's pacts are those who occupy a precarious position: the new proletarians, the sugarcane-cutters who no longer own land. For those people to cut a few extra square metres could mean the difference between mere survival and a reasonable or even comfortable standard of living. Small wonder that the peasants cutting sugarcane are believed to solicit the help of the Prince of Darkness.

The hypothesis of affinity between a precarious status in society and an association with devil or demons is indirectly confirmed by the work of historians. According to Cohn (1975: 252) demon beliefs were primarily relevant for a new town-dwelling elite in Europe. Similar indications are to be found in the works of

Baschwitz (1966: 38), Thomas (1971: 564) and de Waardt (1989: 236–37). In their view ambitious young men were singled out for allegations. Despairing of chances to be successful in a 'normal' way, they would strike a bargain with the Devil. The idea has found its best-known elaboration in the myth surrounding the figure of Faust.

The lure of new prosperity, coupled with anxiety whether there will be any chance of getting access to it, lends power to the evil spirits. Although demons manifest themselves in economic backwaters, their areas of preference are places at the outskirts of a prosperous area; in New England in Salem Village, a periphery of Salem Town, a centre of commercial growth in the region; in Sweden in a sparsely populated area, far from cities, but close to a prosperous mining district; in Suriname the remote Tapanahoni villages, which constituted a periphery linked to a city offering vistas of prosperity. Collective fantasies appear to reflect the main lines of socio-economic cleavage.

Thus, there is ample support for an interpretation that takes the material conditions of existence into account. Yet, the relation between social tensions and the demonic idiom is rarely straightforward or clear-cut. The accusations from people in Salem Village were directed at merchants and their relatives in thriving Salem Town. In the diabolic imagery, the Devil appears in the guise of a rich tradesman. Yet, although the rich were suspects, they were not the prime candidates for execution.

Among the Ndyuka boatmen of the early twentieth century fantasies also reflected economic realities but in a different way. Here the main theme was that of the well-to-do insulating themselves from the destitute by intimating allegations of witchcraft. For most of the twentieth century the prototypical Ndyuka witches were needy old women who had no close relatives to take care of them. Economic forces produced other fantasies as well. Among Ndyuka boat owners intense fears of lagging behind rivals gave rise to nightmarish images of sorcery and witchcraft.

On the basis of carefully interpreted socio-economic data, Ankarloo (1990: 310–12) explicitly argues that witchcraft accusations and witch trials were neither simply a weapon in the hands of the affluent to keep the poor in their places, nor were they only employed as levelling devices against well-to-do farmers. In short, 'there is no support for the theory that the witches were living on the margin of or even outside the community. They were right in the middle of it' (312).

In all cases described, the collective fantasies of the age give us a perspective that supersedes the local community. Isolated farming communities in central Sweden were part of a social arena that included the prosperous copper mining district some 100 kilometres to the south-east. The same holds for Salem Village – its witches hatch their evil plots in Salem Town, a city involved in transatlantic trade networks. Through their imaginings the Ndyuka also participate in a social arena that includes the capital city of Paramaribo, and for some the Netherlands as well, the old metropolis. The symbolism of evil offers us a profound grasp of a society's contradictions, enabling us to move from tensions characteristic of kin group and neighbourhood to a much wider social arena.

Not only the relations between the global and the local are involved. The collective fantasies of evil will also allow us to move from the outer to the inner world, to commute from the economic and political arena to the individual, psychic field of tensions. The occult discourses bridge the gap between the social field and the individual psyche. Psychological processes, whether of a conscious or unconscious nature, and socio-economic realities of the immediate local group and the wider social arena, are intimately linked.

In Salem the conflict is not merely one between rich and poor, but is at the same time an inner conflict, as is borne out by the frenetic, hysterical defence against the material seductions of Satan. As Boyer and Nissenbaum explained (1974: 210):

> The witchcraft testimony itself makes plain that even those who felt most uneasy about those developments [growing prosperity] were also deeply attracted by them. For one of Satan's most insidious guises in Salem Village during 1692 was that of thriving freeholder and prosperous merchant.

In their theatrical performances, Salem's 'witch bitches' struggled fiercely against the enticements of the devil. Revealing for the inner conflict is the readiness of the accusers to flaunt their own witchcraft. Particularly during the period when rich merchants were accused, some girls started to accuse themselves as well, indicating thereby that the danger should not be regarded as external only, but was directly linked to their own psychic motives (Boyer and Nissenbaum 1974: 211).

In Sweden also, a profound fascination with opulence shines through. In the girls' imaginings of the Devil, he wears the grey and grubby farmer's smock while the rest of his clothes, with their remarkable ribbons and gaudy trimmings, seems to have come from a different planet. With the help of the Devil bewitched persons can fly right through window panes, visiting not the humble abodes of peasants, but the town houses of wealthy people.

Among the Tapanahoni River Ndyuka the situational background was similar. Vernon's *aperçu* as to the ambivalence about money, quoted above, reveals the intensity of the desire it is capable of inciting: 'This thing they call money is a terrible thing. As soon as you see it, your whole body begins to tremble' (1985:15).

The demon, Devil and witch beliefs betray the constitutive role of desire in the shaping of collective fantasies. And desire is double-edged in this case: one wants to partake in a more exciting world and yet fears disenchantment. Dream-like scenarios speak of high hopes but doubtful outcomes.

Notes

1. This essay is a revised and condensed edition of two earlier publications (Thoden van Velzen and Van Wetering 1982, 1989). We are grateful to Peter Geschiere and Hans de Waardt for their comments on the first draft of this paper. Much has been written about the subject since 1982. The strong relationship between modernity and witchcraft has recently been powerfully restated by Geschiere (1997).

    Most of the data used here have been gathered in eleven periods of anthropological fieldwork in the Tapanahoni area of eastern Suriname. The first fieldwork in 1961 and 1962 took eighteen months, the other periods varied in duration from some months to some weeks. The shorter trips were undertaken in the period 1965–91; on some occasions both authors worked simultaneously in the same village, in other years at different times in different villages.

2. Freud's style of thinking, Turner discloses (1978: 582), enabled him to arrive at an independent theoretical position. It was not Freud's actual inventory of concepts and hypotheses that provided the inspiration. These, in Turner's view, could not literally or mechanically be applied to the data he collected. Nevertheless, he makes ample use of Freud's ideas and borrows many terms from *The Interpretation*. Recently, Turner's indebtedness to Freud has been re-evaluated. Elliott Oring (1993) has argued that Turner's conceptualisation of symbolism is derived directly from Freud, that it was not merely a style of thinking, but an entire theory that was adopted. This is not the place to delve deeply into the argument, or into the reasons why the extent of Freud's influence upon one of the main anthropological approaches to symbolism was masked. The issue is touched upon here merely to explain the option chosen to turn directly to Freud's work on dream mechanisms, without the mediation of earlier anthropological work.

3. Taussig suggests that the faculties of imagining and understanding of large groups of their own social conditions had been severely impaired: 'The advance of market organisation not only tears asunder feudal ties and strips the peasantry of its means of production but also tears asunder a way of seeing' (1980:

121). We hesitate to subscribe to such a position. In our view, certain social categories, especially those occupying a precarious position in the economic structure of society, will rapidly engender new representations, often of a fantastic and absurd kind, but never inconsequential for society's fate.

4. Maroons are the descendants of slaves who escaped from the plantations in preceding centuries, and built new communities along the rivers in Suriname's rain forest. From very early on – 1800 or even earlier – Maroons participated in the colonial and postcolonial economy.

5. During the 1920s, for many years, Van Lier was in daily contact with Ndyuka of the Tapanahoni area, where he worked as a civil servant (see de Groot 1969).

6. See: Herskovits and Herskovits 1936: 105, Herskovits 1958: 254, Van Lier 1940: 228, Vernon 1980: 4.

7. The most important sources are Green (1974), Lenoir (1973), van Wetering (1992) and Vernon (1980, 1985). During the early 1960s, we collected information about demons at the anti-witchcraft shrine of *Gaan Tata* in Diitabiki on the Tapanahoni River (Thoden van Velzen & Van Wetering 1988). Data on the upsurge of demon beliefs on the Tapanahoni were collected during field work periods in 1987, 1988, 1989 and 1991.

8. The section on the new wave of demon mediumship is taken from Thoden van Velzen (1997).

9. A term taken from Obeyesekere (1990: 237) which we use as a synonym for 'dramatisation ', Freud's third dream mechanism.

10. We are obliged to Nellejet Zorgdrager for a translation of relevant parts from B. Ankarloo's doctoral dissertation (1971), by far the most important source on the social dynamics of the Swedish witch craze. An excerpt of the witches' confessions at Mora appeared in a Dutch booklet (Anonymous 1670); it would later be used by Joseph Glanvill (1681) and Balthasar Bekker (1691–93) for his *Betoverde Weereld* (The Bewitched World). The pivotal place of copper mining in the Swedish economy of the 16th and 17th centuries is discussed by Hekscher (1954: 79) and Mead (1981: 83–87).

11. Bekker's aim was to demonstrate that the evidence furnished by the interrogators was false and absurd. Ankarloo (1990: 317) mentions the parish vicar Elaus Skragge as responsible for the excerpt of 1670 of the Royal Commissioners' report on their investigation in Mora. We have not been able to confirm this. Copies of this booklet in the *Koninklijke Bibliotheek* in The Hague carry no author's name. It is filed under # 9815, section 'Oude documenten'. Bekker's (1691–93) and Glanvill's (1681) renditions of the excerpt are only different in some details.

12. These eighteen sentences were reconsidered by a higher court. There was one acquittal, and four children aged from nine to twelve years received a mitigated punishment. One of the suspects died before judgement had been passed. Twelve condemned persons were executed in Ålvdalen in May 1669 (Ankarloo 1971: 118, 120). The accusers almost invariably were children, varying in age from nine to seventeen years. The witches were mostly women, sometimes the girls' age-mates, but more often their mothers or grandmothers. It seems noteworthy that a result of the long period of war was a high surplus of women (Friberg 1953: 229–41).

13. 'Land use was extensive, with pastoralism, hunting, and slash-and-burn agriculture on sparsely scattered single farms. This is the area of the violent witchcraze in the 1670s' (Ankarloo 1990: 285).

14. It is interesting to note Ankarloo's remark: 'The spatial and temporal distribution of the craze is a matter of great interest. From the nucleus area around lake Siljan in Dalarna the trials spread north and north-east. The mining district in the southern parts of the province [around Falun] was completely spared' (1990: 300).

15. To a large extent the wars were financed by the sale of copper. Most of the ore was extracted from the Falun mine, making it the motor of the Swedish war economy (Roberts 1973, 1979).

16. 'Nothing else than that? Yes, but all of this will undoubtedly be better than what they have in their houses' (Bekker 1691–93, 4: 220).

17. Only very rarely did the judges have recourse to torture; it was forbidden in Swedish legal proceedings (Ankarloo 1990: 290).

18. On collective fantasies as a key concept in anthropology, see Thoden van Velzen (1995).

19. 'The process by which two (or more) images combine (or can be combined) to form a composite image which is invested with meaning and energy derived from both' (Rycroft 1972: 22).

References

Ankarloo, B., 1971, *Trolldomsprocesserna i Sverige*. Stockholm: A. B. Nordiska Bokhandeln.

Ankarloo, B., 1983, 'Das Geschrei der ungebildeten Masse: Zur Analyse der schwedischen Hexenprozesse', in Degn, C., Lehmann, H. and Unverhau, D., eds, *Hexenprozesse: Deutsche und skandinavische Beiträge*. Neumünster: Karl Wachholtz Verlag.

Ankarloo, B., 1990, 'Sweden: The Mass Burnings (1668-1676)' in Ankarloo, B. and Henningsen, G., eds, *Early Modern European Witchcraft: Centres and Peripheries*. Oxford: Clarendon Press.

Anonymous, *Translaet uyt het Sweets, . . . over de ontdeckte toveryen in het dorp Mohra, en d'omleggende plaetsen*, 's Gravenhage, 1670 [Filed in the Koninklijke Bibliotheek, The Hague, section Oude documenten, under # 9815].

Baschwitz, K., 1966, *Hexen und Hexenprozesse: Die Geschichte eines Massenwahns*. München: Deutscher Taschenbuch Verlag.

Bekker, B., 1691–93, *De betoverde Weereld* (The Bewitched World). Amsterdam: Daniel van den Dalen, 4 vols.

Boyer, P. and Nissenbaum, S., 1974, *Salem Possessed: The Social Origins of Witchcraft*. Cambridge, Mass.: Harvard University Press.

Cohn, N., 1975, *Europe's Inner Demons: An Enquiry Inspired by the Great Witch Hunt*. London: Chatto.

Crick, M., 1982, 'Recasting Witchcraft' in Marwick, M., ed., *Witchcraft and Sorcery*. Harmondsworth: Penguin.

Demos, J. P., 1982, *Entertaining Satan: Witchcraft and the Culture of Early New England*. Oxford: Oxford University Press.

Durkheim, E., 1925, *Les Formes Elémentaires de la Vie Religieuse: Le Système Totemique en Australie*. Paris: Librarie Felix Alcan, 2nd edn.

Elias, N. and Scotson, J. L., 1994 [1965], *The Established and the Outsiders*. London: Sage.

Freud, S., 1962 [1900], *The Interpretation of Dreams*. The Standard Edition of the Complete Works of Sigmund Freud. London: The Hogarth Press, vols 3 and 4.

Friberg, N., 1953, 'Dalarnas befolkning på 1600-talet', *Geografiska Annaler*, 35: 145–415.

Geschiere, P., 1997, *The Modernity of Witchcraft: Politics and the Occult in Post-colonial Africa*. Charlottesville/London: University Press of Virginia.

Glanvill, J., 1978 [1681], *Saducismus Triumphatus*. London. [Facsimile edition of the Collected Works of Joseph Glanvill, vol IX. Hildesheim/New York: Georg Olms].

Green, E., 1974, *The Matawai Maroons: An Acculturating Afro-American Society*. Ph.D. dissertation, The Catholic University of America.

de Groot, S. W., 1969, *Djuka Society and Social Change: History of an Attempt to Develop a Bush Negro Community in Surinam, 1917–1926*. Assen: Van Gorcum.

Hekscher, E. F., 1954, *An Economic History of Sweden*. Cambridge, Mass.: Harvard University Press.

Herskovits, M. J., 1958 [1941], *The Myth of the Negro Past*. Boston: Beacon Press.

Herskovits, M. J. and Herskovits, F. S., 1936, *Suriname Folk-Lore*. New York: Columbia University Contributions to Anthropology 27.

Laplanche, J. and Pontalis, J. B., 1988, *The Language of Psychoanalysis*. London: The Hogarth Press.

Lenoir, J. D., 1973, *The Paramaka Maroons: A Study in Religious Acculturation*. Ph.D. dissertation, The New School for Social Research.

van Lier, W. F., 1940, 'Aanteekeningen over het geestelijk leven en de samenleving der Djoeka's (Aukaner Boschnegers) in Suriname', *Bijdragen tot de Taal-, Land- en Volkenkunde van Nederlandsch-Indië*, 99 (2): 131–294.

van Lier, W. F., 1945, *Een en ander over het wisi-begrip bij de Boschnegers*. Paramaribo: Oliviera.

Marwick, M., 1970, 'Witchcraft as a Social Strain-Gauge', in Marwick, M., ed., *Witchcraft and Sorcery: Selected Readings*. Harmondsworth: Penguin.

Mead, W. R., 1981, *A Historical Geography of Scandinavia*. London: Academic Press.

Obeyesekere, G., 1990, *The Work of Culture: Symbolic Transformation in Psychoanalysis and Anthropology*. Chicago: The University of Chicago Press.

Oring, E., 1993, 'Victor Turner, Sigmund Freud, and the Return of the Repressed', *Ethos* 21, 3: 273–94.

Roberts, M., 1973, *Sweden's Age of Greatness: 1632–1718*. London: MacMillan.

Roberts, M., 1979, *The Swedish Imperial Experience: 1560–1718*. Cambridge: Cambridge University Press.

Rycroft, C., 1972 [1968], *A Critical Dictionary of Psychoanalysis*. Harmondsworth: Penguin.

Taussig, M. T., 1980, *The Devil and Commodity Fetishism in South America*. Chapel Hill: University of North Carolina Press.

Thoden van Velzen, H. U. E., 1995, 'Revenants that Cannot be Shaken: Collective Fantasies in a Maroon Society', *American Anthropologist*, 97 (4): 722–32.

Thoden van Velzen, H. U. E., 1997, 'Dramatization: How Dream Work Shapes Culture', *The Psychoanalytic Review*, 84 (2): 173–88.

Thoden van Velzen, H.U.E. and Van Wetering, W., 1982, 'Voorspoed, angsten en demonen', *Antropologische Verkenningen*, 1 (2): 85–118.

Thoden van Velzen, H. U. E. and Van Wetering, W., 1988, *The Great Father and The Danger: Religious Cults, Material Forces, and Collective Fantasies of the Surinamese Maroons*. Leiden: Koninklijk Instituut voor Taal-, Land- en Volkenkunde; Caribbean Series 9.

Thoden van Velzen, H. U. E. and Van Wetering, W., 1989, 'Demonologie en de betovering van het moderne leven', *Sociologische Gids*, 36: 155–86.

Thomas, K., 1971, *Religion and the Decline of Magic: Studies in Popular Beliefs in Sixteenth and Seventeenth Century England*. London: Weidenfeld.

Turner, V. W., 1964, 'Witchcraft and sorcery: taxonomy versus dynamics', *Africa*, 34: 314–24.

Turner, V. W., 1978, 'Encounter with Freud: the making of a comparative symbologist', in Spindler, G. D., ed., *The Making of Psychological Anthropology*. Berkeley: University of California Press.

Vernon,D., 1980, 'Bakuu: Possessing Spirits of Witchcraft on the Tapanahony', *Nieuwe West-Indische Gids*, 54: 1–30.

Vernon, D., 1985, *Money Magic in a Modernizing Maroon Society*. Tokyo: Ilcaa.

de Waardt, H., 1989, 'Met bloed ondertekend', *Sociologische Gids*, 36: 224–44.

Wall, J., 1978, *Tjuvmjölkande Väsen: ii Yngre nordisk tradition* (with an English summary: Magical milk-stealing creatures in later Nordic tradition). Uppsala: Almqvist & Wiksell International.

van Wetering, W., 1973, 'Witchcraft among the Tapanahoni Djuka', in Price, R., ed., *Maroon Societies: Rebel Slave Communities in the Americas*. Garden City (N.Y.): Anchor Press.

van Wetering, W., 1992, 'A Demon in Every Transistor', *Etnofoor*, 5 (1/2): 109–27.

Wolf, E. R., 1999, *Envisioning Power: Ideologies of Dominance and Crisis*. Berkeley, Los Angeles, London: University of California Press.

2

Witchcraft and New Forms of Wealth: Regional Variations in South and West Cameroon

Peter Geschiere

University of Leiden

Introduction[1]

In Africa, globalisation may be mostly *lécher la vitrine* – 'licking at the shop-window' – as Achille Mbembe (1998) puts it so aptly. Yet, the drive towards consumerism is no less intense here. To many Africans, the new consumer goods remain a dream. The happy few who do get access to them, seem to relish them all the more. Cameroon is certainly no exception in this respect. In his fascinating book *L'Esprit d'entreprise au Cameroon*, Warnier writes: 'The taste of Cameroonians for everything which is imported rather than produced locally is proverbial' (Warnier 1993: 163, my translation. See also Rowlands n.d. and Geschiere & Rowlands 1996).[2]

To many Cameroonians, imported goods have become crucial in the definition and the expression of their identity. People use these goods in their own ways to mark their place in the 'material civilisation of success': these goods '... embody the image of what one desires to be' (Warnier 1993: 169, my translation). Many Western observers may view this obsession with modern forms of consumerism in Cameroon, and in Africa in general, with some irony. Yet in Cameroon at least – in contrast to many parts of the West – people are still self-conscious about this phenomenon. Radio

Trottoir is a constant source of jokes on the Cameroonian obsession with 'modern' things: on the fact that, till recently, Cameroon was one of the main importers of French champagne (and it is true that the *préfet* of Abong-Mbang, deep in the 'backward' East Province, used to celebrate his little daughter's birthday with two crates of vintage champagne); on the elite who can only drink the best Scotch whisky; or on the *filles libres* of Yaunde with their war-cry: 'Get lost poor sot, you do not even have a Pajero.'[3]

However, this obsession with modern goods has its reverse in a deep mistrust of where these goods come from. Radio Trottoir is also full of stories on the theme of how arrogance is punished. In some parts of the East, people say that a man who plants a cocoa tree 'will not live to reap its fruits.' And my fellow-travellers during long, long trips in a *taxi-brousse* have often explained to me why there is a grave before each modern house along the roadside: these are the last resting places of the owners who had shown too much ambition by constructing such an impressive house. Indeed, it is only to be expected that such a mixture of fascination and rejection, as in people's perceptions of the new symbols of wealth, is a true breeding ground for all sorts of *bricolages* with the old themes of witchcraft and sorcery.[4]

In Cameroon, as elsewhere in Africa, witchcraft and modernity seem to be closely interconnected. One of the most striking aspects of recent developments in the continent is the often frightening vitality of conceptions of the occult, especially in the more modern sectors of life: in politics and in new forms of entrepreneurship, in sports (football!) and in the schools or the bureaucracy. To many, these conceptions seem to offer the obvious discourse to interpret – or even try to control – the modern changes and notably the new inequalities: the spectacular successes of the few and the failures of the many to get access to the new forms of wealth.[5]

It is important to underline that the resilience of witchcraft fantasies is not just proof of the tenacity of some sort of a 'traditional' relict. The fact that these ideas seem to retain their relevance precisely in more modern settings of society indicates that such a view – apparently quite tempting, since it is so common – is too simplistic. It is true that witchcraft notions inspire gruesome fantasies about how the *nouveaux riches* are finally punished because of their selfish accumulation of the new forms of riches (See Taussig 1980). Yet, it is clear also that these fantasies do not just reflect a 'traditional' refusal of the new forms of wealth. They seem to express, at the same time and often in a most confusing mixture, people's fascination with the goods that symbolise these new riches and the open-endedness of their global flows.

It is, indeed, surprising that until recently anthropologists – despite the discipline's 'traditional' interest in witchcraft and sorcery – had so little to say about the impact of these discourses in modern settings.[6] There are several reasons for this.[7] An important one is, no doubt, that anthropologists have not been very successful – to put it mildly – in deconstructing the current stereotype, mentioned above, of sorcery/witchcraft as a 'traditional' barrier, blocking development and change. This stereotype is also very common in the societies involved. In Cameroon, for instance, I repeatedly heard civil servants admonish the villagers in no uncertain terms that they should stop sabotaging development projects with their *sorcellerie*. Public debates on 'Witchcraft and Development' seem to start from the premise that the first is the 'traditional' counterpoint to the latter. Witchcraft is closely linked to jealousy, and the fear of it would, therefore, discourage people from participating in development projects. This view is also generally shared by Western development experts who are only interested in witchcraft as another 'traditional' barrier to 'Development.'

Classical anthropology, with its static view of 'traditional' societies, largely contributed to this stereotype. Indeed, anthropologists still seem to have considerable difficulty in liberating themselves from this perspective. In 1988, Thoden van Velzen and van Wetering still concluded (1988: 399):

> Despite passionate proclamations to the contrary, most theories and approaches in anthropology will represent a peripheral, (post)tribal or traditional society as 'backward looking'. Particularly when searches for witches are organised and spirits called upon to legitimate political action, a society is diagnosed as being on the defensive, aiming at a restoration of the social relations and values of the past.

Some may prefer to avoid terms like 'post-tribal' or 'traditional societies', but the overall trend of this quote is very apposite. Anthropologists might make more of an effort to convince development experts, journalists and other observers that the stereotype of witchcraft discourses as 'traditional' residues, by definition opposed to change, is one-sided. In Africa there are, as indicated above, many examples where discourses on the occult forces do express a refusal of change. However, there are also many counter-examples showing that such discourses reflect a determined struggle to get access to new forms of wealth. As Thoden van Velzen and van Wetering put it, '(These) collective fantasies are more than harmless 'thought experiments' about modern conditions. They enhance the readiness of disciples to try new courses of action' (1988: 401). The resilience of witchcraft – and fantasies on the occult in general – in modern settings can only be understood from such a perspective.

In earlier publications we – Cyprian Fisiy, my Cameroonian co-author, and I – emphasised the basic ambivalence, crucial in this respect in these discourses between a 'levelling' and an 'accumulative' tenor.[8] They have always 'levelling' implications since they are related to jealousy and thus seem to encourage attacks on inequalities in wealth and power. However, this is often balanced by 'accumulative' implications: the same discourse can also serve to protect or reinforce the accumulation of wealth and power. Moreover, the balance between 'levelling' and 'accumulative' implications may vary in time and space.

This ambiguity becomes especially manifest when these discourses are used to interpret modern changes. Rumours about new and therefore particularly frightening forms of witchcraft – such as the ones discussed below – express a deep distrust of the new forms of wealth. In this sense, they do reflect the stereotype of witchcraft as a 'traditional' barrier against development and progress. However, this should not mask the other side: the effort to gain access to the new forms of wealth by the same discourse. On the one hand, the new rich are associated with the occult in order to make them suspect, but on the other, the rich themselves can use such associations to protect themselves against jealousy and occult aggression. It is precisely because of this ambiguity that these notions become a kind of *passe-partout*, a panacea that can explain anything – including the baffling modern changes. This ambiguity is not particular to witchcraft discourses or to the African context. As Johannes Fabian remarks, referring to Michel Foucault, 'It is precisely their dispersal in many kinds of expression that makes tenets of a discourse 'central', in the sense of being ideologically and practically effective' (Fabian 1990: 39). Their basic fluidity, that allows for all sorts of interpretations, makes these discourses so all-pervasive, even in modern contexts.

Another ambiguity, of special relevance in the context of this collection, is the confusing relationship between notions of 'evil' and 'good' in these fantasies. It is true that rumours about the novel forms of witchcraft of the *nouveaux riches* – and about the occult forces in general – have a highly moralising tenor. Yet, the precise distinction between 'good' and 'evil' is always subject to constant re-interpretation. In practice, these conceptions often have a strikingly a-moral impact. This moral ambiguity is, again, crucial to understand the all-pervasiveness of these discourses, their vicious circles and the ease with which they absorb modern changes.

In Cameroon, such reflections on the new forms of wealth and their relation to witchcraft find expression in rumours about a novel form of witchcraft that bears various names: *ekong, nyongo, famla, kupe, kong.* The basic idea, however, is the same: there is a new type of witches who no longer eat their victims but transforms them into a kind of zombie and puts them to work in 'invisible plantations'. The new riches are supposed to be accumulated by the exploitation of these zombies' labour. People insist on the novelty of this form of witchcraft and they often relate it to the arrival of the Europeans and the introduction of new luxury items. Since colonial times, but especially after Independence, these representations rapidly spread throughout southern and western Cameroon. Precisely because they concern a new form of witchcraft, they created general fear, and uncertainty in all these regions. However, people try to deal with this new threat in different ways. Apparently, some societies are more uncertain than others about how to contain this threat.

Because of this variability, the *ekong* conceptions – and notions of zombie-witchcraft in general – can offer a good starting point for exploring different trajectories in the relation between global commodities and popular discourses on occult forces.[9] Of special interest is that these discourses seem to make a determined effort to relate 'consumption' to 'production.' They speculate, albeit following different scenarios, on the enigmatic origin of new goods. This popular preoccupation with production, even if it is expressed in exuberant fantasies, merits closer attention. In a more general perspective it poses a true challenge in the face of the tendency, now more and more general not only among economists but also among social scientists, to interpret economic changes in terms of consumption or 'the market.'

The Bakweri: *nyongo* witchcraft and the 'banana boom'

For Cameroon, the classical study of the relation between modern changes and transformations of witchcraft is Edwin Ardener's

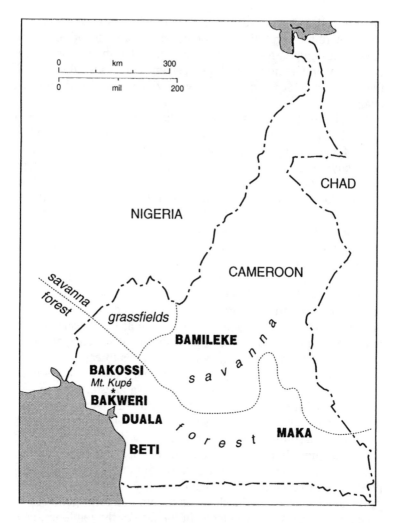

article of 1970. In this study he analyzed how, in the 1950s, the Bakweri broke through the *nyongo* terror and thus could profit from the 'banana boom'.

The Bakweri are a small group (now about 16,000 persons) living on the steep but fertile slopes of Mt. Cameroon, near the coast in Southwest Cameroon. Prior to the colonial conquest (1894), they formed a highly segmentary society, dominated by an egalitarian ideology. Ardener emphasises that there were nonetheless strong tendencies toward accumulation, notably of goats, pigs and dwarf cattle. But such tendencies were restricted by the belief in *liemba* (witchcraft) which was – and still is – closely linked to jealousy. To protect oneself against this threat, the wealth which a family head had accumulated had to be regularly destroyed in big *potlatch*-like ceremonies. It was especially by such ostentatious destruction that a man reinforced his prestige among his fellow-villagers.

The Germans, the first colonisers of Cameroon, quickly discovered that the volcanic soil around Mt. Cameroon was very fertile. Already in the 1880s, they started to appropriate land in order to create large-scale plantations. This process was accelerated after the definitive 'pacification' of the Bakweri in the next decade. The Bakweri themselves were confined to reservations higher up the mountains. Thus, the Germans hoped to force them to come and work on the plantations. However, right from the beginning, the Bakweri showed little enthusiasm to do this. Also after 1914, when the British conquered this part of Cameroon, the Bakweri kept apart from the plantation sector. The consequence was that they were marginalised in their own area. The plantations attracted ever more labourers from elsewhere and especially after 1940 the Bakweri rapidly became a minority in their own villages. The 'strangers' profited much more from the new economic opportunities and the colonial reports began to oppose these strangers' spirit of enterprise to the Bakweri 'apathy'. The latter did not seem capable of defending their own lands or even their women. They sold or rented their land to 'strangers', and their women left them to live in concubinage or even as prostitutes among these same strangers who seemed better able to maintain them. In 1952, when the Ardeners arrived in the region, the Bakweri appeared to be threatened with extinction. This was often blamed on Bakweri 'laziness' and 'apathy', which became fixed elements of the ethnic stereotype of this group and remain such to the present day.

The Bakweri themselves tended to relate their restraint in the face of new economic opportunities to their fear of a novel form of witchcraft, called *nyongo*. *Nyongo* was closely linked to wealth, and it was especially the new rich who were suspected of being *nyongo* witches. Like all witches, they were supposed to kill their own relatives. But the new thing about *nyongo* was that these witches did not eat their victims but turned them into a kind of zombies (*vekongi*). *Nyongo* witches were supposed to transport their victims in a lorry to Mt. Kupé, more than 60 miles to the north of Bakweriland, where they had to work on 'invisible plantations'. A *nyongo* man was to be recognised especially by his modern house with a tinned roof, which he had only been able to build thanks to his profit from the zombies' labour. But a *nyongo* man was always in danger. He had to go on 'selling' his intimates to his co-witches. If he were no longer able to offer somebody, his colleagues would kill him and reduce him to slavery in his turn.

Ardener indicates that these ideas constituted an obstacle to economic initiative. The villagers hardly dared build modern houses. The few houses of this type, built by Bakweri clerks and other 'carpetbaggers', remained empty. Nobody dared pass the night there for fear of the *vekongi* (zombies). The new forms of wealth were considered dangerous since they automatically made one suspected of *nyongo*.

The *nyongo* belief seems to be a good example of witchcraft as a 'traditional' obstacle to development. Therefore, it seems relevant to stress that to the Bakweri this *nyongo* was anything but 'traditional'. On the contrary, they insisted that, before the arrival of the Europeans, their ancestors had not known *nyongo*. It had been introduced by the Duala, the first traders to come into contact with the Europeans. It had been the Duala who had taught Bakweri witches how to turn their victims into zombies and become rich by their labour.[10]

The *nyongo* by itself is therefore a sign of the dynamic of this witchcraft discourse rather than a 'traditional relic'. But other and even more spectacular changes were to follow. In 1951, several Bakweri intellectuals founded the 'Bakweri Cooperative Union of Farmers'. The Cooperative propagated the cultivation of bananas in order to profit from new opportunities, due especially to better means of transport to Europe. In 1953, the first sale of bananas under the auspices of the Cooperative clearly showed how much money could be earned this way. Under these circumstances, the Bakweri proved to be far from 'apathetic'. More and more villagers started to cultivate bananas and ever more money flowed into the villages. As Ardener (1970: 149) puts it: 'the 'banana boom' created an *embarras de richesse*' (See also S. Ardener 1958).

These economic changes reinforced the people's worries about witchcraft. Ardener describes how, in 1955, *nyongo* accusations rocketed. Young men dramatically accused the elders of attacking them with their *nyongo*. Finally a '*nyongo* doctor' in Lysoka village made the village council look for support elsewhere. Money was collected to send a delegation to the Banyangi near Mamfe, 150 miles to the north, in order to buy a new *juju* – a powerful spirit – strong enough to resist the *nyongo*. The delegation returned with the message that the Banyangi wanted more money. But even this extra sum was rapidly collected. Finally, the Banyangi agreed to come with their famous Obasinjom – a powerful *juju* which, incidentally, they themselves had borrowed a few decades earlier from the Ejagham in Nigeria (Ruell 1969: 210).

Seven weeks later, the Banyangi made a triumphant entry into Lysoka: a group of wild dancers in long robes, and in their midst a fearsome crocodile mask – Obasinjom himself. Ardener (1970: 152) described the ensuing events in lyrical terms: 'The marvels of the succeeding days passed expectations'. Witches were flushed out and disarmed in large numbers.[11] The Banyangi trained thirty doctors capable of performing Obasinjom and they left a powerful fetish to protect the village. Other villages followed the Lysoka example and invited Banyangi doctors to found an Obasinjom lodge with them as well. Altogether, the Bakweri would have paid more than £2,000 sterling of the banana money to the Banyangi doctors.

Ardener emphasises that at the very same time a true building craze began. He often could hardly hear his informants' stories about *nyongo* and Obasinjom because of the noisy construction of tin roofs. The *nyongo* ban on modern houses and on individual enrichment in general, was broken. A one informant put it: '*Nyongo* is gone, there is Obasinjom instead' (Ardener 1970: 154).

However, the story did not end with this 'happy scene', so vividly depicted by Ardener. After 1963, the Bakweri farmers lost their privileged access to the British market, because of the unification with former French Cameroon and the new State's association with the EEC. The Bakweri interest in banana cultivation was immediately over. In 1987, when I worked in the area, people suggested that *nyongo* was still there but that it was more or less under control. Obasinjom had not danced for years. According to several people, he was 'something of the past'. However, in 1988 things again changed suddenly. Obasinjom began to make his appearance once more, especially in the mountain villages, to expose *nyongo* witches. Several people related this resurrection to the new austerity measures, announced by President Paul Biya in 1987, the effects of which began to be felt in 1988. Others said simply that they had made Obasinjom come out again 'because there was too much witchcraft'.

An old chief in Buea gave me a more specific explanation. According to him, Obasinjom had come out by himself because he was so angry with the old men who were his guardians: they had become too corrupt and accepted money from the *nyongo* witches 'just like the policemen do'. Consequently, several old witch-doctors abruptly died, victims of Obasinjom's anger. That is why hardly anybody was left who knew the *juju*'s secrets. And indeed, in several villages, people had been obliged to go and buy the *juju* from the Banyangi once more, again at a high price.

When I returned in 1992, the situation had changed once more. Obasinjom had again stopped dancing. According to several informants – mostly young men – this was because people found out that the *juju* was corrupted by the elders who continued to use Obasinjom to enrich themselves. As yet, no new way had been found to combat the *nyongo*.

These dramatic and rapidly changing stories about *nyongo* and Obasinjom – summarised here in a far too schematic form – are characteristic of the ambiguity of discourses on the occult in their relation to modern changes. At first sight Obasinjom seemed to bring a definitive breakthrough in the witchcraft ban on the new riches. According to Ardener, he liberated these from the suspicion of *nyongo*. But one may wonder whether this rupture was indeed definitive. After all, Obasinjom himself does belong also to the shadowy world of the occult. And the more recent developments among the Bakweri indicated that he also could be corrupted by the elders, who are, everywhere in Africa, the true masters of the occult domain.[12]

One wonders also whether Ardener's heavy accent on the conceptual continuity among the Bakweri, despite all the changes, was completely justified. He concluded that the innovations in the sphere of witchcraft, such as the *nyongo* or Obasinjom, had to be interpreted as variable but repetitive emanations of a basic conceptual 'template' which continued to determine the Bakweri reactions. Ardener does indeed sketch a fascinating historical perspective, but his approach seems to neglect the novelty of these transformations in the witchcraft discourse – the fact that they reflected a determined struggle to cope with really new circumstances. This aspect is all the more interesting since the *nyongo* notion followed different trajectories in other regions.

The Maka and the *Sorcellerie des Blancs*

I was fascinated by the stories about *nyongo* and Obasinjom among the Bakweri since I had heard surprisingly similar stories among the Maka, 400 miles away in the forests of the Eastern Province of Cameroon, where I have been doing field-work since 1971. One of the first topics I worked upon in this area was the impact of cocoa-cultivation on the village economy (Geschiere 1982). At that time, several Maka villagers told me that it was only fairly recently that they had dared to start their own cocoa plantations. They made me understand – by more or less hidden allusions – that 'not long ago' people had been afraid to plant a cocoa tree, 'since everybody knew that a man would not live to reap the fruits of a tree he had planted'. The idea was that the witches' jealousy would be lethal to anyone who tried to profit from the new opportunities for enrichment. Moreover, the Maka, like the Bakweri, explicitly focused these fears on the new tin houses. In 1971, people still told mocking stories about rich farmers who did not dare to sleep in the prestigious house they had built because they were afraid of being attacked by their jealous kin. In 1971, everybody agreed that the Maka had overcome these old fears. The villagers did sleep in their new tin houses and many had created cocoa plantations.

However, when I made a short trip further into the interior, to Yokaduma, close to the border with the Central African Republic, I noted that similar fears were still very much alive there. In this more isolated region, the spread of cocoa cultivation had only just started and one of the reasons the villagers gave for this delay was the old adage of a man not living to reap the fruits from a tree he had planted. A comparison of the Bakweri, Maka and Yokaduma examples seems, at first sight, a striking confirmation of the stereotype of witchcraft as a 'traditional' barrier which has to be overcome, in one region after another, before 'Development' can take off. Among the Bakweri, near the coast, this threshold had been crossed already in the 1950s; among the Maka, further into the interior, this occurred later; and in Yokaduma, this transition had not yet really taken place in 1971.[13] But, of course, on closer inspection, such a linear vision turns out to be too simplistic. It rather seems that the logic of the local discourses on witchcraft and inequality imposed their own dynamics on the developments in each of these regions.

When I asked my Maka informants how they had overcome the witchcraft ban against the planting of cocoa trees and the building of modern houses, their reply was simple. Things had changed 'by themselves'. Enterprising villagers had had the courage to plant cocoa trees despite all the warnings, and they had not died. On the contrary, they acquired a new prestige in the village as 'grands planteurs'. Similarly, the Maka had learnt from the example of a few diehards that one could sleep under a tin roof without being bewitched. However, I soon realised that this explanation was too simple. As always when witchcraft is involved, things turned out to be more complicated.

Incidental remarks indicated that the villagers tended to link these grands planteurs themselves to the world of djambe (witchcraft/sorcery). How else could one explain that they had dared to defy the jealousy of the witches? Apparently, people considered a support in the witchcraft world to be indispensable if one wanted to have success in the new cash-crop economy. People linked these farmers' success to a new form of witchcraft, called the djambe of success or the djambe le mintang, that is the sorcellerie of the Whites. By way of explanation for the latter term, my informants said that the wealth of the grands planteurs was due to a new form of enrichment in which the white man excelled: 'Therefore the djambe of the grands planteurs is like your kind of sorcery'.

It is therefore clear that, among the Maka as well as the Bakweri, the acceptance of the new forms of accumulation did not imply a definite breach in the witchcraft belief; it corresponded rather to a transformation of these notions. As among the Bakweri, the new forms of accumulation turned out to be protected by the belief in the occult powers. Yet, there were important differences as well.

Initially, modern developments among the Maka and the Bakweri corresponded in many respects. The Maka also formed a highly segmented society until the colonial conquest (1906–10), and they proved even more difficult to mobilise for the mise en valeur of their area, which came under French rule, after 1914. The French officials never tired of complaining about la douce inertie of the Maka and their esprit réfractaire. To them, the only remedy was l'obligation au travail. Yet despite continuous coercion by the government, it proved to be very difficult to make the Maka produce any surplus for the colonial trade. It was only after 1945 that relations became less strained. Then, the villagers gradually began to plant coffee and cocoa on their own initiative. But despite these resemblances, the interaction between new opportunities and occult forces followed a different path.

The Bakweri imported Obasinjom from outside to break the nyongo terror. The Maka, by contrast, found a solution within their own witchcraft discourse by linking their grands planteurs directly to the djambe (witchcraft). This difference might be related to the very broad meaning of the key notion – *djambe* – which seems to have much wider implications than the parallel Bakweri notion of *liemba*. *Djambe* and *liemba* have many parallels (indeed, they probably stem from the same linguistic root). *Djambe* is also closely linked to jealousy. A *djindjamb* ('one who has *djambe*') is supposed to leave his body by night and fly away to meet his companions. Together they attack their victim in his sleep and eat his heart. Like the *liemba*, the *djambe* seeks out its victims especially among close kin. For the Maka, however, these shocking practices are only one facet of the *djambe* – maybe the most fascinating aspect but certainly not the only one. The Maka speak also about the *djambe idjuga* (the *sorcellerie* of authority), which is indispensable to chiefs, or the *djambe le dombe* (*sorcellerie* of war), which made the great warriors of former times invincible – and which, according to some, still serves football players in their matches against strangers. The word *djambe* is sometimes used in such a general sense – for instance, when a host is praised for his *djambe* because he receives his guests well – that it can only be translated as some sort of special energy. However – and this is crucial to understand the role of *djambe* in daily life – these more positive aspects of *djambe* are intrinsically linked to its dark core of the witches' nightly escapades and their cannibalistic attacks on kin. There may be different sides to the *djambe* but it is one entity. A brief example will illustrate this.

> Mr. Zog was the richest planter of the village where I lived. Several neighbours hinted that he doubtlessly knew his way in the *djambe* world. How else would he have dared challenge the witches with his new kind of wealth? On closer questioning, it turned out that these informants did not really believe Zog had left his body at night to fly away and pursue sinister plans. They rather meant that Zog knew how to defend himself with the *djambe*. However, when several of Zog's relatives fell ill, people began to whisper about Zog's powerful *djambe*. After all, the *djambe* can be used for many purposes, constructive as well as destructive, and one can never be sure how a person will use his *djambe*.

The moral implications of the *djambe* belief are consequently fairly ambiguous. The nightly escapades of the witches are shocking and fearsome (and also terribly intriguing) but the same *djambe* can be put to more positive uses as well. What is more, the only real protection against the witches is to be found within the *djambe* sphere itself, by developing one's own *djambe* or by turning to a *nganga* (witch-doctor). This *nganga* can only protect because he or she has a particularly powerful *djambe*: the *nganga* is 'a witch who has beaten all records'. *Djambe* thus becomes a force that a Maka can hardly do without.

In view of the polyvalent nature of the Maka *djambe* belief, it is not surprising that both the new wealth of the *grands planteurs* and the jealous reactions to their success were easily incorporated into the *djambe* discourse. *Djambe* is viewed as the prime form for the expression of jealousy and the strong levelling tendencies within village society. But it is considered to be equally indispensable for anyone who wants to accumulate power and wealth. The Maka are always ready to associate notables and powerful leaders with *djambe*, if only because especially such prominent people must have some sort of protection against the witches' jealousy. The *grands planteurs* had introduced a new form of wealth into the village and were therefore associated with the *djambe* in a similar way.

Striking in this case is the strong circularity of the witchcraft discourse. The new opportunities for enrichment do not seem to undermine the validity of this discourse; instead, they are easily accommodated within it. The Maka representations of the *djambe* of success in relation to the richer farmers offer a perfect example of a 'catch 22': if a farmer dares to defy the witches' jealousy, he must have his own supports in the world of the *djambe*. This makes one wonder if there is ever an escape from the vicious circles of *djambe*.

The Temptations of Mt. Kupé: The Witchcraft of Wealth and Its Variations

The above suggests that there are indeed different trajectories in the interaction between witchcraft discourses and politico-economic changes. Maka and Bakweri discourses followed their own patterns of change which directly affected the ways people reacted to new opportunities for enrichment. In order to elaborate upon this idea of different trajectories, it is interesting to compare the Bakweri *nyongo* ideas with parallel conceptions among neighbouring societies, for the Bakweri obsession with *nyongo* fits in with a broader regional configuration. Similar notions play an important role throughout the Southern and Western parts of Cameroon – among the Duala and Batanga on the coast, but also among the Bakossi and the Beti in the interior, and with particular force still further inland, in the 'Grassfields' of the Western and Northwestern Provinces (among the francophone Bamileke and the anglophone Bamenda). In all these areas, these ideas mark people's reactions to the new forms of wealth, but their exact implications vary considerably.

In these representations, two places are of special importance. First of all Duala, the main port through which the European trade has penetrated the country since the 16th century, and now Cameroon's metropolis. People often say that Duala is also the place from where this new form of witchcraft originated. Secondly, Mount Kupé, 60 miles from the coast in the land of the Bakossi, which has a sinister magical reputation throughout the country. It is there that the witches put their victims to work in the 'invisible plantations'.

Among the Duala, this form of witchcraft is called *ekong*. According to Eric de Rosny – a French priest who had himself been initiated as a *nganga* (witch-doctor) – it is still highly feared in the city. The basic scenario of *ekong* is vividly summarised by Bureau (1962: 141, my translation):

> A person who is interested in *ekong* goes to visit an *ekoneur* (French for '*ekong* owner' – a commonly used neologism), who puts him to sleep by hypnosis. In his dreams, this person will see a land where money flows and many labourers work for him. An estate owner will offer him his plantations on condition that he offers the life of, for instance, his mother in return. His first reaction will be to refuse. When he wakes up, the *ekoneur* will say to him: 'Now you have seen, now you know what you have to do'. His client will ask for some time to think about it. Some day he will make up his mind.[14]

De Rosny gives an equally vivid picture of the other side – the anxiety of the potential victims (1981: 93, my translation):

> When someone dreams that he is taken away, his hands tied, towards the river or the Ocean while he cannot see the face of his capturers, he knows that he has to see a *nganga* as soon as possible.

Ekoneurs are supposed to steal their victims' bodies from the grave and then 'sell' them to one of their customers. In their magical pursuits they use a huge snake, the *nyungu*, which is linked to the rainbow and brings riches.[15]

One can imagine why in these areas an expression like 'I'll sell you' has a particularly ominous ring. Indeed, de Rosny's informants made a direct link between this idea of 'selling someone' and the old slave trade. The same association can be recognised in de Rosny's dream picture of someone being taken away 'to the Ocean', without recognising his capturers. Actually, the Duala and other people in the area still tend to relate *ekong* to the Europeans. This is what de Rosny found out to his distress when he visited an old *nganga* and a chief in a village near Duala, and offered them both a bottle of whisky. When he wanted to leave, he found to his surprise that the road was blocked by the village youth who abused him and refused to let him pass. Apparently, both the chief and the *nganga* were suspected to have the *ekong*. The rumour that a white stranger had come to offer them a present was enough to resurrect old fears of people being sold to the Whites (de Rosny 1981: 93).[16]

De Rosny's spokesmen made a clear distinction between the *ekong*, 'where one kills and sells someone', and older forms of witchcraft (*liemba* or *ewusu*) where the witches eat their victims. The *ekong* is considered to be something new, special to an urban setting. Nonetheless, the Duala seem to have known the *ekong* long before the colonial conquest (1884). In earlier days, the *ekong* was an association of chiefs, notables and traders: it represented *la classe opulente* (De Rosny 1981: 92). But nowadays, the *ekong* has been 'democratised': it is believed to be within everybody's reach and therefore people are even more afraid of it. De Rosny connects this change with the spread of wage labour and the expansion of the money economy. The power to buy and sell is no longer a prerogative of a few family heads and notables. However, this has not made the economy more transparent. The dramatic fluctuations of cash-crop prices and the uncertainties of the labour-market have become crucial to the survival of ever more people but seem to be utterly uncontrollable and unpredictable. One of the attractions of the *ekong* belief is – still according to de Rosny – that is has 'integrated' the mysteries of the market. It continues to be so generally accepted because it can offer an explanation for the growing inequalities of wealth and poverty.

Although Duala is often mentioned as the place of origin of the *ekong*, its centre is now clearly located on Mount Kupé. This is a densely wooded mountain in the heart of the land of the Bakossi who speak of *ekom* to indicate a similar, new form of witchcraft. S.N. Ejedepang-Koge (1971: 200) describes this *ekom* as an 'association' of witches who frequent Mount Kupé in order to obtain riches. The Bakossi as well believe that one can 'buy' the *ekom* from someone who possesses it already, but for this one has to 'sell' a close relative. Only then can one go to Mount Kupé. There, the initiated will find 'mysterious, closed bundles' which contain riches but also all sorts of misfortune (illness or even death). In the night, the *ekom* people secretly go up the mountain to steal a bundle but they should on no account open it until they are safely back. If one discovers misfortune in one's bundle one must immediately throw it into the river. But one can be lucky and find riches. People call this the 'market of sorcery'.

The missionaries of Basel who, in the 1890s, were among the first Europeans to reach this region, noted already that Mount Kupé had a strong magical reputation throughout the area. But they observed also that this reputation differed for the Bakossi and for the other groups. Initially, they had great trouble in reaching the mountain since their carriers from the coast were so afraid of it that they blandly refused to go on. The Bakossi from their side did everything to stop the Europeans from climbing the mountain. Apparently, they feared that the Whites would appropriate the riches hidden there. In 1893, the missionary Fr. Authenrieth wrote: 'Just as the mountain appears dangerous and ruinous to the coastal tribes, so it is a promise of good luck to the Bakossi people' (quoted in Balz 1984: 327–28).

In the 1970s, Heinrich Balz found that people in certain parts of Bakossiland believed that Mount Kupé's riches were exhausted and that it was no longer of any use to go there (1984: 330). But he found also that among other Bakossi groups, the belief in these riches was still very much alive, having integrated all sorts of modern elements related to the colonial plantation economy. Alobwede d'Epie indicates that the Bakossi even integrated the post-colonial manna of development into the *ekom*. He notes that during the secret meetings on Mount Kupé, 'development projects of great significance are believed to be highly contested for among the different racial or tribal spirits, and the race or tribe whose spirits win, wins the project' (1982: 80).

But here again the segmentary logic of Bakossi society asserts itself (1982: 80):

> For example, a fight breaks out among the spirits of the tribe that won the project so as to determine the clan in which the project would be located. Another fight breaks out among the spirits of the victorious clan to determine the village in which the project would be finally situated.

S.N. Ejedepang-Koge describes the *ekom* in more detail (1971: 202):

> This invisible town on Kupé is something like a labour camp. First of all the ancestral spirits need people who should work to keep the fortunes flowing in such a way that they can be distributed during the *ekom* meetings. Secondly the great men have invisible estates there and they need people to cultivate them. The source of this labour supply is widespread: from all the area surrounding the mountain, from Victoria, Bakweri area, from Duala etc.

Furthermore, Ejedepang-Koge says of these 'invisible labourers' that they are 'enslaved people' but that they are 'very contented' (sic); many of them are recruited among the victims of '*nyongo* witches' in the south. Apparently, the fear of being 'sold' and put to work on Mt. Kupé, so widespread among the Bakweri and the Duala, has its reverse in a kind of wishful dreaming among the Bakossi who believe they are entitled to profit from the magical riches of 'their' mountain. Heinrich Balz (1984: 331) speaks of a 'capitalist or ruling-class dream'. Maybe one should rather speak of an absentee landlord's dream. When the cultivation of cocoa spread in this area, during the 1920s and 1930s, the Bakossi tried to profit in a particular way from the new possibilities for enrichment. Many farmed out their land to 'strangers', mostly Bamileke who descended from the western highlands and who were willing to pay a substantial rent – often one-third of the harvest or even more – to the landlord. In the following decades it seemed possible for the Bakossi to get rich without much effort, profiting from other people's labour. The Bakossi imaginary around Mount Kupé seems to reflect the memory of those happy days which, unfortunately, are over.[17] No wonder that to them the *ekom* is certainly not unequivocally evil. If someone is believed to have enriched himself through *ekom*, this is, according to Balz, 'not criticised, but seen as just good luck' (1984: 331). There is indeed a clear contrast here with the general fear or even panic about *nyongo* or *ekong* among the Bakweri and the Duala.[18]

Famla and Modern Entrepreneurs in the Grassfields

The variations become even more marked if one compares developments in the Grassfields of the west and the north-west, among the Bamileke and the Bamenda. This area is of particular interest since it is from here that, especially after Independence, a new bourgeoisie of entrepreneurs emerged who are generally supposed to dominate the national economy of present-day Cameroon. Similar notions of the new witchcraft of wealth, here mostly referred to as *famla* or *kupe*, spread somewhat later in this area where they acquired particularly strong capitalist overtones. They are often associated with notions of debt and with the rotating credit associations, the famous *njangi*, which in this area gained particular momentum.

Nowadays, people quote examples of big businessmen's *njangi*, in which millions of francs CFA (the standard currency unit for West African countries) are accumulated. So much money is circulating, particularly in the Bamileke *njangi*, that this endangers the cash-flow through the official banks.[19] But these *njangi* are also supposed to have a more sinister side. People tell horror stories how, through them, one can be recruited into a *famla* coven without knowing it. A man goes to town and accepts a beer from some strangers. Suddenly he realises that he has to do with a *famla njangi* but then it is already too late. He has contracted a debt which he can only pay off by 'selling' a close relative.

Famla has become a major issue of debate in present-day Cameroon, precisely because of its supposed link with the success of the Bamileke – and to a lesser degree Bamenda – businessmen. Unfortunately, it has been very little studied in a systematic way.[20] It is clear that, in these societies as well, this witchcraft of the wealthy is considered to be a new and highly shocking phenomenon. Here also *famla* or *kupe* rumours can create outbursts of panic. Mbunwe-Samba (1996), for instance, cites several cases from villages in the Grassfields where such rumours triggered a true avalanche of accusations. It is striking, however, that in other contexts the fact of being associated with *famla* does not seem to have serious consequences for the people concerned. Warnier (1993) remarks that many of the big Bamileke entrepreneurs are the object of strong *famla* rumours; but he adds, quite surprisingly, that these rumours hardly seem to affect their position. Young Bamileke often complain that the *famla njangi* have become so strong that it would be futile to try and attack them.[21] The only way to escape them would be to migrate. To many, *famla* seems to have become a normal aspect of modern entrepreneurship.

A series of case-studies from this area, presented by Mbunwe-Samba (1996) and Fisiy (in Fisiy and Geschiere 1991), highlight a recurrent pattern. People react sharply against *famla* when it is supposed to be active within the village. Then the *fon* (chief) will mobilise the associations of his court to chase suspected *famla* witches from the village. However, when a successful entrepreneur returns to the village and dedicates his new wealth to the *fon* – by offering him an important present or buying a title at his court – he is accepted. In several of these cases this even concerned persons who only a few years earlier had been chased out of the village. In Fisiy's words: the chief still has the power to 'whitewash' the suspected wealth of the new rich and the occult powers behind it. He can still act as a crystallisation point for reintegrating his successful 'sons' abroad into the structures of the chieftaincy. The *fon* is still credited with the moral authority to neutralise the dangerous powers of the new rich and thus allay fears about the proliferation of new witchcraft threats.

The broader institutional setting of these societies is very different from that of the forest area. The Grassfields societies have a strong hierarchical tradition. The *fon* (or *fo*) was and is the centre of social life in all respects. Around his court are organised a number of more or less secret associations, the most important one being a kind of police society, often called *kwifoyn*. Relation to these associations is a complex system of graded titles controlled, again, by the *fon*. Warnier (1985) emphasises the importance of long-distance trade and the accumulation of wealth abroad for people's status in these societies, also in the precolonial period. However, individual success in trade was only acceptable if it was backed by the authority of the *fon*. Indeed, the strict control of the *fon* over outside relations and wealth was the very basis of his power. This model proved to be highly resilient in colonial times. The present-day role in post-colonial times of the chiefs and their associations in containing *famla* rumours and in re-integrating the new urban elites into the local structures continues this tradition.

This central position of the chiefs goes together with another interesting difference with the forest societies: the strong tendency to try to 'compartmentalise' the witchcraft discourse. Many elements in this discourse are the same as in the forest: witchcraft is supposed to reside in someone's belly, witches are supposed to fly away at night to betray and devour their kin during nocturnal banquets. However, in the Grassfields societies there seems to be a conscious effort to overcome the ambiguity and the circularity of this discourse, and to institutionalise clear-cut distinctions, especially between permitted and illegitimate uses of the occult forces. As is to be expected, the *fon* play a crucial role in this. Just as in the forest area, the chiefs themselves are closely associated with the occult. However, in the Grassfields, there is a heavy emphasis on all sorts of institutional boundaries between the chief and the evil expressions of occult power. In principle, it is the chief who decides whether these powers are used in an acceptable or unacceptable way. If someone is suspected of having access to sources of occult power without the blessing of the *fon*, this is automatically seen as a-social and therefore marked as 'witchcraft.' And the *kwifoyn*, the chief's secret police association, is supposed to deal with it in its own secret ways. However, the pursuit of wealth by a subject who has the blessing of the chief can never be witchcraft. On the contrary, this is supposed to strengthen the chief and thus the community as a whole.[22] To put it in simpler terms: in the last instance it is the chief who decides who is a witch and who is not. He has the moral authority to clarify someone's true identity.

Yet, as is only to be expected when witchcraft is at stake, this last conclusion must certainly be nuanced. It is, for instance, a moot point whether the Grassfields chiefs will retain enough moral authority to exercise this kind of control in the future as well. The eagerness with which many chiefs try to share in the wealth of their successful subjects – by creating all sorts of pseudo-traditional titles at their courts which the *nouveaux riches* can buy, but also by privatizing and selling their customary land rights – makes people wonder whether the chief still controls the new elite or whether the roles are reversed (see also Fisiy 1992). Warnier (1993) characterises the Bamileke chieftaincy as a 'shell' which is emptied and refilled by the new elites. Goheen quotes a highly evocative image expressing the doubts of the people of Nso (one of the largest north-western chiefdoms) about the collaboration of their chiefs with the new elites (1996: 145 and 161). People wonder whether these *nouveaux riches* will be 'the chief's new leopards' who, like the notables of former days, will accompany him at night when, transformed as a lion, he prowls the country in order to protect it against evil. Or will they prove to be 'sorcerers of the night' who corrupt his court from the inside?[23]

The *Kong* Spreads Panic in the South

More recently, the forces of Mount Kupé have made themselves felt in the southern forest area of the country. Among the Beti (around Yaunde and further to the south) people have already referred for some time to the *kong*. Again it concerns a new form of witchcraft, associated with the selling of relatives but also with the Whites and their new forms of wealth.[24] Until very recently this occult force was still little known among the Maka in the East. Since a few years the *kong* is assumed to be at work among them too. In those regions, the unrest is all the greater because of a striking uncertainty about what sanctions to apply against this new danger. I have already emphasised the strong circularity of the witchcraft discourses in these areas. Completely in line with this, people seem to suspect the *nganga*, who should be in principle protectors against the *kong*, of being involved in it themselves. The consequence is a great hesitance as to how to deal with this new threat. People seem to feel defenceless against it.

During a brief stay in Kribi, a small port on the coast of the forest region, a few questions were enough to trigger a true avalanche of rumours and dramatic stories about the new witchcraft excesses.[25] Everybody – both village elders and young employees in town, both Catholic priests and the State attorney – complained about the proliferation of sorcery and witchcraft, which seemed to be out of control. People spoke of *kong* but also of similar contracts to enrich oneself on a truly international scale. The priest of Bipindi told us how he had cured a boy who had sold himself to *L'Oeil du Tigre* (The Tiger's Eye), a notorious sorcerer from Europe. The priest himself had seen how white phantoms, sent from Europe by this sorcerer, were attacking the poor boy since he no longer wanted to honour his obligations. Other informants made us understand that Mount Kupé was now only a relay station in the traffic of zombies to Europe and beyond.

A striking symptom, revealing the great uncertainty created by such rumours, was that people had recourse to very young healers. In the Bisima – supposedly an anti-witchcraft movement which has been active in the area for about 15 years – it is not exceptional that boys of sixteen begin to practice as *guérisseurs*.[26] An excommunicated priest, Father Many from Lolodorf, had founded a new anti-witchcraft movement which only recruited young boys, often pupils, called *zomeloo*, some of whom had considerable renown throughout the area.[27] Our informants in Kribi were themselves also somewhat surprised by the rapid ascent of such young 'healers'. Normally, the elders are supposed to control the domain of the occult forces. However, according to some, the latter no longer used their forces to heal, but only to destroy. Others implied that, these days, the elders tended to keep their secrets to themselves and refused to pass them on to the next generation. Others again believed that the young folks, with their modern forms of knowledge, despised the secrets of their elders. But everybody agreed that the elders' failure had created a gap and that sorcery thus threatened to run wild. Such sombre prophecies were often accompanied by references to other groups – the Bassa or the Bamileke – where elders and chiefs still knew how to restrain the occult forces.

This uncertainty seems to inspire a frantic search for ever new sanctions and forms of protection. For some time, the Bisima seemed to be capable of combatting the *kong*, but nowadays many people believe that this movement is corrupted as well. Thus, people are more and more inclined to invoke the help of outside institutions such as the State with its *gendarmes* and its law-courts, or the churches with their priests and their exorcism rites.[28]

Again, there is a clear contrast here with the examples from the west and the north-west, discussed above. There, these new forms of witchcraft also invoke great unrest but people seem to know at least what kind of sanctions to apply.

Conclusion

A common feature of these stories is that they hardly correspond to the stereotype of witchcraft as a 'traditional' barrier against change and innovation. On the contrary, there is a proliferation of constantly new forms of sorcery/witchcraft which seem to express a determined effort to appropriate the new riches. To the Bakossi, *ekom* has become a means of appropriating development projects; to the Bamileke, *famla* has become a normal trait of modern entrepreneurship; in the forest areas of the south, where such entrepreneurship is less developed, the *kong* takes on a bureaucratic appearance.[29]

Clearly, the relation between the occult and the new forms of power and wealth is the *leitmotif* in all these examples. But it is equally clear that the reactions to these new forms of witchcraft are strikingly different. General uncertainty and even panic in Kribi; an appeal to the chiefs and his notables in the Grassfields; the introduction of a *juju* from elsewhere to eradicate the *nyongo* among the Bakweri; a quest for healing among the Duala, where the *ekong* associations have apparently completely lost their more or less prestigious aura from pre-colonial times: these various scenarios represent different choices and different patterns of articulation between local arrangements and modern developments.

The great uncertainty in Kribi suggests that in this region conceptions of the new riches can hardly break out of the vicious circles of the witchcraft discourse. Among the Bakweri it seemed for some time that Obasinjom, the *juju* imported from elsewhere, was capable of breaking through the witchcraft ban on the new forms of wealth. However, recently, his force seems to be corrupted by the same forces he is supposed to combat. In the Grassfields, the chief and his court appear to offer a more solid institutional support for efforts to 'domesticate' these occult forces and to 'socialise' – or 'whitewash' – the new forms of wealth. In those regions, the rumours of *famla* and *kupe* hardly seem to undermine the success of the modern entrepreneurs.

One can wonder, however, whether it is not too simple to reduce the differences discussed in this chapter to a simple opposition between societies with and without 'real' chiefs. It seems that deeper differences are at stake.

This might be illustrated by a brief but very interesting argument during a recent Ph.D. defence at the University of Yaunde, where I had the honour to preside over the jury. The thesis concerned was about funeral rites among the Ewondo (a Beti group). An elderly jury member, himself from another Beti group, praised the candidate, especially because he had so well analyzed the precarious position of urban elites when they had to assist a funeral in their village of birth. The professor resumed the ambiguity of the elite's position by the following striking phrase: '*C'est comme ça chez nous: celui qui émerge doit s'excuser constamment auprès de ceux qui n'émergent pas*' (It is like this with us: those who ascend must excuse themselves constantly with those who do not ascend). The jury member at my left, a colleague from the north-west, was clearly as struck by this phrase as I was. He bent over and whispered in my ear: 'Did you hear that? That is precisely the difference with relations among us. It is because of this that those Beti have to eat the State. How else could they satisfy their own people?'[30]

A striking element, which might help to understand what is at stake here, is the recurrent link between witchcraft and kinship. In all the examples above, witchcraft originates from kinship: the witches are supposed to attack their own kin and the therapy of the victims requires first of all a reparation of the kinship relations. Even in cities like Duala, where the family ties seem to be drastically weakened, the accusations and the therapies of *nganga* always primarily address relations within the family.[31] However, the daily meanings of kinship relations – the discourses and the practices – vary from one region to another. In their analysis of the ascent of entrepreneurs from the Grassfields, Rowlands (n.d.) and Warnier (1993) emphasise that these societies know special arrangements to protect themselves against 'the strategies of disaccumulation' – that is, against the levelling forces – that characterise so many kinship systems. In these Grassfield societies as well, people are certainly obliged to share with their kinsfolk, but there are clear limits. Warnier speaks of 'a solidarity according to merit' and 'a diking-in of kinship'.[32] Among the Beti, the Maka or the other segmentary forest societies, on the contrary, it seems that there are no limits to the levelling impact of the kinship ideology. In these regions, the new forms of wealth and the commodities that express them still constitute an unresolved problem.

The various examples above indicate also that it is too easy to simply equate the occult or even 'witchcraft' with 'evil.' On the contrary, precisely the fact that good and evil seem to be inextricably mixed in these visions can help us understand why they retain such a hold on people's minds. Elsewhere I tried to show that its highly moralizing tenor can explain why the anthropological discourse on witchcraft led to this quite surprising neglect of the modern dynamics of these representations (Geschiere 1997: 215–25).[33] Above, we saw that the fantasies about the new forms of witchcraft of the *nouveaux riches* can express both people's fear and fascination with the new commodities. This is what makes them so all-pervasive and still so convincing in present-day circumstances. In this sense, these new fantasies seem to prolong witchcraft's basic capacity to undermine and corrupt all clear-cut distinctions, notably the one between good and evil. The strong Manichean tenor of the Western world-view, implicit in much anthropological discourse, seems to be an obstacle for dealing with such ambiguity.

Another recurrent trait of these macabre stories is that they all try to relate 'consumption' to 'production': they all speculate about the enigmatic origin of these desirable commodities. On the one hand, they express the popular uncertainty about these origins; this is what makes these goods so suspect. Yet, at the same time, they indicate, at least in some instances, how these goods can be 're-produced' in order to liberate them from their suspect aura. In the above examples from the Cameroonian Grassfields, the chiefs are still supposed to be able to 'whitewash' the new riches.

However, it is clear that, also in this context, this remains a highly precarious enterprise – just like any attempt definitively to distinguish good and evil when witchcraft is concerned. Because of their eagerness to co-opt the *nouveaux riches*, the chiefs themselves risk to be accused of being 'witches.' In a more general perspective, these stories can therefore be seen as reflecting wider criticisms, unfortunately increasingly scarce, of a global economy that seems to be based only on demand and consumerism. Consumption, prised loose from production, has qualities of a dream, and a weird one at that.

Notes

1. This text takes up some of the themes discussed in an article I published with Cyprian F. Fisiy (now at the World Bank, Washington) in *Critique of Anthropology* (1991, 11, 3: 251–278) and in chapter 5 of my book on *Witchcraft and Modernity, Politics and the Occult in Postcolonial Africa* (1997). Cyprian Fisiy's contributions and creative comments have been essential to this text as well. Moreover, I greatly profited from the opportunity (September 1995) to discuss an earlier version at the Yale Program in Agrarian Studies (notably from comments by Angelique Haugerud, Pauline Peters and James Scott). Many others – but mainly Jean-François Bayart, Achille Mbembe, Birgit Meyer, Peter Pels, Janet Roitman, Eric de Rosny, Mike Rowlands and Mick Taussig – have generously helped me along in my long-term struggle with these obsessive themes.
2. 'Le goût des Camerounais pour tout ce qui est importé plutôt que produit localement est légendaire.'
3. The Pajero is the Japanese car which has replaced the Mercedes as the main status symbol of the Cameroonian elite.
4. A brief note on terminology might be required here. I have serious misgivings about using terms like witchcraft, sorcery or *sorcellerie*. In general, these terms are awkward translations – for too pejorative – of African notions which have much wider implications. Thus, a broad world-view in which all man's environment is animated by spiritual forces risks being reduced to an ugly, evil core. A more neutral translation, like 'occult forces', might be preferable. The problem is, however, that these Western terms have now generally been appropriated by Africans (also in public discussions in newspapers, on the radio or the TV). Therefore I prefer to retain these terms, despite such misgivings. Moreover, I do not follow the classical – but much contested – distinction between 'witchcraft' and 'sorcery', proposed by Evans-Pritchard on the basis of his Azande material, since it is hard to apply to the Cameroonian societies discussed here and to the modern dynamics of representations of the occult in Africa in general.
5. See J. & J. Comaroff 'Witches ... embody all the contradictions of the experience of modernity itself, of its inescapable enticements, its self-consuming passions, its discriminatory tactics, its devastating social costs' (1993: xxix). It must be emphasised, however, that, in a broader perspective, Africa is certain not particular in this linking of modernity and notions of occult forces. See J. & J. Comaroff 1999 on 'modernity's enchantment' and the proliferation of

'economies of the occult' throughout our modern world. See also Geschiere 1999 and forthcoming. I will return to this more general perspective below.

6. At the end of the 1980s, Fisiy and I could still write that it was very difficult to find parallel studies to relate to in our efforts to analyze the interaction of witchcraft conceptions on new forms of accumulation, national politics or the role of the State (Fisiy & Geschiere 1990 and 1991). However, recently, there has been a sudden interest in these topics in African studies, especially among anthropologists (see J. & J. Comaroff 1993 and 1999). For Cameroon, one can mention, moreover, the pioneering studies of Ardener (1970) and Rowlands & Warnier (1988). However, we found our main landmark outside anthropology in de Rosny's fascinating book (1981; See also de Rosny 1992 and Desjeux 1987). Seminal studies outside Africa are by Kapferer (1983 and 1997) and Taussig (1987). In general, one must say that anthropologists have waited surprisingly long before picking up the topic of witchcraft in modern settings and its baffling effects in many parts of present-day Africa (as in other continents). There was – and is – a regrettable tendency to leave this topic to journalists, philosophers, theologians and others.

7. See Geschiere 1997 (Afterword, 'The Meanderings of Anthropological Discourse on Witchcraft') on the impact of classical anthropology in this respect, with its functionalist, highly moralizing overtones and its focus on local relations.

8. See Fisiy and Geschiere 1990 and 1991, Geschiere 1982 and 1995. See also van Wetering 1973, Rowlands and Warnier 1988, Mary 1983.

9. An attempt at comparison inevitably raises the thorny question of the units to compare. In this article we compare regions or ethnic groups, units which are by definition vague. Moreover, it seems that in South and West Cameroon an interregional sorcery discourse is emerging which blurs the boundaries between local cultures. The aim of this article is precisely to analyze how a similar set of ideas – concerning the links between wealth, witchcraft and the labour of victims, turned into zombies – has undergone diverging transformations in various regions. The intention is not to oppose clearly demarcated units but to study different regional trajectories of a similar set of ideas. Unfortunately it is beyond the scope of this chapter to make a comparison with similar representations elsewhere in Africa (see for example Meyer 1995 on southern Ghana, Bastian 1993 on eastern Nigeria, Bockie 1993 on Lower Zaire). It would be highly worthwhile to make such a comparison precisely because, in all those cases, representations with a similar basic pattern have varying effects in daily life.

10. Data gained during interviews in Buea during 1987 and 1988. E. Ardener (1970) says also that the *nyongo* was something new to the Bakweri. Below we shall discuss certain transformations which accompanied the borrowing of these notions from the Duala.

11. As father Tatah H. Mbuy (1989: 7) puts it, Obasinjom 'fished and tamed the witches'.

12. It is not very clear how exactly Obasinjom intervened in the relation between elders and juniors (as elsewhere in Africa, a key relation among the Bakweri). At first sight, Obasinjom seems to be a weapon of the juniors against the elders. Ardener says explicitly that it was because of the juniors' accusations against their elders that the latter agreed to send for Obasinjom. But several informants gave as their opinion that Obasinjom had always been controlled by the elders.

According to them the elders sent for Obasinjom in order to protect themselves against the juniors' accusations and to legitimate their wealth. It is clear in any case that in the course of time the elders succeeded in gaining control over Obasinjom. Such a pattern of elders gaining control over an anti-witchcraft movement, originally directed against them by the juniors, seems to occur elsewhere also (see, for instance, Rey 1971 and Dupré 1982 on the *njobi* movement in the Mossendjo area of Congo-Brazza; see Löffler 1983 on the same movement in Gabon).

13. Elisabeth Copet-Rougier reports on the Kako (or Kaka) to the North of Yokaduma: 'Until the 1980s, nobody dared to build a roof in sheet-metal because to do so was a mark of great success, and was too dangerous' (1986: 65).

14. See also Mallart 1981: 115. Eric de Rosny (oral communication) doubts that hypnosis plays a role since this practice is not very current among the Duala. But to him also, the notion that one must 'sell' a parent to have access to the riches of the *ekong* is the basic pattern in these representations.

15. As discussed above, the Bakweri use a related term *nyongo* to indicate the whole *ekong* complex (which would have been introduced among them by the Duala). Apparently, the Bakweri use the term *nyongo* in a somewhat different way: to them it is also related to wealth, but I did not encounter any link with a snake or with the rainbow. The Bakweri sometimes use also the term *ekongi* as a general term for this kind of witchcraft (see also Ardener 1956).

16. In these regions the expression *la sorcellerie des Blancs* has therefore a much less positive ring than among the Maka, who often oppose the *sorcellerie des Blancs* and the *sorcellerie des Noirs* (the first is to *construire* while the second is to *détruire* – see above). According to Pool (1994), the Mbum of the limits of the Grassfields (near the Nigerian border) make a similar contrast. In the regions touched by the *ekong* little remains of the positive association of Whites and witchcraft.

17. Levin (1980 and 1987) paints a fascinating picture of a kind of 'whisky galore' among the Bakossi during the spread of cocoa cultivation: 'The period most vividly remembered is the postwar period of high cocoa prices and nothing to spend money on. People recollect buying cases of smuggled Spanish gin and brandy and consuming it in long drinking bouts. Shouting and singing echoed through the cocoa farms throughout the night; pits were dug to bury the empty bottles. No farmer had to work. For one-third of the crop, a share-cropper would tend the farm' (Levin 1980: 321). He adds that after 1960, the dream was over. Then there were more possibilities to invest money (especially in schooling, since people became aware of the potential value of school certificates); so people needed ever more money. On the other hand, they began to realise that by renting their land to strangers, they risked to losing their control over it (see also Ejedepang-Koge 1971). In the post-colonial era, the Bakossi have been involved in a rather desperate struggle to keep their lands in the face of an ever stronger encroachment by especially Bamileke immigrants. Heinrich Balz (1984) explains the Bakossi readiness to have strangers work on their lands by the fact that in this area slavery had only just disappeared when the spread of cocoa began. The imaginary around Mount Kupé and the *ekom* seems, therefore, to correspond to this practice of exploiting other people's labour, first as slaves and later as share-croppers.

18. Compare, however, de Rosny's remark (1981: 92) quoted above, that, in precolonial times, *ekong* among the Duala used to be associated with respected traders and notables and did not yet have 'the odious character it has acquired

nowadays'. Apparently, the interpretations of these images can also vary strongly over time.

19. In the 1980s, the bankruptcy and subsequent closure of several banks were generally attributed to the large-scale withdrawal of cash from the official circuits by the *njangi*. See also Warnier (1993) and Warnier and Miaffo (1993) on the role of the *njangi* in the rise of the entrepreneurs from the West and the Northwest. Warnier remarks that, among the Bamileke, *famla* is sometimes described as 'a *njangi* of the rich' (1993: 198). See also Rowlands 1993 and n.d.

20. Warnier (1993), Warnier and Miaffo (1993) and Pradelles de Latour (1991) all mention *famla* but only briefly. Mbunwe-Samba, who produced the longest text on it, has an original explanation why it is so little studied: 'The word *famla* has gained such a mystical force that no one will dare write or talk about it lest he/she dies' (1996: 75).

21. The *famla* can therefore be viewed as a hidden script in the epos of *Le dynamisme bamiléké* (the title of a book by Jean-Louis Dongmo – 1981 – on the economic fervour of the Bamileke). It is clear that the massive migrations of Bamileke to other parts of the country have played a crucial role in the economic ascent of this group. But juniors often tend to associate these migrations with *famla* and with the new rich who re-invest the money, accumulated in the diaspora, in the home country; for a junior, the only solution to evade this pressure would be to migrate in his turn.

22. See Goheen's recent study (1996) on Nso (the largest chiefdom of the Northwest) for a detailed treatment of the complex relation between the *fon* and *sem* (occult power, in some contexts equated with witchcraft, but never so in relation to the *fon*). See especially her nuanced analysis of the role of such ideas in the precarious pact of the *fon* with the new elite.

23. See also the interesting text by Basile Ndjio (1995) on a recent series of performances of the *Ngru*, a Bamileke purification ritual. Apparently this old ritual was suddenly revived in 1994, simultaneously in several rural chieftaincies in the West Province but also in the Bamileke quarter in the city of Duala. Ndjio interprets the staging of the ritual as a somewhat desperate attempt by the chiefs to restore their authority, severely undermined by their close collaboration with the regime. Typically, the chiefs were strongly supported in organizing this ritual by the 'external elites' and the administrative authorities. Equally typical is the ambivalent role of the *nganga* as a kind of brokers between these groups. A year later, Ndjio returned to these places and found that, although the chiefs and some notables were still satisfied with having staged the ritual, the people in general were more sceptical. Many talked about it as a swindle that served only to enrich the chiefs and the *nganga*.

24. See Mallart 1981 and 1988, Nomo n.d., Yombi 1984, Fisiy 1990 a and b.

25. I worked in this area together with Cyprian Fisiy (my aforementioned co-author). This region is populated by various ethnic groups. The Batanga, related to the Duala, are generally considered to be the autochthons of the coastal area. In the interior one finds 'Pygmies' (or rather Bagyeli), Ngumba (related to the Maka) and Fang. Since the last century, there is a strong influx from 'Beti' groups coming from the north (Ewondo and especially Bulu).

26. See Yombi 1984 and Fisiy 1990a and b. We did not succeed in getting a clear picture of this Bisima. According to some, the movement was related to the *miengu* (water spirits) of the Batanga; others said that it came rather from the

Fang in Gabon and Bata, and that it was related to the Bwiti-Fang (see Mary 1983 and Fernandez 1982).

27. See also Bayart (1996: 136). According to our information, Father Many had been exorcising evil spirits already for some time. He was only excommunicated when he started to use, moreover, his personal powers to heal people. It is, incidentally, quite surprising that his young assistants were called *zomeloo*. In Ewondo, this term is a kind of honorary title, sometimes translated as 'Master of the Word' and strictly reserved for elders (see Mebenga 1991 and Ngoa 1968). Laburthe-Tolra (1977: 1401) gives *zomoloo* or *zomoloa*, translated as *grand juge* and relates this title to the *So* ritual, a key institution in the old Beti order. The transfer of this titles to young boys might be characteristic for their increasing role in sorcery and witchcraft. Some informants from this area emphasised indeed that the juniors were more and more overtaking the elders, even in this domain.

28. See Fisiy & Geschiere (1990) and Geschiere (1997), on a new judiciary offensive against witchcraft by the State courts in East Cameroon and its highly problematic effects. In relation to the role of churches in this respect, it is to be noted that, during the last decades, notably Pentecostalist churches have been very successful in the Kribi area, much more so than in other regions of Cameroon. In general, until quite recently, the spread of such independent churches remained very limited in Cameroon – as compared to other parts of Africa – for reasons I do not fully grasp (possibly one reason is the strict control of the one-party regime over society, especially under Ahidjo). Recently, authors such as Meyer (1995 and in this volume) and Marshall (1991 and 1993) have emphasised that especially Pentecostalist sects, with their strong emphasis on the role of the Devil and their highly physical purification rituals, seem to be capable of breaking through the circularity of the witchcraft discourse emphasised above.

29. Several informants told us that *kong* witches work with a list. Each time they cross a name from their list by their magic means – for instance, with a finger dipped in a magic potion – the person concerned dies (Fisiy 1990a and b, and *Procès-verbal de la gendarmerie national, compagnie d'Ebolowa, brigade d'Olamze*, nr. 364, 24-12-1985. I thank Fisiy for showing me these files).

30. See also a similar quote from a conversation of Warnier with a Bamileke entrepreneur, who made exactly the same contrast (Warnier 1993: 90). See also Franqueville (1987: 239 and 275) on the contrasts between *le familialisme beti* and the relations of Bamileke migrants to their home village.

31. See de Rosny 1981 and 1992. The young healers from Kribi were the only ones among our informants who claimed that modern forms of witchcraft were no longer linked to kinship and the family. To them, this was precisely one of the really new aspects of 'modern' forms of witchcraft. However, in the few witchcraft cases we could study in more depth in this area (unfortunately our time was limited), there was always a link with tensions within the family. Many studies on other parts of Africa emphasize also this continuing link of witchcraft/sorcery with kinship (see, for instance, two very interesting studies by Meyer 1995 on the Ewe in South Ghana and Bastian 1993 on the Ibo of East Nigeria – Bastian briefly mentions the opinion of some Ibo that, nowadays, witchcraft seems to surpass the framework of kinship but she does not discuss this further; clearly in this case as well it is seen as a novel development).

32. In practice, this means making a distinction between relatives who show that they merit help and others who 'don't honour the help received' and whom a rich entrepreneur described to Warnier as *les délinquants* (Warnier 1993: 75). See also Jan den Ouden who makes a simple but very helpful opposition between *helping* and *sharing*: 'among the Bamileke ... to give help is quite different from letting others share your prosperity' (1987: 18). A fundamental contrast with the Beti and other forest societies is also that, in most Grassfields societies, a father's heritage goes to one son only (often the oldest); in most forest societies, on the contrary, all sons share in the heritage, so that it is often dispersed on the father's death.

33. See Gluckman's well-known comparison of the belief in witchcraft to the Anglican anthem 'See that ye love one another fervently' (Gluckman 1955: 94), or Marwick's characteristic of witchcraft as a 'social strain-gauge' (Marwick 1965). See also Douglas' ironical comment (Douglas 1970). This approach neglects people's fascination with these occult forces, and the idea in many parts of Africa that they can be controlled and are even indispensable to the accumulation of wealth and power. See, for instance, what is said above about the *nganga* ('witch-doctor') among the Beti or the Maka, who is supposed to be able to heal only because (s)he has such a highly developed *evu/djambe* (local terms, generally translated as 'witchcraft') in his/her belly.

References

Alobwede d'Epié, C., 1982, *The Language of Traditional Medicine – A Study in the Power of Language*. Thèse d'Etat, University of Yaoundé.

Ardener, E., 1956, *Coastal Bantu of the Cameroons*. London: IAI.

Ardener, E., 1970, 'Witchcraft, Economics and the Continuity of Belief' in Douglas, M., ed., *Witchcraft Confessions and Accusations*. London: Tavistock.

Ardener, S., 1958, 'Banana Co-operatives in the Southern Cameroons', *Nigerian Institute of Social and Economic Research: Conference Proceedings*, p. 10–25, Ibadan.

Balz, H.,1984, *Where the Faith Has to Live: Studies in Bakossi Society and Religion*. Basel: Basel Mission.

Bastian, M., 1993, "Bloodhounds Who Have No Friends': Witchcraft and Locality in the Nigerian Popular Press', in Comaroff, J. and Comaroff, J., eds, *Modernity and Its Malcontents: Ritual and Power in Postcolonial Africa*. Chicago: University of Chicago Press.

Bayart, J.-F., 1996, *L'illusion identitaire*. Paris: Fayard.

Bockie, S., 1993, *Death and The Invisible Powers: The World of Kongo Belief*. Indiana University Press.

Bureau, R., 1962, *Ethno-sociologie religieuse des Douala et apparentés, Yaoundé: Recherches et Etudes camerounaises*, 7/8.

Comaroff, J. And Comaroff, J., eds, 1993, *Modernity and Its Malcontents: Ritual and Power in Postcolonial Africa*. Chicago: University of Chicago Press.

Comaroff, J. And Comaroff, J., 1999, 'Occult Economies and the Violence of Abstraction', *American Ethnologist*, 26: 279–301.

Copet-Rougier, E., 1986, "Le Mal Court': Visible and Invisible Violence in an Acephalous Society, Mkako of Cameroon', in Riches, D., ed., *The Anthropology of Violence*. Oxford: Blackwell.

Dongmo, J.-L., 1981, *Le Dynamisme bamiléké*. Yaoundé.

Desjeux, D., 1987, *Stratégies paysannes en Afrique noire: le Congo*. Paris: L'Harmattan.

Douglas, M., 1970, 'Introduction: Thirty Years after "Witchcraft, Oracles and Magic"', in Douglas, M., ed., *Witchcraft Confessions and Accusations*. London: Tavistock.

Dupré, G., 1982, *Un ordre et sa déstruction*. Paris: ORSTOM.

Ejedepang-Koge, S. N., 1971, *The Tradition of A People: Bakossi*. Yaoundé.

Ejedepang-Koge, S. N., 1975, *Tradition and Change in Peasant Activities*. Yaoundé.

Fabian, J. 1990, *Power and Performance: Ethnographic Explorations through Proverbial Wisdom and Theater in Shaba, Zaire*. Madison: The University of Wisconsin Press.

Fernandez, J. W., 1982, *Bwiti: An Ethnography of the Religious Imagination in Africa*. Princeton: Princeton University Press.

Fisiy, C. F., 1990a, *Palm Tree Justice in the Bertoua Court of Appeal: The Witchcraft Cases*. Leiden: African Studies Center.

Fisiy, C. F., 1990b, 'Le monopole juridictionnel de l'Etat et le règlement des affaires de sorcellerie au Cameroun', *Politique Africaine*, 40: 60–72.

Fisiy, C. F., 1992, *Power and Privilege in the Administration of Law: Land Law Reforms and Social Differentiation in Cameroon*. Leiden: African Studies Center.

Fisiy, C. F. and Geschiere, P., 1990, 'Judges and Witches, or How is the State to Deal with Witchcraft? – Examples from Southeastern Cameroon', *Cahiers d'Etudes Africaines*, 118: 135–56.

Fisiy, C. F. and Geschiere, P., 1991, 'Sorcery, Witchcraft and Accumulation: Regional Variations in South and West Cameroon', *Critique of Anthropology*, 11 (3): 251–78.

Franqueville, A., 1987, *Une Afrique entre le village et la ville: Les migrations dans le sud du Cameroun*. Paris: ORSTOM.

Geschiere, P., 1982, *Village Communities And The State: Changing Relations Among The Maka of Southeastern Cameroon*. London: Kegan Paul.

Geschiere, P., 1995, *Sorcellerie et politique en Afrique – La Viande des autres*. Paris: Karthala.

Geschiere, P., 1997, *The Modernity of Witchcraft, Politics and the Occult in Postcolonial Africa*. Charlottesville: University Press of Virginia.

Geschiere, P., 1999, 'Globalization and the Power of Indeterminate Meaning: Witchcraft and Spirit Cults in Africa and East Asia', in Meyer, B. and Geschiere, P., eds., *Globalization and Identity: Dialectics of Flow and Closure*. Oxford: Blackwell: 211–36.

Geschiere, P., forthcoming, 'On Witch-doctors and Spin-doctors: The Role of "Experts" in African and American Politics', in Meyer, B. and Pels, P., eds., *Magic and Modernity*. London: Routledge.

Geschiere, P. and Rowlands, M., 1996, 'The Domestication of Modernity: Different Trajectories', *Africa*, 66 (4): 552–55.

Gluckman, M., 1955, *Custom and Conflict in Africa*. Oxford: Blackwell.

Goheen, M., 1996, *Men Own the Fields, Women Own the Crops: Gender and Power in the Cameroon Highlands*. Madison: The University of Wisconsin Press.

Kapferer, B., 1983, *A Celebration of Demons*. Indiana University Press.

Kapferer, B., 1997, *The Feast of the Sorcerer: Practices of Consciousness and Power*. Chicago: University of Chicago Press.

Laburthe-Tolra, P., 1977, *Minlaaba, histoire et société traditionnelle chez les Bëti du Sud Cameroun*. Paris: Champion.

Levin, M. D., 1980, 'Export Crops and Peasantization: The Bakosi of Cameroon', in Klein, M., ed., *Peasants in Africa: Historical and Contemporary Perspectives.* Beverly Hills: Sage.

Levin, M. D., 1987, 'Family Structure in Bakosi: Social Change in an African Society'. PhD. diss., Princeton University.

Löffler, I., 1983, 'Hexerei, Staat und Religion in Gabun', *Peripherie*, 12 (3): 77–88.

Mallart Guimera, L., 1981, *Ni dos, ni ventre.* Paris: Société d'ethnographie.

Mallart Guimera, L., 1988, *La forêt de nos ancêtres.* Thèse d'Etat, Paris X.

Marshall, R., 1991, 'Power in the Name of Jesus', *Review of African Political Economy*, 52: 21–38.

Marshall, R., 1993, "'Power in the Name of Jesus': Social Transformation and Pentecostalism in Western Nigeria 'Revisited'", in Ranger, T. And Vaughan, O., eds, *Legitimacy and the State in Twentieth Century Africa.* Basingstoke: Macmillan.

Marwick, M., 1965, *Sorcery in Its Social Setting: A Study of the Northern Rhodesian Cewa.* Manchester: Manchester University Press.

Mary, A., 1983, *La naissance à l'envers, essai sur le rituel du Bwiti Fang au Gabon.* Paris: L'Harmattan.

Mbembe, A., 1998, *Provisional Notes on the Postcolony.* Berkeley: University of California Press.

Mbunwe-Samba, P., 1996, *Witchcraft, Magic and Divination: A Personal Testimony.* Bamenda (Cameroon), Leiden: African Studies Center.

Mbuy, T., 1989, *Encountering Witches and Wizards in Africa.* Buea.

Mebenga, L. T., 1991, 'Les Funérailles chez les Ewondo, thèse de 3ème cycle', University of Yaunde.

Meyer, B., 1995, 'Translating the Devil, An African Appropriation of Pietist Protestantism – The Case of the Peki Ewe in Southeastern Ghana, 1847–1992'. Ph.D.thesis, University of Amsterdam.

Ndjio, B., 1995, 'Sorcellerie, pouvoir et accumulation en pays bamiléké: Cas du *Ngru*', unpublished paper, Yaunde, Cameroon.

Ngoa, H., 1968, 'Le mariage chez les Ewondo, étude sociologique', thèse de 3ème cycle, Paris.

Nomo, n.d., *L'Evu dans la tradition eton.* Yaoundé.

den Ouden, J., 1987, 'In Search of Personal Mobility: Changing Interpersonal Relations in Two Bamileke Chiefdoms, Cameroon', *Africa*, 57 (1): 3–27.

Pool, R., 1994, *Dialogue and the Interpretation of Illness: Conversations in a Cameroon Village.* Oxford: Berg.

Pradelles de Latour, C. H., 1991, *Ethnopsychanalyse en pays bamiléké.* Paris: EPEL.

Rey, P.-P., 1971, *Colonialisme, néo-colonialisme et transition au capitalisme.* Paris: Maspero.

de Rosny, E., 1981, *Les yeux de ma chèvre, Sur les pas des maîtres de la nuit en pays douala.* Paris: Plon.

de Rosny, E., 1992, *L'Afrique des guérisons.* Paris: Karthala.

Rowlands, M., 1993, 'Economic Dynamism and Cultural Stereotyping in the Bamenda Grassfields', in Geschiere, P., and Konings, P., eds, *Les Itinéraires de l'accumulation au Cameroun.* Paris: Karthala.

Rowlands, M., n.d., 'The Domestication of Modernity in Cameroon'.

Rowlands, M. and Warnier, J.-P., 1988, 'Sorcery, Power and the Modern State in Cameroon', *Man (N.S.)* 23: 118–32.

Ruell, M., 1969, *Leopards and Leaders.* London: Tavistock.

Taussig, M.,1980, *The Devil and Commodity Fetishism in South America*. Chapel Hill: University of North Carolina Press.

Taussig, M., 1987, *Shamanism, Colonialism and the Wild Man, A Study of Terror and Healing*. University of Chicago Press.

Thoden van Velzen, H.U.E. and van Wetering, W. V., 1988, *The Great Father and the Danger: Religious Cults, Material Forces and Collective Fantasies in the World of the Surinamese Maroons*. Dordrecht (Holland): Foris.

Warnier, J.-P., 1985, *Echanges, développement et hiérarchies dans le Bamenda précolonial (Cameroun)*. Stuttgart: Steiner.

Warnier, J.-P., 1989, 'Traite sans raids au Cameroun', *Cahiers d'Etudes africaines* 113: 5–32.

Warnier, J.-P., 1993, *L'Esprit d'entreprise au Cameroun*. Paris: Karthala.

Warnier, J.-P. and Miaffo, D., 1993, 'Accumulation et ethos de la notabilité chez les Bamiléké' in Geschiere, P. and Konings, P., eds., 1993, *Les Itinéraires de l'accumulation au Cameroun*. Paris: Karthala.

Van Wetering, W., 1973, 'Hekserij bij de Djuka: Een Sociologische Benadering'. PhD. diss., University of Amsterdam.

Yombi, A.B., 1984, 'La Répression de la sorcellerie dans le Code pénal camerounais: le cas du Kong dans le Ntem', *Jahrbuch für afrikanisches Recht*, V: 3–12.

3

The Devil, Satanism and the Evil Eye in Contemporary Malta

Jon P. Mitchell

University of Sussex

Introduction

This chapter compares two types of evil in contemporary Malta – the Devil and the evil eye, or *ghajn*. The distinction between the two would seem to conform to Pocock's separation of 'strong' and 'weak' versions of evil (1985). While 'strong' evil is absolute and inexplicable, 'weak' evil is an understandable malevolence brought about by human agency (44).

In Malta, the Devil is a representation of inexplicable, motiveless and chaotic power – a mysterious, inhuman and hostile power located outside the person and threatening to act upon it. This 'strong' evil contrasts with the 'weaker' *ghajn*, which originates inside the person, and is linked to the very human tendency of envy. Prevalent in various forms throughout the world, the evil eye is based on the assumption that in certain circumstances envy is turned into a supernatural power that brings harm or misfortune to its object (Dundes 1981). The eye is seen as the conduit for this power, which can destroy the very things that a person envies. Like witchcraft in other contexts, the evil eye can be seen as a *post hoc* explanation of illness or accident in terms of the supernatural agency of others.[1]

In the early 1990s,[2] these two types of Maltese evil were transforming. There was broad consensus that while the *ghajn* was becoming a thing of the past, the power of the Devil was expanding.[3]

This chapter seeks to explain why this might be so, linking the explanation to two main contexts. First, the context of an inherent Maltese ambivalence towards 'tradition' and 'modernity', that was perpetuated by the Catholic Church. Second, a shift in the way religiosity was constituted, and particularly the expanded role of bodily experience. These contexts combined to produce transformations of evil that would seem to contrast with certain modernist assumptions – not least those of Pocock.

Writing on contemporary Britain, Pocock argues that the invocation of 'strong' evil is increasingly a thing of the past – reserved for ecclesiastical circles or secularised to provide a demonology of notorious criminals or political dictators. He therefore contrasts absolute evil in 'primitive' society with that of the modern: 'In primitive society evil is attributed ultimately to monsters that cannot exist, whereas in our society it is attributed to monsters that do' (Pocock 1985: 56).

The Maltese situation would seem to contradict this observation. Whilst in no senses could Malta be described as 'primitive', it appears to have maintained or even entrenched its commitment to 'monsters that cannot exist'. Indeed, the conjunction of factors seems to produce a kind of contradiction or double-bind, whereby getting rid of the 'weaker' malignancy of the *ghajn* merely ushers in another, stronger, power of evil – the Devil.

'Tradition' and 'Modernity' in Malta

Like many of the ethnographic examples in this volume, this chapter describes a situation in which accounts of and images of evil serve as a means by which people objectify socio-economic uncertainties and mediate the ambivalence of social and political change. The argument picks up from that of the Comaroffs (1992, 1993) and Taussig (1980), who highlight the use of indigenous or indigenised images of evil – in the form of witchcraft or the Devil – to mediate the contradictions and anxieties inherent in a rapidly changing economic setting. The Comaroffs in Southern Africa and Taussig in South America demonstrate the extent to which images of evil can be used by indigenous peoples to marshal conflict or resistance to the encroaching cultural forms of capitalism. As Kahn (1997) has argued, such a proposition implies – at worst – a romanticisation of 'indigenous' culture as pristine and uncorrupt and therefore uniquely placed to forge a critique of capitalism. At best, it reinforces distinctions between the 'West' and the 'rest', suggesting that the former are entirely mystified by capitalism's culture. As such, it ignores the long tradition of anti-capitalist thought within the capitalist 'West'. Ambivalence towards capitalism, then, is not the preserve of areas such as Southern Africa or South America. It also has a long tradition in Europe.

Although making this important point, Kahn's main concern is with 'non-Western' images of capitalism. He highlights the ways in which global Islam has tried to negotiate capitalist economics, and how that negotiation is manifest in contemporary Malaysia, where versions of pro- and anti-capitalist, or anti-Market discourse have emerged since the 1980s. In particular, he shows how 'admiration for the economic and developmental potential of Market forces coexists with a demonisation of instrumentalism and materialism in a vision of the West as 'transcendental evil' (93–94). I identify a similar process on the fringes of Europe – in Malta, where a long-established Roman Catholicism has attempted a similar negotiation between the beneficial and the negative elements of capitalism. In examining ambivalence towards capitalism in a 'Western' context, it returns to the agenda Kahn sets out.

Unlike the Southern African and South American – or even Malaysian – examples, Maltese ambivalence towards capitalism is not related to its recent introduction, but to recent developments in its history. Of particular importance is the political-economic consolidation of Europe, and the possibility of Malta's accession to the European Union (EU). Malta is very much on the edge of Europe, wondering whether it should be in or out. The last three general elections in Malta (1992, 1996 and 1998) have largely been fought over the issue of EU accession, and arguments about 'Europe' display an inherent ambivalence. On the one hand it has become associated with an increased availability of consumer goods, and on the other hand with an increase in taxation and surveillance of the economy. Similarly, it has become associated with an expansion of 'modern' thinking through education, at the same time as a dangerous erosion of 'traditional' morality.

Rather than objective categories, I treat 'tradition' and 'modernity' as aspects of indigenous Maltese discourse. One could argue that they are inherently opposed, with tradition standing for Maltese Catholicism and modernity for European rationalism – each trying to establish hegemony over the Maltese. Although there is perhaps some truth in this, both 'tradition' and 'modernity' involve an inherent ambiguity. 'Tradition' is associated with the

morally approved Catholic tradition, but also with the less acceptable, backward or superstitious tradition from which beliefs such
as the *ghajn* are derived. There are therefore both positive and
negative connotations of 'tradition'. Similarly, 'modernity' has both
positive and negative aspects. On the one hand, it is associated
with enlightenment and education, on the other hand with excess,
and the erosion of 'traditional' morality. Such ambiguities ensure
that Malta is not just on the margins of Europe, but also places
itself on the margins of modernity. An early 1990s attempt to locate
Maltese society on a gradient of tradition and modernity concluded
that Malta was 'neo-traditional' – 'traditional' because maintaining
a Catholic morality, 'neo-' because also incorporating a modernist
orientation to economy and rationality (Abela 1991). In invoking
the Catholic 'tradition', Malta places itself both inside and outside
European modernity. Catholicism is used as a means of legitimis-
ing the calls for accession to Europe, but also a means of resisting
it, or keeping it at arm's length. It is used by those who promote
accession, as evidence of an enduring European-ness. Because
Malta is Catholic, so the argument goes, it belongs in Europe. But
the Catholic pantheon also provides a central metaphor in the critique of European modernity – the Devil.

Malta's marginal position, inside and outside both Europe and
modernity, explains the accounts of an increasingly potent Devil,
and a decline of the *ghajn*. On the one hand, the Devil can be seen
to mediate or objectify Malta's marginal position, and the inherent
sense of vulnerability this necessarily involves. He embodies a concern for the preservation of the positive, approved and correct version of Catholic 'tradition', as threatened by the negative or
excessive elements of modernity. On the other hand, the *ghajn* represents the negative, incorrect or non-standard 'tradition' of the
superstitious. This belief is vulnerable both to the official teachings
of the Church, but also to the invocation of education inherent in
the positive aspects of modernity – that modernity will bring
enlightenment and an increased 'rationality'.

Thus while on the one hand, traditional Catholicism is heralded
as the potential saviour of Maltese morality against the negative
effects of European modernity, on the other hand, the positive
effects of European modernity are seen as a potential deliverance
from non-Catholic tradition, or superstition. While the tradition of
Catholicism remains strong, that of non-Catholic belief is eroded,
making the 'traditional' belief in the evil eye 'irrationally' traditional
– as opposed to the 'rational' traditionality of the Catholic Church.

Belief and Bodily Experience

The rise in Devil power and fall of the *ghajn* can also be seen in the context of broader transformations in Maltese religiosity. The rise of Catholic organisations such as the Catholic Charismatic Renewal (see Theuma, chapter five of this volume) have ushered in an increasingly 'Pentecostal' focus for Maltese belief, invoking the direct power of the Holy Spirit over the person. This in turn lends new currency to the experiential, with belief increasingly drawing upon the bodily feelings associated with the presence of the Holy Spirit. This focus on experience, although a central feature of more 'marginal' movements such as the Catholic Charismatic Renewal, is also prevalent in the mainstream Church (Mitchell 1997). Indeed, bodily experience and 'feeling' might be described as central to Maltese belief. For example, the regular rituals of holy communion are not only rites of commemoration (Connerton 1989: 47, Halbwachs 1992: 99) but also significant experiential moments. Informants described a tingling sensation or feeling of warmth as they ingested the host during communion – a bodily feeling both signalled by and signalling the presence of the power of God (Mitchell 1997: 90–91).

This focus on experience gave increased currency to forms of belief that were directly experienced by the person, or felt by the body. This was the case with the power of the Devil, but not so with that of the *ghajn*. In contrast to the 'stronger' version of evil embodied in the Devil, the power of the 'weaker' *ghajn* is located inside the person, and is a consequence of human agency. The Devil, for its part, originates outside the person, and is a wholly supernatural agency – non-human, even anti-human. This difference in the source or location of the malignant powers signals an important difference in the way Maltese people experience them. Paradoxically, although the Devil's power originates outside the body, it is a felt power. Accounts of possession by the Devil or his demons describe in detail the various somatological symptoms of the Devil's presence. That of the *ghajn*, by contrast, is not felt, despite originating *within* the body. Accounts of the *ghajn* stress the fact that there are no symptoms experienced by people who possess it, only by those who are their victims. Possessors of the evil eye are not conscious of this supernatural agency, although as with witchcraft there may be local disputes about the consciousness or unconsciousness of such power (see Evans-Pritchard 1976: 56–64, Ginzburg 1984: 39–48).

The bodily experiences entailed in the presence of the Devil's power are cognatic with experiences of the powers of goodness. An increased emphasis on the experiential nature of human relationships with God also leads to a focus on the experiences brought about by the power of the Devil. Thus, although the Devil has been central to images of Maltese evil for many centuries (see Borg, chapter eight of this volume), his contemporary prevalence is marked by the new manifestations of Satanic ritual and possession. This new focus on the experiential, however, means that versions of evil – such as the *ghajn* – which are not directly experienced, become less convincing, and ultimately lose salience. If the focus of belief shifts towards the bodily feelings caused by the direct action of grand, mysterious powers – of good or evil – then beliefs which *don't* involve these feelings, among them the *ghajn*, increasingly fail to convince. The transformations of evil, then, the increase in Devil powers and decrease in the *ghajn* relate not only to Maltese ambivalence towards 'traditional' and 'modern' ways of life, but also to differences in the locus of power which in turn mean differences in the ways they are experienced.

Speak of the Devil

The fieldwork on which this chapter is based was conducted in Valletta, the capital city of Malta, in the parish of St Paul's Shipwreck. During two years in Malta (1992–1994) I examined social relations in the parish, focusing particularly on how the specifically local concerns of Valletta's people articulated with those of the nation. As in the population of St Paul's parish, Valletta is socially differentiated. In particular, there is a distinction of social hierarchy between those regarded as members of 'polite' society – *il-pulit* ('the polite') – and those who are not. This differentiation maps onto a spatial distinction between the topographically higher parts of the parish – *il-fuq* (lit. 'the up') – and the lower parts – *l-isfel* (lit. 'the down') – and therefore relates to residence, but also to occupation, wealth and social connections in the wider national political and social milieus (Mitchell 1998a, forthcoming). There are also significant distinctions on the basis of age and gender in Valletta, which shape the contours of discussion about the practitioners of Satanic ritual and belief in the *ghajn*.

Like the results of much anthropological fieldwork, a good deal of the data I collected was taken from everyday conversations that I participated in and listened to in various locations – bars, coffee shops, sitting rooms and the sacristy of the parish church. These observations were supplemented with more directed interviews and discussions with both laity and clergy. During these conversations and interviews, a profound concern was expressed for Malta's future. It was often framed in terms of the imminent threat of a seeping and erosive 'modernity' threatening Maltese society and morality. Particular *foci* were the increased emphasis on personal material gain, sexual promiscuity and the rising tide of recreational drug use. These three potential threats were associated with a fourth – the presence and power of the Devil and Satanism.

These four main elements comprised a matrix of the Devil's activity. The Devil, materialism, sex and drugs were often seen as causally related, but in different ways (see Fig. 1). There were two main trends. First, there were accounts of Satanic practices, in which materialism led to pacts with the Devil made during rituals involving sex and drugs. These rituals were aimed at summoning the power of the Devil, and were said to be performed in remote rural areas, wealthy neighbourhoods or the new entertainment centres geared towards the tourist industry. They were said to involve a variety of proscribed sexual activities, animal and sometimes human sacrifice, and the widespread use of drugs. Second, there were accounts which stressed a different line of causality. In these examples, rather than the Devil's power being courted or invited, it was said to have entered people's lives – and indeed their bodies – of its own accord. The focus was on the various 'windows' of opportunity the Devil had. Again, materialism, sex and drug abuse were linked, with each being seen as both cause and consequence of the others – drug abuse leads to materialism and sexual promiscuity, materialism leads to sexual promiscuity and drug abuse or sexual promiscuity leads to drug abuse and materialism. This type of account focused on the possession of people's bodies by the Devil or his demons, and the feelings associated with his presence and expulsion.

In general, accounts of Satanism were more common than those of possession, although the two were not mutually exclusive. The former presupposed the latter in a way that contrasted with La Fontaine's observation that in contemporary Britain, Satanism may be invoked by those who do not necessarily believe in the Devil (1998: 7). Although as in the British tales, the spread of Satanism in Malta might involve various types of exploitation or abuse, it is primarily the Devil himself that is the object of anxiety, not the abuse people suffer during his worship. In the Maltese context, the reason why Satanism is dangerous is because it invokes the very real power of the Devil.

Figure 1: Lines of Causality in Accounts of the Devil

SATANISM:	Materialism	> >	Devil Pact	> >	Sex/Drugs
POSSESSION:	Sex/Drugs/Materialism	> > > >	> >	> >	Possession

Conversation about the *ghajn* was rather less common, and people showed a marked reluctance to discuss its power or prevalence. It was seen as backward, a thing of the past. People who did talk about it were often embarrassed, and became the objects of derision. When I began to ask questions about the *ghajn*, the immediate response was *temmen bl-ghajn?* – 'do you believe in the *ghajn*?'. The question was asked with a smile, and a hint of incredulity. As a 'modern' Northern European, I could not possibly believe in such an outdated superstition. Yet this reluctance to discuss the *ghajn* was not only a product of my presence as an outsider. As I show below, my Maltese informants were also reluctant to discuss the *ghajn* among themselves. There appeared to be a clear hierarchy of acceptable concerns in early-1990s Malta, and this mirrored official Church teaching on evil, the *ghajn* and the Devil.

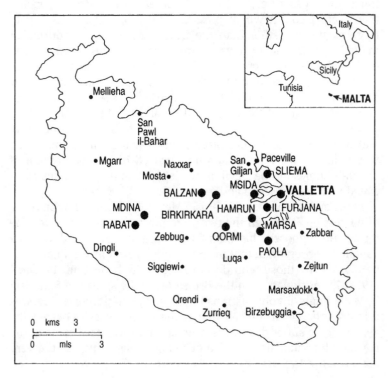

The Devil Came Down to Malta

Although the invocation of Satanic activity – both ritual and possession – is firmly anchored in contemporary Maltese society, the
Devil has been present since the arrival of Christianity.[4] The division between good and evil is central to Christian theology, and
has led to the equally fundamental characterisation of this opposition in the figures of God and the Devil. The Devil, as God's logical opposite and spiritual adversary, is a necessary point of
reference for the contemplation of goodness. As John Wesley put
it, 'No Devil, no God' (Forsyth 1987: 8). The origins of this opposition lie in the incorporation of Essene and Zoroastrian dualisms
into Jewish theology by the early Christians (Russell 1981: 36–40).
A later, Manichean dualism spurred Augustine to link evil in the
world to the very human activity of sin, made inevitable in the
notion of original sin (Farmer 1987: 29).In this sin lay the origins
of all evil, and the foundations of the eternal conflict or combat
between good and evil, light and dark, God and the Devil (Forsyth
1987: 399ff). By linking evil with sin he made the Devil a control-
lable power – dangerous, but ultimately weaker than the power of
God. Although evil is an abstract force, it is objectified in Augustine
and other early Christian writers in the form of a legion of demons
or fallen angels led by the Devil himself (Russell 1981: 36). As
such, the Devil becomes a kind of Ur-symbol of a multiplicity of
evil spirits which are increasingly subsumed under a singular
image (Stewart 1991). Under this over-arching evil are also subsumed non-standard beliefs such as those in the *ghajn*, and abject
heresies. Both figure significantly in the history of Maltese evil.

For most of Maltese history, evil lurked across the sea in the
Islamic world, whose philosophers and theologians Aquinas had
refuted in his *Summa contra Gentiles* (Aquinas 1956). However,
there was also an internal evil, as manifest in the proliferation of
witchcraft, sorcery and magic which preoccupied the Maltese
Inquisition, set up in 1561 and not dissolved until 1800 (Cassar
1993, Bonnici 1990). In its latter years, there was also concern
about the increasing influence of the rationalist *philosophes,* and
with the advent of British colonial rule in 1800 a new set of heresies arrived, in the form of established Protestantism and Freemasonry (Agius 1995, Sant 1992). The latter continues to preoccupy
the popular imagination in Malta, and is seen by some as the origin
of Satanism. With the development of party politics in Malta, in the
late nineteenth and early twentieth centuries, a new opponent to

the Church emerged – in the form of socialism (Frendo 1979). This became the central preoccupation for Catholicism not just locally, but also globally.

Under the colonial constitutions Maltese politics became heavily polarised, resulting in the current opposition between a broadly Christian Democratic Nationalist Party, and a Socialist Malta Labour Party. Independence came in 1964, and during the Labour Government of 1971 to 1987 links were established with Gadaffi's Libya and the Eastern bloc – suggestive given the Church's historical attitude to Islam and Socialism. The administration pursued a policy of austerity, imposing high import taxes that made consumer goods both expensive and hard to come by. In 1987, Labour were replaced by the Nationalists, who promised greater access to goods, an end to the links with Libya and the Soviets, and Malta's entry into Europe. Europe had come to stand for all things 'modern'. Not only consumer goods, but also education and democracy were held up as potential goals for Malta under a Nationalist Government.

The application to join the EU – tabled by the Nationalists in 1989 – brought with it EU subsidies, and privileged access to the European market. This enabled the importation of consumer goods in unprecedented quantities, and led to a rapid rise in consumption. Consumer spending rose from 306 million in Maltese pounds (Lm) (roughly £612 million sterling) in 1983 to Lm461 million in 1990 – a rise of 50 per cent (Tonna 1993: 5). With the loss of British Naval income, the Government promoted the tourist industry as a means of generating foreign exchange. The nation's gross earnings from tourism rose from Lm138.2 million in 1988 to around Lm241.9 million in 1994. Meanwhile, total tourist arrivals rose from 745,943 to 1,176,223 (National Tourism Organisation of Malta 1995). The expansion of tourism has had a considerable impact on local life, and although the overall economic benefits are welcomed, there are also frequent Maltese complaints about the intrusive nature of tourism, and its effects on the island's environment (Boissevain 1996, Boissevain and Theuma 1998).

On the whole, the increased affluence was popular in Malta, although by 1996 it became clear that EU membership would also have less palatable economic consequences. In the election of that year, the big issue was tax reform, and particularly the introduction of VAT as part of the streamlining of the Maltese economy with EU expectations. Apart from an increase in the cost of living, the move meant unprecedented surveillance of an economy historically characterised by *laissez faire*. It was one of the main factors in the 1996 Nationalist loss to the Euro-sceptic Labour Party. As disillusionment with the project of EU accession developed, so did anxiety about modernisation and economic development more generally. Again, this mirrors developments in Catholicism on a global scale.

With the collapse of the Eastern bloc in 1989, and the apparent death of socialism, the Church, which had hitherto seen capitalism as the saviour of Catholic morality, began to question its excesses. In his 1991 encyclical, *Centesimus Annus*, Pope John Paul II argued that the new ideological struggle was against unbridled capitalism. He proposed as an ideal, a society that 'is not directed against the market, but demands that the market be appropriately controlled by the forces of society and by the state, so as to guarantee that the basic needs of the whole society are satisfied.' (Pope John Paul 1991: 74). In this plan, Church and state would temper the excessive tendencies of capitalism and ensure that it preserved correct moral standards. Although there may be an economistic contradiction in this message (Lenches 1993), its moral position is clear – capitalism is a good thing, but too much of a good thing is bad.

In Malta, this new orientation was manifest in escalating concern for the excesses of *materializmu* ('materialism'). *Materializmu* was seen as a major threat to the moral health of Maltese culture and society, and particularly that of its central 'traditional' institution – the family. In a pastoral letter to the Maltese nation in August 1992, the Bishops of Malta and Gozo expressed concern for the state of the family in the light of recent trends in *materializmu* (*The Times of Malta* 15/08/92: 5):

> Today, unfortunately, many future spouses and young married persons are alienated by a false desire for money because of the great debts they incur to have a home lacking nothing before thinking of children, something which could also harm their union in marriage.

The threat of increased *materializmu* was linked to an overall decline in morality. A newspaper editorial in the same month continued the theme (*The Times of Malta* 25/08/92: 4):

> Maltese society as a whole, has fallen victim to placing material values before spiritual ones. Under the excuse of freedom of thought and conscience, and of pluralistic permissiveness, many have gone much further than the bounds of liberty would allow.

Outside public culture there was also widespread concern about the negative effects of materialism. In particular, the parents of teenagers worried about their children's spendthrift attitude and apparently escalating appetite for expensive Italian clothes, music and alcohol. These in turn were associated with increased sexual activity and potential exposure to drugs. Unwanted pregnancy, abortion and Satanism made up the package of moral threats signalled by the increase in affluence and *materializmu*, and present in the Maltese popular consciousness of the early 1990s. *Materializmu* went hand in hand with the power of the Devil. Its effect was to isolate people from the proper moral context in which they ought to live their lives – the family – and make them vulnerable to possession by the Devil. It also led them to enter into Devilish pacts or actively pursue the Devil's power through Satanic ritual.

Satanic Rituals

The Maltese Church was at pains to demonstrate the enduring power of the Devil. It published a number of pamphlets and booklets outlining the threats of the Devil, and publicised this message in the newspapers. Such publications, and subsequent press reports and interviews were widely read throughout Malta, and supplemented existing knowledge about the Devil's presence. In St Paul's parish, concern about the Devil was promoted in particular by one of the local canons, who I shall call Father Joe. He was a prominent local figure, but also wrote in the national newspapers and often spoke at national prayer meetings and rallies. Through him, many of the local people learned of the dangers of modern life, and the threat of the Devil. Connections between the laity and the clergy in Valletta are strong. The clergy are often friends, advisors and confidantes even outside their official role as confessors and absolvers of sin. Father Joe was regarded as a particularly good advisor. He had long connections with the parish, and was widely trusted, particularly as a source of information and reassurance.

Father Joe saw the Devil as a very real and immediate threat – particularly to young people, and the future. I discussed this threat with him after a parish committee meeting. During the meeting he had been doodling on a scrap of paper, drawing crucifixes, followed by swastikas. I was curious about these drawings, and asked him about their significance. He said that he had just seen graffiti in the form of a swastika spray-painted onto the main door of the church, and asked the sacristan to clean it off. The vandals were Satanists, he said, trying to attack the Church by putting their mark on it. This was quite typical nowadays, with the rise of the Devil. He explained that the swastika was a perverted form of the crucifix, and in drawing the two together, he was working through that perversion, to try and understand it better. Such a process of discernment is central to the clerical preoccupation with the Devil's mystery. It mirrors the activities of inquisitors and witch-finders in earlier years, for whom signs of *Maleficium* became reinterpretable as diabolic or heretic activities, thus permitting a proliferation of 'signs' of the Devil (Sanders 1995: 166). Once discernment becomes a preoccupation, almost anything can be identified and discerned as evidence of Satanism (La Fontaine 1998: 49–55). Indeed, La Fontaine points out that levels of actual Satanic ritual practices are extremely low despite strong moral panics in both USA and UK during the late 1980s (46–49). The same is undoubtedly true of early 1990s Malta. Actual levels of Satanic activity were probably negligible or perhaps even non-existent, but this is not the point. The point is that there was substantial fear of the apparently rising tide of Satanism and the Devil's power, that gained momentum in part through the identification of particular 'signs'. In the process, the swastika, which in other contexts might be associated with neo-fascism or simply mindless graffiti, became significant evidence of the Devil's presence.

In this process of identifying or discerning Satanism, a kind of bricolage of clichés emerged which, significantly, saw its origins in external cultural forces that were taking over and threatening the integrity of Maltese life. In discussions with a group of Father Joe's parishioners, the origins of Devil-worship in Malta were explained to me. This conversation took place with a group of – mostly married – men in their thirties and forties, over a drink on the Sunday night after the swastika had appeared on the church door. Like Father Joe, they were concerned that the perpetrators were Satanists. For them, Satanism was prevalent, and increasing. It had come to Malta through music, they said. First punk, then heavy metal music, had been introduced to the Maltese youth, in whom it had encouraged a respect for or even worship of Satan. One had only to look at the t-shirts many young people wore, and the covers of the compact discs on sale, to see their Satanic content. This account was corroborated by the exorcist Elias Vella, in a press interview that cited the usual cliché of subliminal messages in the music of various heavy metal bands which, when played backwards, revealed statements such as '"Satan is my Lord", "Hail to Satan" etc' (*The Sunday Times (Malta)* 11/07/93).

With the encouragement of foreign music, Malta's youth were increasingly motivated to hold Satanic rituals in remote parts of the countryside. The evidence of these rituals was identified in the landscape, in the form of a variety of signs. One man said that when he had been walking in the countryside he had seen a cave with the remains of a fire and charred animal bones. That was just hunters, came a reply, but the first man persisted – there was a skull and crossbones daubed on the wall nearby, which was surely evidence of Satanism. Another said that he had recently been walking in the old British cemetery, and many of the graves had been opened or vandalised. 'They use the bones for the black mass', he said.

Accounts of who 'they' were varied, but as with the kinds of accusation associated with witchcraft (Sanders 1995: 73ff), 'they' were generally 'not people like us'. However, unlike witchcraft accusations – and unlike those associated with the *ghajn* – Satanic rituals were not, for these men at least, associated with women. Rather, they were associated with wayward 'youth' – *zghazagh* – a category that gained increasing currency throughout the late 1980s, and which the central institutions of Maltese society, the Church and the two main political parties, attempted to co-opt by setting up youth organisations that helped to give direction to this otherwise problematic category of person.

Concerns that Maltese *zghazagh* were involved in Satanic practices fed into the overall discourse of declining morality in the face of European 'modernity'. For this group of men in their thirties and forties, Maltese youth were flighty and irresponsible, showing a lack of commitment to 'traditional' ritual practices such as the annual parish *festa* – 'saint's feast'.[5] They habitually berated the decline of Maltese society and the egotism, materialism and *libertinagg* – 'taking liberties' – of the youth. Alongside this perception of an increasingly individualistic Maltese youth went concerns over youth drug abuse and sexual promiscuity. These concerns were epitomised by attitudes towards the coastal resort town of Paceville, the streets of which are lined with bars and night-clubs that attract young people from all over Malta on weekend evenings. Paceville was regarded as a centre of material excess, with entertainment and consumption of alcohol, sex and drugs contributing to a new culture of gratification. As one man put it, 'It's a place that encourages you to want more and more. It's no surprise those youths end up in trouble.'

Significantly, Paceville was also regarded as a centre of Satanic practices, or at least a centre for the organisation of such practices. While there, young people were lured into participating in Satanic rituals, it was argued, with promises of sexual or material success.

These inter-generational tensions were matched by ones that reaffirmed the tensions and antagonisms between 'polite society' – *il-pulit* – and those who were neither as wealthy nor as well-connected. The men with whom I discussed the causes and consequences of Satanism, and indeed with whom I spent most of my two years in Malta, fell into this latter category. They were mainly skilled or semi-skilled workers for government or private companies in Valletta and elsewhere, and often expressed a resentment or antagonism towards those who were better off or more influential. At times, this resentment verged on a kind of conspiratorial assumption that the whole of Malta was run by a central 'clique' – *klikka* – of interconnected *pulit* who organised their lives for maximum personal gain and, although apparently governing a democratic state, were in fact unaccountable to the people – *il-poplu*.[6] This sense of conspiracy was consolidated by an assertion that many of the wealthiest and most influential Maltese – either businessmen or aristocracy[7] – were involved in Satanic practices.

Again, the focus was on materialism and the anti-social consequences of greed, with a direct link being made between the accumulation of wealth and influence, and Satanic practices. Often, narratives of elite Satanism related back to the historical concerns over Freemasonry, a link articulated in both press accounts and everyday conversations. According to these narratives, the aristocratic and other elites were either driven to maintain their wealth and position, or had achieved them in the first place, by entering into pacts with the Devil. As explained by one Valletta man:

> They meet up in the countryside . . . near Wardija [a remote area close to some of the wealthier Maltese villages] and meet up with the Devil. They sell their souls to the Devil, in return for help with their material and financial needs.

This image of a contract links the supernatural with the material. If wealth and influence is accumulated through formal and informal contracts, so does their means of accumulating it – the support of and power of the Devil. Not all *pulit* were seen as guilty of entering into these contracts. Others had achieved their position through hard work and application, but there were some, and perhaps an increasing number, who had turned to the Devil for help.

This focus on personal moral corruption and personal gain was born out in discussions with another, different group with whom I discussed the issue of Satanism. These were young college students, themselves often from *pulit* families, and therefore potentially doubly culpable in the eyes of the older Vallettans – they were both 'youth' and 'elite'. For them, Satanic practitioners were also drawn from these groups, and therefore from their own group, but their stories of Devil worship avoided a blanket vilification. Rather, they focused on personal respectability and demarcated a boundary of moral acceptability in pursuit of material or political goals. For them, the accumulation of wealth or influence was not problematic *per se*, but there were problematic ways in which it could be achieved. This mirrors the Church position that capitalism is not inherently bad, but could lead to bad things if done improperly.

For example, one evening I was sitting having dinner with a group of students in their early twenties, both men and women. They were discussing the success of one of their colleagues in a recent round of examinations, and his subsequent injury in a car crash. One of them remarked how amazed he had been when Godwin had done so well in the exams. He hadn't done a scrap of work, and had been out in Paceville virtually every night during the revision period. 'He had help', replied another, with a knowing look, 'He's "of the Devil"' – *ta'xitan*. That was why he had done so well, but also perhaps explained his accident. It was the Devil telling him that he couldn't be complacent about the commitment he had made.

The group explained how the student had been ostracised at College following these events, because of the suspicion that he had achieved success by immoral and supernatural means. Their concerns clearly demarcated an area of acceptable and moral success, in contrast to the immoral and unacceptable pursuit of success through Satanism or other means.

Blaming the student's car accident on the Devil signalled a predominant perception of the Devil as fundamentally untrustworthy. Although one could enter into a contract with the Devil, these were contracts that he would always benefit from more than you. As one informant put it, 'you can believe in the Devil, but he can't be trusted. God, on the other hand, is both believed and trusted'. The idea of God as both believed in and trusted has its origins in the notion of creed, or *credo*. This comes from the Latin *credere*, which also gave rise to the notion of credit and the necessity of trust in economic activity (cf Gambetta 1988). If, via the notion of *credo*, belief can be split into the trustworthy and the untrustworthy, so through the idea of trust, can capitalist economics. Just as *credo* signals a distinction between good and evil at a supernatural level, so credit signals a distinction between good and evil economics or accumulation. For whilst at one level, credit is necessary for the functioning of the market, and giving trust in others' activities is a positive valuation of their integrity, an over-dependence on credit – and particularly the active creation of credit in others – is negative. This message was central to John Paul II's 1991 Encyclical, and is fundamental to Maltese ambivalence towards capitalism, modernity and Europe. It linked notions of unacceptable economic activity and unacceptable accumulation with those of unacceptable – even sinful – ritual practices.

In descriptions of what Satanists got up to in their rituals, there was an emphasis on desecration, or perversion. Father Joe told of how young Satanists had started stealing consecrated hosts from communion services to be used in the Satanic mass. In Catholic theology, the consecrated host is the body of Christ, so abusing the host is abusing Christ himself. In the rituals attended by Satanists, the desecration of Christ's body was matched by desecration of their own. In accounts of the rituals, reported in the press as confessions of former Satanists, drug abuse and 'beastly sex' figure prominently. In a society dominated by Catholic morality, in which sex is generally considered sinful outside procreation, the invocation of oral sex, group sex and bestiality was extremely shocking. Whether or not these reports of Satanic ritual were 'true', they nevertheless had both an effect, and a meaning. Their effect was to prompt something of a moral panic. The Church began to organise all-night prayer vigils on full moon nights, which were believed to be particularly popular for Satanists. Their meaning was to communicate particular anxieties about modernity and excess.

Just as the Pope's new ambivalence towards capitalism was based on the condemnation of excess, so the proliferation of the Devil's activity in Malta was related to excess. *Materializmu* was a guiding force, giving rise to temptation. Temptation took many forms – sexual, chemical, material – and was seen as central to the Devil's designs. Although not directly responsible for temptation, the Devil nevertheless profited from it (Vella 1992: 15). Temptation created windows of opportunity through which the Devil could enter, to possess the individual: 'Among those windows through which Satan easily enters one could name: violence, hatred, drugs, drink, prostitution etc' (Ibid. 23).

Satanic Possession

If accounts of Satanic ritual saw a causal movement from greed and materialism to Devil pacts that involved sex and drugs, accounts of possession involved an inversion of this causal sequence (see Fig. 1, p. 84). In this account, sex, drugs and materialism were seen as opportunities that the Devil might seize upon to enter the person and possess them.

The symptoms of possession are not always conclusive, and a great deal of time and energy is put into discerning the difference between physical or psychological illness, and possession. A general listlessness was often cited, or a lack of capacity to enjoy life, leading to an urge to commit suicide, as well as hostility towards and even fear of sacred items (such as the crucifix, holy water or consecrated oil), speaking in religious tongues, sudden violent outbursts and the vomiting of green or black substances (*Sunday Times (Malta)* 11/07/93). Many of these symptoms are consistent with those of drug addiction, and it is with this 'window' that possession by the Devil is particularly associated.

Since the 1970s, drug addiction and its associated problems of crime and delinquency have been a major preoccupation for the citizens of Malta in general, and Valletta in particular (Mitchell 1998a). The various derelict houses and abandoned tenements are popular places to shoot up and crash out. The groups of junkies who congregate in these places are regarded with suspicion and fear, and sometimes represented in demonological terms as *taxxitan* ('of Satan'). At a much more general level, however, drug addiction was referred to as possession by the Devil. At prayer meetings organised by Catholic Pentecostalist groups, ex-drug addicts would describe the pain of their possession, as well as outline the details of Satanic activities (see Theuma, chapter five of this volume).

This image of possession was born out by my Valletta informants, including one young man, an example of the wayward *zghazagh*, who had been a drug addict. He was keen to emphasise that his experience of possession during addiction was more than mere metaphor. His addiction to drugs *was* possession by the Devil:

> Listen, Jon. I was taken over. I had Satan inside me. Really. At the time it was fantastic. You can't believe what the feeling was like. But it was painful too – and hard to get over. Really hard. When the Devil gets into you, it's hard to get him out.

To understand the movement from using the Devil and possession as a metaphor for drug addiction, to an interpretation of addiction *as* Satanic possession, we must understand that statements about belief in the Devil's power are *constitutive* rather than *representational*. A number of anthropologists, following Austin's (1962) formulation of 'performative' speech acts, have argued that statements of belief, rather than representing some inner state of being actually *produce* that state (Csordas 1989, Harding 1987, Stromberg 1993). For example Csordas, in an analysis of healing services among Charismatic Christians in the USA, describes how people come to acknowledge and therefore experience evil spirits as a result of the 'discernment' of the presiding Reverend (1989: 13–14). Before coming into the service, many of the participants were unaware of being possessed by spirits, but once the Reverend had identified them, a range of experiences such as coughing, choking, vomiting or a feeling of electric shock, confirmed their presence. Through these experiences, themselves brought about by the words of the Reverend, the participants came to believe they were possessed. By identifying the possession linguistically, the spirits were brought into existence, or put another way, the speech act performed by the Reverend *produced* the spirit.

A similar process can be seen in the constitution of Satanic possession in Malta. Not only during healing masses organised by the Catholic Charismatic movement, but also during drug rehabilitation programmes, drug addicts are encouraged to view their affliction and its symptoms as evidence of the Devil's presence. The young man quoted above described to me his experiences at a Church-run drug rehabilitation unit. He'd gone in looking for help, he said, and because he felt out of control. He was getting desperate and thought to himself that he was likely to 'do something stupid', by which he meant damage either himself or members of his family. He referred to the therapy programme as one of strict regimentation, with a strong emphasis on bodily discipline. There was also a strongly religious element, he said, and with time he began to see that his feelings of loss of control, of depression and fear, were signs of the Devil's presence. The process allowed him to reconstitute the bodily symptoms of addiction as feelings caused by Satanic possession. He explained to me that he had been sceptical to start with, but it gradually became clear. The therapy programme, like the healing service of Csordas's American Charismatics, constituted a belief in the intrusive and threatening powers of the Devil (see also Borg, chapter eight of this volume).

This constitutive process transforms the Devil from a mysterious and distant figure to an immediate physical and spiritual threat. Above all, it identifies the Devil's power as a *felt* power, with a distinct array of symptoms and a recognisable cure – exorcism. Although my drug addict friend never referred to a process of exorcism explicitly, the identification of his problem as one of possession suggests that alongside the regime of detoxification and rehabilitation there was also a process of exorcism. In identifying his malady as also a supernatural one, he simultaneously identified his body as a site of spiritual struggle in which an intrusive evil power needed to be exorcised by a benevolent good one. This focus on bodily experience was gaining increased currency in early-1990s Malta, with the Charismatic movement growing and other forms of experiential religious practice, most notably the parish saints' feasts or *festi*, escalating in scale and popularity (Boissevain 1991, 1992). Boissevain interprets this escalation in terms of an increased salience of the ludic. One might equally argue that it also represents an increased importance of the experiential (see Mitchell 1998b).

These phenomena represent an increased significance of the bodily element in religious experiences of good, but the same can also be said of experiences of evil – the two go hand in hand. That the bodily threat of Satanic possession was becoming increasingly immediate is demonstrated by the rehabilitation of the Church office of exorcist, which was re-established in the early 1990s after a period of thirty years during which there was no exorcist in Malta. This increased focus on the experiential in early-1990s Maltese religiosity had the opposite effect on people's belief in the *ghajn*. Where the Devil as immediate bodily threat increased, the *ghajn* as property of the body was in decline.

The Decline of the *Ghajn*

The decline of the *ghajn* can partly be explained in discursive terms. Whilst Church discourse was committed to preserving the existence of the Devil as an orthodox belief, the *ghajn* was regarded as superstition. As Burke (1978) has pointed out, the Church's definitions of superstition effectively make it a residual category. Anything that falls outside the acceptable canon of orthodox beliefs becomes superstition, by definition. But it is also assumed that such non-standard belief is systematic and shared.

Along with the notion of heresy, then, superstition implies a dis-
crete, autonomous tradition, separate and perhaps opposed to that
of the Church, which must be stamped out. This acknowledgement
of an alternative tradition to that of the Church is central to an
understanding of the transformations in evil belief of early-1990s
Malta.

In Malta, superstition is associated with beliefs which come
from the non-Catholic tradition of folklore. In general, this tradition
is not particularly well articulated, and the category of folklore is
used to describe a range of non-standard beliefs and practices –
from the burning of palm or olive leaves at Easter to expel demons,
to the telling of fortunes by wise women, or *sahhara*, to the use of
protective amulets against the *ghajn*. They were regarded as obsolete beliefs, only maintained by the elderly and in remoter parts of
Malta; interesting, perhaps, as part of the national heritage, and for
presentation to tourists, but no longer part of everyday life. The origins of such 'folklore' are of little concern to the wider public,
although Maltese folklorists have identified various continuities
between local practices and Semitic, or Arabic, folklore (Cassar-
Pullicino 1992). The beliefs and practices are disapproved of by the
Church. Another St Paul's priest, Father Peter, explained that practices associated with divination and fortune telling are considered
particularly problematic, because they amounted to a human
attempt to 'play at God'. For Vella, they constitute another 'window
of opportunity' for the Devil (*The Sunday Times (Malta)*
11/07/93).

However, alongside these discursive reasons for a decline in the
ghajn there were other considerations relating back to the issue of
bodily experience and the extent to which the *ghajn* was considered a *felt* power. Paradoxically, although the *ghajn* was said to
originate within the body, in contrast to the external power of the
Devil, it could not, in and of itself, be felt. People who had it were
not aware of the fact. Rather, its presence could only be deduced
by its effects. One Valletta woman in her fifties explained the *ghajn*
to me as follows:

> Jealousy is in the heart. That's where sin comes from, but for some
> people, the jealousy comes out and hurts others. *Imsieken* ['Poor
> things'] I call them. It's not their fault, and they don't even know
> they've got the *ghajn*.

This power can cause damage to others or their property, but is
uncontrollable and unfelt. For this reason, in an environment

which gave increasing significance to felt experiences of the super-natural, the *ghajn* was increasingly superseded by the Devil as a significant power of evil – a felt power of evil.

However, it was not only this contrast between Devil as felt and *ghajn* as unfelt that marked the demise of the *ghajn*. It was also discouraged by the Church, and disapproved of in an everyday context, where discourses on modernity and education prevailed, as well as those on Catholicism. We have already seen how my apparently believing in the *ghajn* provoked incredulity among the people of Valletta. In other contexts, it became even more clear that debates about the *ghajn* were also debates about modernity, sophistication and education.

Again, social differentiation was important in debates about the *ghajn*. It was widely held by both the Valletta men and the students with whom I had freely discussed the Devil, that belief in the *ghajn* was a thing of the past. It was only believed by certain 'ignorant' people – *injurant* – old people, particularly women, and some of those who lived in the 'lower' part of Valletta – *l-isfel*. As with dis-cussions about the Devil and Satanism it was wrapped up with ideas of social hierarchy. In this context, though, the debates revolved around a politics of distinction as much as antagonisms between *pulit* groups and *il-poplu* – 'the people'(see Bourdieu 1984, Stewart 1991). The debates were also different in form. Where accusations of Satanism were the subject of denigration in discussions about the Devil, a *belief* in the *ghajn* was sufficient to classify a person as *injurant*. While the one discourse acknowl-edged the phenomenon, and then looked round to see who was guilty of it, the other denied its existence and looked round to see who was stupid enough to believe in it.

Significantly, although the woman quoted above clearly did believe in the *ghajn*, it was obvious from other discussions that many older women were equally sceptical about it as their younger male neighbours. One afternoon I had been sitting talking with a group of elderly women, about the various types of non-standard belief that had used to be common in Malta. When I introduced the *ghajn* as a topic of discussion, they denied its existence, citing Father Joe as an authority who had assured them it didn't exist. As the conversation wore on, they began to cite anecdotes in which their neighbours or friends had cited the *ghajn* as the cause of breakages, accidents and illnesses. Conversation focused on one particular woman, who always wore small gold amulets, in the form of chilli peppers and hands formed in the sign of the horns –

with index and little finger protruding, and the middle two fingers held back with the thumb. These were worn as protection against the *ghajn*. She was *injurant* ('ignorant'), they said. Wearing all those amulets made it look like she was accusing them of having the *ghajn*. She was *pastaza* ('rude/rough'). The focus here was not so much on the non-Catholic element of such 'superstition', but on its being evidence of 'ignorance', or lack of education. This is where the denial of belief in the *ghajn* becomes linked to discourses of modernity.

Conclusion

Although associated with the evils of the Devil and Satanism, modernity and capitalism were not considered unequivocally evil. Modernity could be a source of positive change, not only because it provided access to consumer goods and labour-saving devices, but also because it brought rationality and scientism. As well as threatening Catholic tradition, modernity provided a more acceptable challenge to superstitious or folkloric tradition. Following Independence, such a challenge was increasingly available, through the expansion of education, both formal and informal. In particular, the 1970s increasingly saw education being made available to the mass of society, rather than a wealthy, privileged few. Compulsory primary education for all had been introduced in 1946. In 1970 a policy of secondary education for all was introduced, and consolidated in 1974 with the Education Act that made education compulsory for all Maltese aged 6 -16 (Zammit Mangion 1992: 104). Malta's one University also expanded, with student numbers rising from 730 in 1978 to 3,564 in 1992 (*Malta Year Book 1994*). This massification has made education itself a valued commodity, and with it has come a denigration of 'traditional' beliefs and practices such as those associated with the *ghajn*. They were increasingly categorised as 'superstitions', to be eradicated, rather than preserved.

Like the preservation of 'traditional' family values, the eradication of 'superstition' was promoted by the Church, but its denial also became an important part of the Maltese self-image. By and large, Maltese of the early 1990s would distance themselves from 'superstitious' beliefs in order to avoid their being seen as 'backward'. Denying belief in the *ghajn* became part of their own narration of themselves as 'modern' (see Stewart 1991).

To be even considered for accession to Europe, Malta must be modern, rational, developed. It must therefore abandon such superstitious and folkloristic beliefs that associate it not only with Europe's past but also, more problematically, with the Arab world. Such is the motivation behind the denial of *ghajn* belief, and its subsequent decline. To be modern is to be free from such problematic associations, but also to be incorporated into a wider capitalist economic system that provides prosperity and the opportunity for consumption of foreign goods – the trappings of modernity. However, modernity is not all good. It encourages excess, greed, materialism and temptation. The latter, particularly when associated with sexuality and drugs, give an opportunity to the Devil, who can take people over to possess them for his own purposes. Apprehensions of modernity, then, fuel both a decline in belief in the *ghajn* and an increase in that of the Devil. Moreover, these discourses on modernity articulate with those of established Catholicism, to achieve the same end. The Church is ambivalent about capitalist development, and as such promotes the association of modernity's excesses with the Devil and Satanism. However, it also supports the rationalist invocation of education in the denigration of superstitious *ghajn* beliefs. These transformations of evil are a product of Malta's position on the edges of Europe, simultaneously preoccupied with becoming European and concerned at the threat Europeanisation, capitalism and modernity might pose to traditional Catholic life.

Yet there is another reason why the transformations I have outlined in this chapter might be occurring. This is linked to the relationship between belief and experience. Belief in the Devil and belief in the *ghajn* attribute feelings in different ways, and also locate the power of evil in different places. While the Devil's power is outside the body, it can enter and take over the body, causing various changes. These symptoms are felt by the possessed body, and are indices of the Devil's power itself. By contrast, the power of the *ghajn* is felt neither by its agent nor its victim. As we have seen, those who possess the *ghajn* may be unconscious of the fact, and those who are subject to it only know the fact because something happens that is interpreted as a manifestation of the *ghajn*. Put another way, the *ghajn* explains misfortune, while the Devil *is* misfortune. It seems to me that this distinction in the experiential aspect of the Devil and *ghajn* belief serves as a phenomenological precondition for the transformations I am engaged in explaining. Because the *ghajn* is not felt, it is vulnerable to the modernising discourses that seek to rationalise it out of existence, whereas the Devil, as a felt power, is strong and strengthening. The developments in Catholic belief create a context in which its discourses of evil, tradition and modernity are brought to bear on the Maltese population with an immediate, experiential force. In conditions of anxiety and ambivalence, this force can be discerned in the transformations of evil.

Notes

1. The attribution of misfortune to the supernatural agency of others has been a classic theme in the anthropology of malevolence, particularly in the sphere of witchcraft, which has broadly been seen as an explanation for or rationalisation of misfortune (Evans-Pritchard 1976, Marwick 1982, Briggs 1996). According to this argument, misfortunes such as sudden illness, crop failure or other accidents are blamed on the malevolent powers of a neighbour. Witchcraft accusations therefore have the twin function of giving explanation for apparently random occurrences, and providing a channel for the airing of neighbourhood grievances. This is no less the case with the *ghajn*.
2. Fieldwork was carried out from 1992 to 1994, funded by an ESRC Research Studentship. I am grateful to them, and to Paul Clough, Joel Kahn, Hildi Mitchell and Charles Stewart for their comments on earlier versions of this chapter.
3. As should be clear from this statement, I am less interested in whether the Devil or the *ghajn* actually *were* changing in prevalence, than what it means for my Maltese informants to *say* that they were. If we assume, after Needham (1972) and Asad (1983) that belief is a discursive practice, then changes in the prevalence of belief must also be seen in a discursive context.
4. According to the Acts of the Apostles, Christianity arrived in Malta with St Paul in 60AD. See Mitchell 1998c.
5. For a detailed discussion of Maltese *festa* see Boissevain 1965 and Mitchell 1996.
6. For a more detailed discussion of relations between *poplu* and *pulit* see Mitchell 1998a. The process described here mirrors that identified by Geschiere in Cameroon, where the ruling elite become associated with a shady clique of witches (1997: 5).
7. Malta has an aristocracy that dates back to before the arrival of the Knights of St John (1530). The oldest title was given by Ludovic, King of Sicily in 1350 (Malta Year Book 1994: 369). Although they no longer have a direct role in politics, they are nevertheless an acknowledged presence as a slightly aloof and wealthy elite. See also Montalto (1979).

References

Abela, A. M., 1991, *Transmitting Values in European Malta*. Malta: Jesuit Publications.

Agius, R., 1995, *The Genesis of Freemasonry in Malta*. Malta.

Aquinas, T., 1956 [1955] *On the Truth of the Catholic Faith*. 5 vols, trans. A.C. Pegis, J.F. Anderson, V.J. Bourke, C.J. O'Neil. New York: Doubleday.

Asad, T., 1983, 'Anthropological Conceptions of Religion: eflections on Geertz', *Man*, N.S. 18 (2): 237–59.

Austin, J. L., 1962, *How to do Things with Words*. Oxford: Clarendon Press.

Boissevain, J., 1965, *Saints and Fireworks: Religion and Politics in Rural Malta*. London: Athlone.

Boissevain, J., 1991, 'Ritual, Play and Identity: Changing Patterns of Celebration in Maltese Villages', *Journal of Mediterranean Studies*, 1 (1): 87–100.

Boissevain, J., 1992, 'Play and Identity: Ritual Change in a Maltese Village', in Boissevain, J., ed., *Revitalising European Ritual*. London: Routledge: 137–54.

Boissevain, J., 1996, 'But We Live Here!: Perspectives on Cultural Tourism in Malta', in Briguglio, L., Butler, R., Harrison, D. and Leal Filho, W., eds, *Sustainable Tourism in Islands and Small States: Case Studies*. London: Cassell: 220–40.

Boissevain, J. and Theuma, N., 1998, 'Contested Space: Planners, Tourists, Developers and Environmentalists in Malta', in Abram, S. and Waldren, J., eds, *Anthropological Perspectives on Local Development*. London: Routledge: 96–119.

Bonnici, J., 1990, *Storja ta'L-Inkwizizzjoni ta'Malta*. Malta, 3 vols.

Bourdieu, P., 1984, *Distinction: A Social Critique of the Judgement of Taste*. Trans. Richard Nice. London: Routledge.

Briggs, R., 1996, *Witches and Neighbours: The Social and Cultural Context of European Witchcraft*. London: Harper Collins.

Burke, P., 1978, *Popular Culture in Early Modern Europe*. London: Temple Smith.

Cassar, C., 1993, 'Witchcraft Beliefs and Social Control in Seventeenth Century Malta', *Journal of Mediterranean Studies*, 3 (2): 316–34.

Cassar-Pullicino, J., 1992, *Studies in Maltese Folklore*. Malta: Malta University Press.

Comaroff, J. and Comaroff, J., 1992, *Ethnography and the Historical Imagination*. Boulder: Westview.

Comaroff, J. and Comaroff, J., eds, 1993, *Modernity and its Malcontents*. Chicago: Chicago University Press.

Connerton, P., 1989, *How Societies Remember*. Cambridge: Cambridge University Press.

Csordas, T., 1989, 'Embodiment as a Paradigm for Anthropology', *Ethos*, 18 (1): 5–47.

Dundes, A., ed., 1981, *The Evil Eye: a Folklore Casebook*. New York: Garland.

Evans-Pritchard, E. E., 1976, *Witchcraft, Oracles and Magic Among the Azande*. Oxford: Oxford University Press, abridged ed.

Farmer, D. H., 1987, *The Oxford Dictionary of Saints*. Oxford: Oxford University Press, 2nd ed.

Forsyth, N., 1987, *The Old Enemy: Satan and the Combat Myth*. Princeton: Princeton University Press.

Frendo, H., 1979, *Party Politics in a Fortress Colony*. Malta: Midsea Books.

Gambetta, D., ed, 1988, *Trust: Making and Breaking Cooperative Relations*. New York: Blackwell.

Geschiere, P., 1997, *The Modernity of Witchcraft: Politics and the Occult in Postcolonial Africa*. Charlottesville: University of Virginia Press.

Ginzburg, C., 1984, 'The Witches' Sabbat: Popular Cult or Inquisitorial Stereotype?', in Kaplan, S., ed, *Understanding Popular Culture : Europe from the Middle Ages to the nineteenth century*. Berlin: Mouton: 39–51.

Halbwachs, M., 1992, *On Collective Memory*. Trans. Coser, Lewis, A. Chicago: Chicago University Press.

Harding, S. F., 1987, 'Convicted by the Holy Spirit: the Rhetoric of Fundamental Bapitist Conversion', *American Ethnologist*, 14 (2): 167–81.

John Paul II, Pope, 1991, *Centesimus Annus*. Vatican.

Kahn, J. S., 1997, 'Demons, Commodities and the History of Anthropology', in Carrier, J., ed., *Meanings of the Market*. Oxford: Berg: 69–98.

La Fontaine, J., 1998, *Speak of the Devil: Tales of Satanic Abuse in Contemporary England*. Cambridge: Cambridge University Press.

Lenches, E. T., 1993, 'Centesimus Annus: Towards a New Capitalism', *International Journal of Social Economics*, 20 (3): 27–50.

Malta Year Book. 1994.

Marwick, M. G., ed., 1982, *Witchcraft and Sorcery: Selected Readings*. Harmondsworth: Penguin, 2nd ed.

Mitchell, J. P., 1996, 'Gender, Politics and Ritual in the Construction of Social Identities: the Case of *San Pawl*, Valletta, Malta'. PhD diss., University of Edinburgh.

Mitchell, J. P., 1997, 'A Moment with Christ: the Importance of Feelings in the Analysis of Belief', *Journal of the Royal Anthropological Institute*, 3 (1): 79–94.

Mitchell, J. P., 1998a 'The Nostalgic Construction of Community: Memory and Social Identity in Urban Malta', *Ethnos*, 63 (1): 81–101.

Mitchell, J. P., 1998b, 'Performances of Masculinity in a Maltese *Festa*', in Hughes-Freeland, F. and Crain, M., eds, *Recasting Ritual: Performance, Media, Identity*. London: Routledge: 68–91.

Mitchell, J. P., 1998c, 'A Providential Storm: myth, history and the story of St Paul's shipwreck in Malta', in Brinkhuis, F. and Talmor, S., eds, *Memory, History and Critique: European Identity at the Millennium*. Utrecht: University for Humanist Studies.

Mitchell, J. P., forthcoming, *Ambivalent Europeans: Ritual, Memory and the Public Sphere in Malta*. Chur: Harwood.

Montalto, J., 1979, *The Nobles of Malta 1530–1800*. Malta: Midsea Books.

Needham, R., 1972, *Belief, Language and Experience*. Oxford: Blackwell Publishers.

Pocock, D., 1985,'Unruly Evil', in Parkin, D., ed., *The Anthropology of Evil*. Oxford: Blackwell: 42–56.

Russell, J. B., 1981, *Satan: the Early Christian Tradition*. Ithaca: Cornell University Press.

Sanders, A., 1995, *A Deed Without Name: the Witch in Society and History*. Oxford: Berg.

Sant, C., 1992, *Bible Translation and Language: Essays into the History of Bible Translation in Malta*. Malta: University of Malta.

Stewart, C., 1991, *Demons and the Devil*. Princeton: Princeton University Press.

The Sunday Times (Malta).

Stromberg, P. G., 1993, *Language and Self-Transformation : A Study of the Christian Conversion Narrative*. Cambridge: Cambridge University Press.

Taussig, M., 1980, *The Devil and Commodity Fetishism in South America*. Chapel Hill: University of North Carolina.

The Times of Malta

Tonna, B., 1993, *Malta Trends 1993: The Signs of the Times*. Malta: Discern.

Vella, E., 1992, *Ix-Xitan u L-Ezorcizmu*. Malta: Curia.

Zammit Mangion, J., 1992, *Education in Malta*. Malta: Studia Editions.

4

'You Devil, go away from me!' Pentecostalist African Christianity and the Powers of Good and Evil

Birgit Meyer

University of Amsterdam

In the diversity of his metamorphosing forms, his secrecy, incongruities, and fiery splendor, the devil is the arch-figure of [. . .] a twofold movement of attraction and repulsion. As the figure of the impure sacred, he irradiates the wild energy of this vortex. As the Great Imitator he opposes not only God but the possibility of ontological anchoring of steadfast meaning that he constantly dangles before us. As the paramount sign of evil, he was always a little too interesting and a little too seductive to be trapped by Christian *ressentiment* into a simple dialectic of Otherness.

(Michael Taussig 1995: 395)

Introduction[1]

Visitors to Ghana can hardly overlook the omnipresence of Christianity. Especially in the urban areas, but also in the countryside there are innumerable – predominantly Pentecostalist – churches.[2] They actively engage in proselytising efforts through posters and banners, magazines, street sermons, radio programs, the organisation of open air services – so-called Crusades – and by making use of loud-speakers during regular prayer meetings. It is impossible for the people in the neighbourhood to close themselves off from Christian propaganda. What is especially salient in this

Pentecostalist appropriation of public space is the popularity of the image of the Devil. The central message is that the present world forms a stage for the final fight between Satan and God, into which all people, albeit unconsciously, are involved on one or the other side. In the representation of this war, images of evil receive much more attention than their divine counterparts. For it is asserted that, although Satan and his allies will eventually lose, at the moment the 'powers of darkness' will do their best to win souls among the living in order to take along in their defeat as many people as possible. It is not considered enough to merely attend church and pray – in Pentecostalist circles the active fight against Satan stands central. The cry 'You Devil go away from me!' – a cry which materialises on stickers and posters and which even is the refrain of a popular song – aptly captures the Pentecostalist attitude towards evil. As good can only be the result of the defeat of evil, the 'powers of darkness' deserve special attention. They have to be invoked and called by their names in order to be defeated.

This essay addresses the Ghanaian preoccupation with evil powers through a historical and ethnographical study of the genesis of popular Christianity among the Peki Ewe in south-eastern Ghana. Taking as a point of departure the encounter between nineteenth-century German Pietist missionaries and the Ewe, it will be shown that the evangelical encounter not only occurred in the context of social and economic transformations, but actively stimulated the emergence of new forms of beliefs and ethics which were indispensable in bringing about such change and in which the image of the Devil held a central place. This dialectical relationship between social-economic transformations and religious imagination will be investigated further through an analysis of current popular Christianity, and the increasing popularity of Pentecostalism, in Peki. It will be argued that recurrence to images of Satan – a process which occurs above all in Pentecostally oriented churches – should not be regarded as a residue of traditional thinking, but as part and parcel of people's engagement with modernity. The image of the Devil is at the centre of an imaginary space through which people may address modernity's temptations and malcontents.

Christian Villages and the Freedom not to Share

The first missionaries of the Norddeutsche Missionsgesellschaft (NMG), a Pietist German mission society, settled among the Ewe in the mid-nineteenth century. They opened their first mission post in Peki Blengo, about 150 km from the coast in the inland (see Meyer 1999: Chapter 1).[3] Later they founded more posts all over the area inhabited by the Ewe, who lived on both sides of the colonial border that came to be drawn between the British Gold Coast and German Togo. Paradoxically, although at home the missionaries belonged to a conservative movement, in the African context they became the first agents of 'civilisation' and modernity the Ewe were confronted with.

Propagating 'civilisation' through missionisation, they instigated the establishment of Christian villages (called *Kpozdi* – literally translated as 'on the hilltop') with a school, church and small houses for nuclear families. They taught people to read and write and offered new skills such as carpentry, masonry and teaching. After colonial rule had been established in the course of the first decade after 1884, the NMG also propagated the cultivation of cash crops such as cotton, coffee and, last but not least, cocoa, which became the main export crop from 1900 onwards. Although for the mission all these activities were rather ordinary, not particularly modern and fully in line with the Pietist ideal of a rural way of life, they appeared to the Ewe as an avenue towards 'civilisation'. Many felt attracted to convert.

The price to be paid for 'civilisation' was submission to the NMG's strict regime. All inhabitants of *Kpodzi* had to be baptised and had to live in conformity with the congregational order which requested that Christians draw a strict boundary between themselves and the 'heathen' village (see Meyer 1996: 205ff). They were to abstain from any religious ceremony performed by their non-Christian relatives – since religion was entangled with all domains of life this request amounted to a far-reaching separation from their family in the 'heathen' village – and were to live up to what the mission defined as a Christian way of life. They inhabited new types of houses, wore different clothes, used Western medicines,[4] sang to European tunes, held different feast-days, and instead of the traditional taboo days, the 'rest' days of the local gods (*trɔwo*), they observed only the Christian Sunday. For the Christians, polygamous marriages were forbidden and preferably they were to intermarry.

Through the influence of the mission, which both materially and ideologically promoted the Christian family as the appropriate place for individual growth, the nuclear family became the main unit of production, distribution and consumption. The mission set new directives for the distribution of income. In line with nineteenth-century bourgeois Western ideas about the family, the husband was expected to maintain his children while his wife should confine herself to housework and childcare rather than engaging in trade as her non-Christian fellows would do. As a Christian couple was not required to share their income with members of their non-Christian extended family, the mission stimulated the emergence of a new social class which was economically and socially much less dependent on kinship ties with the extended family than had hitherto been the case and which was able to spend a considerable amount of money on Western goods.[5]

It appears that the strong emphasis on the nuclear family at the expense of ties with more distant relatives, which freed Christians from the duty to share their wealth with less fortunate family members, was one of the attractions of Christianity. This is illustrated by the following complaint of a native teacher about his congregation: 'Some people seem to hide among the Christians in order to find the opportunity to spend their money undisturbed.'[6] While in non-Christian society witchcraft (*adze*) fears worked as a levelling mode which ensured that the wealthy would not engage in unconstrained accumulation,[7] it seems as if in *Kpodzi* the wealthy – and this is what most Christians in the early days actually were, at least compared to non-Christians – felt protected against witchcraft attacks inflicted upon them by less fortunate, envious relatives. Here they could spend their money on all those things which they and the missionaries considered indispensable for a 'civilised', and for that matter Christian, way of life.

Witchcraft and the Unequal Distribution of Wealth

In order to understand the appeal of Christianity, it is important to deal briefly with the complex of witchcraft, from which Christians hoped to dissociate themselves through their conversion and settlement in *Kpodzi*. According to Jacob Spieth, an NMG-missionary who wrote a substantial part of Ewe ethnography,[8] *adze* was one of the most feared powers in Ewe land. *Adze* was said to be active at night; it was a light, shining apparition. It could take possession of human beings with or without their consent. Such a person became *adzetɔ*, that is, a witch.[9] At night, *adze* would pass through closed doors and suck blood from people whilst they slept. In turn, the victim would fall sick two days later and even die if the cause of the disease remained undetected (Spieth 1906: 544–45). It was the witches' 'dearest longing . . . to make somebody poor. If he becomes rich, they destroy him. If he has children, they kill them all. Secretly they destroy everything he has' (ibid: 300).

Spieth did not specify which people were considered potential witches. However, through interviews with old people I discovered that *adzetɔwo* (pl. of *adzetɔ*), who could be either male or female, directed their destructive power against members of their own family whom they envied. In particular, the paternal aunt, *tasi*, was considered a potential witch. If her brother's children fared better than her own, or worse still, she did not even have offspring herself, she was suspected of bringing them down out of jealousy. Other potential *adzetɔwo* were old people. When young children in the family kept on dying whilst the old people continued to live, they were suspected of feeding on the blood of the young. Another category considered prone to witchcraft were poor people envying rich family members who failed to share their wealth with them. The important point regarding witchcraft suspicions is that they have to be understood in the context of conflicting relationships. 'And those who long for things too much and those who hate people bitterly, black people use to regard these people as witches', an evangelist remarked pointedly (Staatsarchiv Bremen 7,1025–56/8: 239–40; original in Ewe).

Although *adze* could also be operative among very close friends, it expressed above all tensions in family relationships and, as such, formed the 'dark side of kinship' (Geschiere 1994). The fear of *adze* represents the fear that the people with whom one was closely related secretly sought one's downfall. It articulated the fact that the family was not only functional for the reproduction of life, but also a potential source of destruction. It is important to note that secrecy was a central aspect of *adze*. People were reluctant to talk about it – this might also be a reason for Spieth's comparative neglect of the phenomenon – and kept their suspicions to themselves. As long as suspicions did not develop into accusations, there was no direct remedy against *adze*. One could try to protect oneself against it, but there was no ritual whereby the conflicts between the two family members involved could be settled.

It was because of this impossibility that *adze* was seen as an extremely destructive force against which people tried to protect themselves as best as they could. However, I was told that occasionally people were indeed openly accused of witchcraft and required to submit themselves to an ordeal. If found guilty, they had to pacify their victims and undergo a purification ritual in whose course *adze* was taken away from them. I assume that this did not happen very frequently, because one would otherwise find occasional descriptions of such ordeals in the mission journal, the *Monatsblatt der Norddeutschen Mission,* Hamburg 1840ff/Bremen 1851ff (MB), or in non-published reports which the missionaries and the Ewe mission workers produced for the NMG's headquarters in Germany. Since this is not the case, I suspect that *adze* was very much confined to an invisible, secret realm and hence it was almost impossible to restore the strained relations between an assumed witch and its victims. The only thing to be done against this aggressive evil power was personal prophylactic protection measures.

One possibility to achieve this protection was to consult the priests of the local gods (*trɔwo*); alternatively people could address individual experts in magic and medicine (*dzotɔwo*). The second option became increasingly popular by the beginning of the twentieth century. Although it is difficult to assess an increase in the fear of witchcraft (see below), the reports, which Ewe evangelists wrote in order to keep the NMG informed about what happened in the congregations, give me the impression that both witchcraft and anti-witchcraft measures became a matter of growing concern. One report by an Ewe-evangelist, for instance, emphasised that the *dzotɔwo* actually claimed and were considered to be the most powerful people because they 'have a special kind of dark power' and would 'scare' and be able to 'catch witches . . . by using witchcraft power' (Stab 7,1025–56/8: 233–35; original in Ewe). Thus, *dzo* was presented as surpassing all other powers and hence as the best remedy against *adze*. Other Ewe mission workers also used to note the tremendous power attributed to *dzo*[10] and the widespread fear of *adze*.[11]

In my view, the relative weakening of the power of the *trɔwo* in favour of *dzo* marks a trend from more collective to more individualist forms of religion. Although people could consult *trɔ* priests individually if need be, the worship of a *trɔ* was defined as a collective cult integrating a whole family, clan, or even town. *Dzo*, by contrast, was a purely individual matter. In order to be protected by *dzo* there was no need to participate in any organised worship. One just had to buy *dzo* strings from a specialist and have them tied around one's body. The predominant popularity of *dzo* suggests a need for individual forms of protection in addition to, or even at the expense of participation in collective cults.

In my view the reason for the increasing need for individual protection lies in the increasing fear of *adze* and also destructive *dzo*, two evil powers stemming from unresolvable, secret conflicts between human beings. Of course, conflicts between humans occur any time and any place. However, there are indications that the Ewe's incorporation into the colonial political and economic system (especially through cocoa cultivation, but also other modern professions) resulted in a very unequal distribution of wealth which in turn gave rise to envy – the main motive of people employing *adze* against others.[12] Those who made profits were afraid that less prosperous, jealous family members would seek their downfall. Therefore, they felt that they needed effective protection against *adze.* This not only explains the increasing importance of *dzo*, but also the popularity of anti-witchcraft movements such as the Dente cult (Maier 1983), and last but not least, the popularity of Christianity to which we shall now turn again.

The Institutionalisation of a Dualistic Attitude Towards Good and Evil, God and the Devil

As we have seen, Christianity's new individualist ethics clearly liberated Christians from existing obligations to share their riches and from the fear of being bewitched if they failed to do so. Life in *Kpodzi* therefore was attractive to all those who wanted to accumulate and spend more money for themselves than was possible in the context of the non-Christian village. The fact that converts experienced *Kpodzi* as a relatively safe place out of bounds, however, did not imply that they would no more believe in the power of witchcraft as such. As I have shown elsewhere, the NMG-missionaries continuously talked about Ewe gods and spirits – witchcraft included – as being agents of the Devil: these beings were represented as Christian demons who had been dragged along by Satan when he had been expelled from heaven and who had established themselves as evil spirits on the land, in the water, and in the air (see Meyer 1992). Through this narrative, Ewe religion was constructed in terms of really existing 'heathendom', the lowest form of religion beyond which the missionaries strove to lead the Ewe. For them, Ewe religion was defined by the fact that:

> it is the Satan and his angels, who let themselves be adored in the heathenland. He is the prince of this world, and a divine hour of their salvation first has to be prepared and has to come, before they can be free from his power. (MB 1857:319/20, my translation)

It appears that Ewe converts immediately took up the missionary dualism of God and Satan and that the discourse of salvation
and liberation from satanic power appealed to them. Reports
abound in which converts reject Ewe religion as 'satanic' and
'backward'. The missionary Jacob Spieth summarised this succinctly in his essay on conversion: 'If we could ask the almost
6,000 Christians of Ewe-land from where they come, they would all
reply: "We come out of the dark, where we stood under the power
of Satan"' (1908:1). By casting their experiences in this way, Ewe
converts could dissociate themselves from previous forms of worship and the social relations it implied, which they all regarded as
backward, and open themselves up for 'civilisation' or, as the Ewe
expression had it, *ŋku vu* (open eyes). Both terms were crucial in
Ewe converts' discourse. To be 'civilised' and to have 'open eyes'
translated almost naturally into the way of life upheld in *Kpodzi*,
where new patterns of production, distribution, consumption, and,
last but not least, worship prevailed – where, in other words, the
opening up towards the modern market economy as both consumers and producers, and conversion to Christianity went hand in
hand.

Yet, all this does not imply that those entities which had been
recast as agents of Satan would no more play a role in Christians'
lives. Rather, the image of Satan enabled them to talk about the
religion they had left behind in favour of Christianity. For them the
old gods and witchcraft remained a threatening and complex reality which had great importance in their lives, rather than a stage
which they fully left behind once and for all, as the missionaries
would have hoped. This common stance is illustrated in the critical remark of Theodor Sedode, an Ewe teacher, who referred to
what he considered to be a 'superstitious' conceptualisation (Baeta
and Sedode 1911: 16, my translation and emphasis):

> When I once asserted in a baptismal lesson that there are no idols, one
> grey man looked at me astounded and replied: 'Surely there are idols,
> but the God of the Christians is more powerful than all of them.' *Like-
> wise, the existence of sorcery, sorcery power, witches and all sorts of evil
> spirits is believed in firmly, which limits very much the Christian faith
> and makes superstition persist.* The best console themselves with the
> words: God is more powerful, and since I belong to God they cannot
> harm me.

The image of the Devil offered converts the possibility to keep on
addressing Ewe religion, which they understood as a matter of 'the

past' but which nevertheless still played a role in their daily lives.[13] This image was the focal point in a newly evolving Ewe Christian imaginary space. Although this invisible space was conceived to be the arena of the war between God and Satan, much more energy and passion was being put into the imagination of evil than into the imagination of good.[14] The imagination of evil certainly depended on divine revelation – for it was only possible to talk about Satan if one's eyes had been opened by God and one had adopted a dualistic stance – but the point is that in both missionary and Ewe converts' discourse the dark side of this dualism received much more attention. Actually, Christianity's imaginary space formed a stage for the dramatisation of all those things which were relegated to the dark side of life, without however ceasing to influence people in one way or the other. Through the image of Satan, Ewe Christians could view forbidden and dangerous zones – albeit from a Christian missionary perspective. They became voyeurs, looking from a safe distance.

The Powers of Evil and the Church

Or not so safe. The fact that a great number of Ewe Christians 'relapsed into heathendom', as missionary discourse put it, indicated that it was not at all easy to live up to the standards of the church order.[15] Through the image of the Devil, Ewe religion – Christianity's Other – was still there and remained a reality to return to. Elsewhere I have shown in some detail (1996) that the main reason for Ewe Christians to 'turn back' was the fact that missionary Christianity failed to offer adequate remedies against evil. In line with Protestant tradition, the missionaries fully subscribed to the doctrine of faith in God and prayer alone and hence were against the performance of particular rituals in order to change the course of things. This anti-ritualist attitude stood in stark opposition to Ewe religion, where rituals played an important role, especially in cases of affliction. For that reason, Ewe Christians experienced a continuously frustrated need for elaborate practices to counter evil.

This need persisted throughout the history of Ghana's Evangelical Presbyterian Church – EPC – and until today. When I enquired about the period after 1918, that is, the period no longer covered by extensive mission reports, I learned that there had been quite a few cases of people, among them even pastors and teachers, who secretly owned *dzo* and went to church at the same time. While it was impossible for a Christian to take part in the worship of a *trɔ* without being seen by the congregational authorities, it was much more easy to possess *dzo*. As Dr Seth Bansa pointed out in a 1992 interview, *'Trɔ* is a public thing. If you belong to it, then the other group would know. You would be excommunicated. But *dzo* is secret. So you can belong to that, and nobody knows it. And you can belong to the Christian church'. The attitude of Christians who were relying on magic as well as church attendance was termed *'Yesu vie, dzo vie'* – 'a little bit of Jesus and a little bit of magic'.

In the Peki church diaries I consulted in the course of my research, only a small proportion of the real extent of this attitude is visible, since many people succeeded in 'relapsing' without being detected. Unless the congregational authorities found out, a person could still receive the Lord's Supper and participate in 'heathen' customs at the same time. And once Christians were no longer confined to *Kpodzi*, but lived everywhere in town, ultimate control was difficult. In case people were accused of owning *dzo*, they would try to defend themselves by stating that it was not 'magic', but mere 'medicine' (*atike*), thereby trying to persuade the church authorities that these materials had not been blessed by a *dzotɔ* (healer, diviner) and were just ordinary barks and medicinal plants. Although there was a core of staunch members respecting the church order, many members turned into more or less 'nominal' Christians who were baptised because the church stood for 'civilisation', but who at the same time failed to observe all the regulations.

The belief in *adze* continued to exist among the members of the congregations. Though this is difficult to prove, I have the impression that in Peki, too, fears of being bewitched increased with prosperity. In any case, many people told me that formerly, when people were living from the produce of their farms and had no extra cash income, witchcraft had been much less prevalent. An often-heard complaint was that people became increasingly 'greedy' in the course of time and that this individualist accumulation of wealth gave rise to feelings of envy among others who would be so jealous about the success of their relatives that they secretly sought their downfall through *adze*. For instance, the car accident of a wealthy Peki trader from Blengo as he was returning home with some goods from Accra in 1928, was attributed to witchcraft. Clearly here the fear of witchcraft hardly worked as a levelling mechanism, but rather enticed the wealthy to protect themselves as efficiently as possible, either through the purchase of protective *dzo*, participation in anti-witchcraft cults, membership in a Christian church – or a combination thereof.

The fact that this subject was hardly mentioned in written church documents only illustrates that witchcraft was a taboo topic. For instance, one old lady, the late Mrs Felicia Ansre, who grew up in *Kpodzi*, recounted that although she did not believe in the existence of witches herself, many fellow Christians were afraid of them. Her enlightened viewpoint was not generally shared. Alice Mallet, another elderly woman from a staunch Christian family, recalled her father, the Reverend Barnabas Mallet explaining to her: 'If you don't believe in *adze*, you don't believe in God. In this world, there are two things: the good spirits and the evil spirits. What Jesus called Beelzebub is *adze.*' He prayed privately with members of his congregations (though a native of Peki, he was mainly posted in the Togo area) who regarded themselves as witches or supposed that they had fallen victim to witchcraft attacks.

Alice Mallet's statement reveals that the belief in the existence of witchcraft was not only held by less educated church members, but also by pastors. Whether witchcraft existed or not was a matter about which converts had different opinions, but the subject was not expanded upon or even treated in public, only in private. Although spiritual beings of the non-Christian religion thus remained a reality to most Christians, these spirits were not spoken about explicitly in services. They were bracketed within the category of *Abosam* – the Devil. The church made no attempt to offer any public discourse dealing with the fears represented by, for example, *adze*, nor did it provide any protective rituals apart from private prayer and the sober public church services.

The fact that many Christians were concerned about witchcraft is also confirmed by a report (1932) of the Christian Council of Gold Coast,[16] to which the Ewe Evangelical Church belonged. According to the council, such beliefs were very common throughout the colony. Though it did not deny the existence of witchcraft as such, it recommended exposing all 'charlatans' claiming falsely to be able to perform witchcraft and discouraged consulting 'witch doctors' (a task undertaken by the *dzotɔwo*; 1932: 6). The latter advice was in line with the British colonial government's view of witch-finding as a criminal offence – a view which probably led people to believe that the colonial state and the church protected witches (see also Geschiere 1997: 15). Apart from asserting that for

Christians there was no need to be afraid (Christian Council of the Gold Coast 1932: 7), no practical means of protection against witchcraft were recommended. Though this report only consists of a brief statement, it reveals that despite the fact that fears of witchcraft were a matter of great concern in Christian congregations, no special remedies to counter this threat were offered.

In my view, the continuing (and probably even increasing) fear of witchcraft can help explain the popularity of secret *dzo* referred to above. Since there was no proper church discourse and ritual complex dealing with evil spirits such as *adze*, church members who wanted to maintain their wealth, or receive any other protection, were virtually obliged to consult Ewe specialists in secret. For mere prayer to God, the power of good, was not considered enough by most Christians. As far as spiritual protection was concerned, missionary Christianity was hence still of little value, whereas at the same time, by offering the image of the Devil it contributed to the emergence of an imaginary space that could easily accommodate witchcraft and magic. While this space became increasingly charged with destructive energy and fear, missionary Christianity failed to offer adequate practices to counter evil, and thereby – to remain in the thermodynamic image – discharge the heat that was generated in that space. They were considered unable to engage divine power in the active struggle against the 'powers of darkness', or, as critics claimed: 'there (in the EPC), they don't know how to pray.'

The Powers of Evil and African Independent and Pentecostalist Churches

The African independent churches which started to emerge in Gold Coast on a massive scale from the 1930s onwards took issue with the ritual poverty of Protestant missionary Christianity. For some decades in Peki these churches, which had quite low prestige and mainly attracted people with quite low education, existed alongside with missionary Christianity as it was given form in the Evangelical Presbyterian Church (EPC). This situation changed by the end of the 1950s, when a prayer group was established within the local congregation. This group emphasised the importance of healing through prayer, and its leader, John Sam Amedzro, devoted much time and energy to the exorcism of evil spirits. As the group drew increasingly close to Pentecostalist practices, which are characterised by a strong emphasis on the Holy Spirit, conflict arose between this group and the EPC authorities (see Meyer 1999: Chapter 5). In 1960 the prayer group seceded from the EPC and became independent as The Lord's Church – *Agbelengor*. Later in the 1980s, when the church sought to associate itself with the Pentecostal movement it took the name of The Lord's Pentecostal Church.

With this exclusion, however, problems were not solved for the EPC. Members still experienced the EPC's incapacity to deal with evil as a major problem and shifted, albeit temporarily and in secret, into Pentecostally oriented churches. Moreover, the worshipping style in the EPC, which by and large reproduced the nineteenth-century missionary model, was increasingly experienced as too 'stiff', running counter to African forms of expression. In attempting to avoid the loss of ever more members to rival churches, by the end of the 1970s the EPC decided to deal with both problems by beginning to Africanise its liturgy and accepting a Pentecostally oriented prayer group within the church.

In order to extend the project of Africanisation to the doctrine, in the 1980s the church leader Noah K. Dzobo started to develop an African theology that would do justice to African culture and religion (see Meyer 1992, 1999: Chapter 5). While most local EPC pastors simply ignored this new theology, the prayer group opposed this positive valuation of Ewe religion. To its members, the determined, positive incorporation of tradition boiled down to an invitation of Satan himself into the church. In this conflict, Pentecostalisation was opposed to Africanisation. That the conflict took place along these lines should not, however, blind us to the fact that the proponents of Pentecostalisation stood much closer to traditional worship than they themselves were prepared to acknowledge. Exactly because they regarded local gods and spirits as actual agents of Satan, they strove to exclude them with vigour, thereby placing themselves in a tradition of Africanisation 'from below' which was developed by the first Ewe converts and which had much in common with African cults propagating radical cleansing (see Meyer 1992 for a more detailed analysis).

The members of the prayer group eventually split away from the EPC and formed a church of their own: the Evangelical Presbyterian Church 'of Ghana' (EPC 'of Ghana'). This choice of name shows that the secessionists regarded themselves as the true custodians of the missionary heritage. In its attempt to renew the church, the EPC 'of Ghana' placed itself in the missionary tradition of diabolising 'heathendom' and, at the same time, took current Pentecostalism, which has been growing phenomenally all over Ghana since the 1980s, as a model.

Much can be – and indeed has been – said about the reason for the rise of African independent or so-called spiritual churches and the recent Pentecostal-Charismatic revival (e.g. Jules-Rosette 1994; Gifford 1994; Marshall 1991, 1993, 1998; Van Dijk 1992), in which many formerly 'spiritual' churches also participate.[17] Most important to my argument here, is the fact that these churches relate to the imaginary space which evolved around the image of the Devil in a distinct way – that is, in a manner which is markedly different from mission churches such as the EPC. Rather than turning away from the image of the Devil and 'heathendom' once and for all – as is required by mission churches – Pentecostally oriented churches continuously dwell on the boundary between Christianity and 'heathendom' and regard it as their main task to fight the Devil in all his different shapes and manifestations. Here considerable emphasis is placed on the image of Satan, and all the folds and corners of the realm of darkness are scrutinised in the light of divine revelations. As agents of Satan regain their separate name and iconography, the domain of darkness is increasingly differentiated. Far from being a tabooed topic, as is the case in the mission churches, it is placed right at the centre of Christian belief.

This is clear from a brief examination of what attracts people to *Agbelengor* and the EPC 'of Ghana'. While the EPC expects its members not to deal with the satanic in any detail, these churches offer an elaborate discourse on evil spirits, which is expressed through sermons, songs and prayers, and a strong emphasis on rituals of liberation from, and protection against, evil forces (see Meyer 1999: Chapter 6). Both churches relate to people's ideas about the existence of evil spirits in an affirmative way and encourage believers to trace their problems to demonic sources. When I enquired why people had left the EPC for either *Agbelengor* or the EPC 'of Ghana', I often heard that this had to with the perceived incapacity of the EPC to deal with all sorts of evil spirits, that is old gods, witchcraft and a host of other spiritual beings. Rather than telling people not to bother about these beings and to leave the domain of the Devil well alone, Pentecostalist churches passionately engage in a painstaking struggle against evil spirits, thereby offering them a space to manifest themselves.

On a regular basis, they offer so-called deliverance prayers, in the course of which preachers investigate whether a person, consciously or unconsciously, is in the grip of a Satanic entity. They find out by laying on hands, an act through which the Holy Spirit is supposed to enter a person and force any other entity dwelling in the person concerned to manifest itself and, eventually, leave. As I have described in some detail elsewhere (Meyer 1998a), the deliverance ritual implies a symbolic cutting of blood ties whereby a person is separated from all potential influences from the extended family and is hence recreated, or to phrase it in Pentecostalist terms: *born again*, as an individual subject. The work of the Holy Spirit is to bring about individualisation. In other words, Pentecostalism is actively involved in the symbolic production of modern individuals who exert control over their personal lives, rather than identifying themselves as a part of webs of family relations (which are represented as potentially evil and destructive). With this emphasis on separation from the extended family and personal responsibility, these churches clearly stand in the tradition of the construction of Christian life in *Kpodzi* as I have sketched it above. Part of their appeal certainly lies in their promise to create and safeguard modern individual identity. At a time when the poor – by lack of a better alternative – increasingly appeal to an ethics which emphasises the obligation of the wealthy to share with their wider family, it is not surprising that the Pentecostal promise of individualisation is attractive especially to those who long to accumulate for themselves and succeed in modern society. Clearly, those interested in Pentecostalism are people who are (trying to be) socially upward mobile or already have become somewhat successful (see Meyer 1998a).

Yet Pentecostalist churches do not only deal with evil spirits through exorcism and subsequent symbolic individualisation of the afflicted. It appears that evil spirits and the social ties for which they stand continue to matter even in the lives of *born again* Christians as well as in Pentecostal church services. As Pentecostalist discourse is focused on the cosmic war between Satan and God, the imaginary space with its mysterious landscapes and populations of uncanny monsters permanently holds a central place. Even those people who do not suffer any affliction are continuously confronted with its existence, very much in the same way as they realise in daily life that the ideal of individualisation is actually difficult to attain in a society in which the extended family remains sociologically important.

During the services there is, for instance, a lot of scope for the giving of testimonies. On these occasions, people are invited to relate to the congregation their experiences and confessions of involvement with evil spirits and the ways in which God miraculously saved them. Such testimonies are seen as windows to the otherwise invisible realm of the 'powers of darkness', which were eventually overcome by divine power. In the context of Pentecostalism personal experiences with occult forces are thus transformed into publicly told narratives which are thought to provide a glimpse into the realm of Satan and the extent of his power, which is confirmed as considerable, yet in the last instance inferior to that of God. Very much in line with Protestant tradition, those who confess will place much emphasis on their encounter with satanic forces and represent themselves as eye-witnesses of the domain of the occult. It is because of these experiences that they can claim to be especially qualified to lead the congregation in the cosmic war between the powers of good and the powers of evil. Next to personal confessions (see Meyer 1995b), pastors also make use of a plethora of Pentecostally-oriented journals, magazines and booklets, which appear in great quantity in the capital Accra and which easily find their way even into the remotest corners of Ghana. The testimonies and confessions in these products are represented as important sources of information about the Devil and his agents. In this way, Pentecostalist churches do not merely relate to ideas which live among the people; rather, they actively appropriate them and take part in the production and elaboration of Christianity's imaginary space. Here lies, in my view, the key to the success of this type of churches.

Pentecostalism and Modernity's Demons

As Pentecostalism is always prepared to link up with popular stories which are around, its imaginary space is highly dynamic and easily absorbs new images and people's latest obsessions. It does so by reproducing these stories – to put it in Pentecostal terms – as new revelations, that is, as insights into the operations of the 'powers of darkness'. The catechist in the EPC 'of Ghana', Emmanuel Brempong, explained this accumulative understanding of the occult as follows: 'When the knowledge about Jesus increases, then the knowledge about demons also increases.' Growing insight into the realm of occult forces is represented as a consequence of faith: true *born again* Christians cannot help but confront the Devil in all his tempting, yet deceptive, shapes. As Pentecostalism keeps up with the latest demonic obsession, the imaginary space that is being constructed and explored in its discourse – and attempted to be controlled through the deliverance ritual – is not only found to be inhabited by well-known powers such as old gods, witchcraft and magic, but also by a number of relatively new occult forces. While in the initial period of missionisation the Christian imaginary space that was woven around the Devil was, above all, concerned with the diabolisation of so-called 'traditional religion', nowadays diabolisation is extended to new occult forces which operate through money and commodities. For an increasing number of Christians, the predominant problem is not merely protection against demons such as witchcraft, which directly threaten their socially upward mobile position. The new problem they perceive is that engagement with modernity – especially in the market economy – implies that one may passively or actively become involved with demons. A shift can be discerned from an emphasis laid on the demonisation of matters which prevent people from being successful in modern life towards an increasing demonisation of the very means by which success as achieved.

Modernity itself is more and more perceived as being enchanted, rather than disenchanted, as Western agents of 'civilisation' and modernisation have continued to claim. For instance, I heard a lot of stories pertaining to what is called *adzegã*, that is, 'witchcraft money'. People who want to become rich are said to spiritually sacrifice a family member in exchange for very quick material gain. They do so by consulting a native doctor in the countryside, who asks them to mention the name of a close relative, whose image would subsequently appear in a mirror or on the surface of a calabash filled with water. By destroying this image, a person is killed in spirit, and natural death, for instance through a car accident, is supposed to follow soon. As a result of this sacrifice, the person who committed this crime 'in spirit' will be rewarded with a large amount of money. Usually this money is said to be produced by a small snake that has to be kept in a secret room or on the body. This snake requires regular sacrifices in order to keep the money flowing. Once a person failed to worship the snake properly, the animal will turn against his master and bring about misery (see Meyer 1995b for a more detailed analysis).

People in Peki knew several places in Ghana where this type of wealth – elsewhere called *Nzima Bayi* or witchcraft from Nzima (Debrunner 1961: 184) – could be achieved. There were rumours that certain rich people in Peki may have gone in for this, but of course, this could not be proven. Though no inhabitant of Peki ever confessed to having become rich in this way, this type of witchcraft story caught the imagination of many people. *Adzegā* entails a new type of *adze*, which makes a person actively seek riches rather than destroy a prosperous relative, as was the case with 'traditional' *adze*. As explained above, whereas formerly witchcraft fears would above all worry those who failed to live up to the obligation to share with poorer relatives, the new form of witchcraft is actively employed for the production of money.[18] It is a clear illustration of the dynamic capacity of the notion of witchcraft to develop as part and parcel of modernity (Geschiere 1997).

As Pentecostalism has the same dynamic capacity, stories about satanic riches are easily incorporated into its imaginary space and become matters about which pastors and members have something to say. During my stay in Peki, a booklet called *Delivered from the Powers of Darkness* (1988) by the Nigerian Emmanuel Eni, a member of the Pentecostalist Assemblies of God, was highly popular among leaders and members of *Agbelengor* and the EPC 'of Ghana'. In this book, Eni makes elaborate confessions about his work for Satan, which included his assistance in achieving money in the way described above (ibid.: 23ff). These 'revelations' were talked about and connected with others, which people had heard during public confessions made in deliverance services and Crusades.

Although this particular way of becoming rich is condemned as a satanic shortcut which will, in the end, be at the cost of even one's own life, prosperity as such is considered a divine blessing. Both *Agbelengor* and the EPC 'of Ghana' devoted explicit prayers to wealth and subscribed to the so-called Prosperity Gospel (Meyer 1998b: 311–12), which is popular among Pentecostalists all over Ghana and which represents poverty as an evil spirit that has to be exorcised. For that reason the recurrence to the narrative of *adzegā* or satanic riches certainly does not entail an idealisation of poverty and extended family relations. By incorporating such a story, in which the striving for wealth is represented in opposition to the family – after all, the money is generated in exchange for the life of a close relative – Pentecostalist discourse offers people the possibility to reflect on their ambivalence with regard to the ways in which one can succeed in the modern market economy. By encountering this narrative in the framework of the Christian imaginary space, members can safely fantasise about and face their hidden desires of unlimited greed and selfishness without actually giving in to them. Thus, rather than positing itself in opposition to money and the modern market economy, Pentecostalism offers room for the expression of second thoughts or – to use the expression of Comaroff and Comaroff (1993) – modernity's malcontents, and at the same time provides safe and morally sound ways for people to relate to modernity. Here the image of the Devil is employed to demonise certain aspects of modernity and, at the same time, assert Pentecostalism's ability to draw on divine power in order to overcome him.

This attitude also pertains to another fertile complex of narratives that relates to the bottom of the sea.

This area is considered to be the realm of *Mami Water* spirits, that is, mermaids (and sometimes mermen) who may appear on earth in the shape of beautiful – in many cases white or Indian – strangers and entice human beings to become their spouses. Those who give in to *Mami Water* spirits visit this area in their dreams. Once married to a *Mami Water* spirit, a person is no longer allowed to marry a human being and can no longer have children, but in exchange for sacrificing the capability of sexual reproduction will receive riches from the bottom of the ocean. Here one finds a world of beautiful golden buildings, well-dressed people who enjoy Western luxury and drive flashy cars – a sort of Cockaigne or, as many people explained to me, America. Yet, this world is not just a faraway place, for *Mami Water* spirits are said to do their utmost to bring commodities which are produced under the sea to the local markets. These commodities are, above all, jewellery, pomades, perfumes, clothes, artificial hair and cosmetics, but also such items as food, radios, cars, and so on. By purchasing such a thing, people risk linking themselves with *Mami Water* spirits, who will start visiting them in their dreams and try to tempt them into establishing a spiritual marriage by arousing sexual desires.

There are a number of shrines for *Mami Water* along the coast in neighbouring Togo and one on the bank of the Volta River, not far from Peki.[19] Here *Mami Water* devotees are initiated by established priests and priestesses who actively engage in a worshipping cult and who represent it in quite different terms than popular imagination. Above all, they claim that *Mami Water* spirits can help people to get children, thereby denying that riches and fertility necessarily exclude each other. The *Mami Water* imagery, however, clearly surpasses the cult itself and catches the imagination of a very large number of people. Therefore it does not come as a surprise that the *Mami Water* narrative, which circulates along the entire African coast (Drewal 1988; Fabian 1978; Wendl 1991; Wicker n.d.), has also been taken up by Pentecostalists who have incorporated it into their imagination of the Satanic, claiming that *Mami Water* spirits are agents of the Devil.

This imagery has become increasingly popular since the early 1990s. Members of *Agbelengor* and the EPC 'of Ghana' told me that these relatively new occult forces have recently become a problem comparable to or even worse than *adze*.[20] I observed that while in Peki *adze* attacks were the chief concern of middle-aged women, the new spirits mainly take hold of younger people who dream of being successful in life. Many of them were really obsessed with this spirit, which clearly stands for a fascination with the pleasures of capitalism, but also for its dangers. The catechist of the EPC 'of Ghana' Emmanuel Brempong openly talked about the confusing experiences he underwent after purchasing a pair of underpants on the local market. Since the day he began wearing them, he had been harassed by sexual dreams in which he had intercourse with beautiful ladies, though in daily life he was alone. Only after some time he realised that the dreams were caused by the underpants. Having thrown them away, he slept undisturbed by seductive women. Obviously I was not the only person to whom he related this experience. Many members of the church told me his story which he had recalled in public several times. Other people also talked about strange experiences related to the purchase of certain commodities. Especially the young were warned continuously not to wear particular sorts of dresses and jewellery, as they might come from the bottom of the sea. During deliverance sessions I witnessed how a preacher scolded a young girl because of her earrings in the shape of strawberries, her butterfly belt and her little necklace with a heart. Again and again people were warned not to eat, wear and use just anything, but to be aware continuously that objects might have 'strange origin', that is, come from the bottom of the sea. In Eni's book, too, there are long passages about the dangers of the market and the way in which Satan is the true Lord of the realm of the *Mami Water* spirits.

People were warned about the possible danger inherent in goods, but not asked to be abstinent as such. Rather, one was to employ a remedy to neutralise the pollution – prayer. All church members were called to predicate a brief, silent prayer over every purchased commodity before they enter their homes. They were to ask God to 'sanctify' the thing bought, thereby neutralising any diabolic spirit imbued in it. Only in this way would it be possible to prevent the destructive powers incorporated in the objects from damaging their owners' lives (for a more detailed analysis see Meyer 1998b).

Again we encounter Pentecostalism's peculiar attitude towards modernity. On the one hand, the *Mami Water* imagery is affirmed and further explored, on the other hand a safe path towards consumption is offered. In the same way as Pentecostalism condemns particular shortcuts to wealth but promotes prosperity, it warns against the possible dangers of commodities, but endorses consumption of luxury goods as such. In doing so, Pentecostalism claims to be able to function as a gatekeeper to modernity. With its guidance and prayer, people will make it in the modern market economy without losing their souls to satanic forces. Here modernity as such is represented as a deceptive and dangerous maze whose demons can easily destroy those who involve themselves all alone, in their own way. What Pentecostalism claims to achieve is to render powerless modernity's demons, that is, to disenchant modernity. This happens above all through prayer, particularly by calling on the Holy Spirit to fill members with his power, thereby rendering them immune to possible attacks by the 'powers of darkness'. In a way, through countless sermons and prayer services, Pentecostalism calls upon the image of the Devil in order to assert its ultimate power to conquer him.

As this disenchantment takes place under the condition of a previous enchantment, Pentecostalism offers members to think – or perhaps better, imagine – on two levels. On the one hand, they can enter the imaginary space and mimetically visit the sites of ultimate selfishness and hedonistic indulgence in pleasure. On the other hand they are led beyond these 'powers of darkness' without losing their ambitions to lead a more prosperous and successful life. Through the peculiar dialectics of enchantment and disenchantment which is operative in Pentecostalist discourse, followers are able to express their moral ambivalence about the modern market economy, and find ritual means to open themselves up to it and participate as modern consumers.

The Attraction of the Devil and the Power of Pentecostalism

These views are of course not confined to the locality of Peki. Pentecostalism being a powerful force all over Christian Ghana,

Pentecostalist churches rise in both urban and rural areas at the expense of mission churches and so-called spiritual churches. Although important differences exist between denominations – especially between Pentecostalist churches of the older type, such as the Assemblies of God and the Church of Pentecost, and those of the charismatic type which were founded by independent Ghanaian prophets in the 1980s (see Gifford 1994; Van Dijk 1997) – I deem it justified to speak of an emergent Pentecostalist complex. It articulates a distinct set of ideas and practices which attract an increasing number of people who are dissatisfied with the versions of Christianity they practised up until now. The emergence of this Pentecostalist complex is being facilitated by popular written media such as newspapers and magazines and electronic media such as video and audio tapes, movies and songs which all combine in a chorus delivering the central message. As I already suggested in the introduction, what I find most salient in all these cultural products is the tremendous importance attributed to the image of Satan.

Against the background of the case investigated in this essay, I want to suggest that one important reason for Pentecostalism's appeal lies in its capacity to let people face the Devil in order to defeat him. As I have shown, the encounter with the satanic is represented as a condition for the victory of divine power. Pentecostalism does not only relate to existing obsessions which figure in popular stories, but recreates them as Christianity's Other and makes it possible to relate to them in a new way. As the Devil and consorts are assigned a place in Pentecostalism's imaginary space under the condition of a dualism, which assigns ultimate power to God, it is possible for believers safely to confront satanic machinations. The more one grows in faith, the more one is able to gain insight into this otherwise impenetrable and dangerous domain. The more one is filled with the power of God, the more one is obsessed with evil.

But why this obsession? To which experiences does Pentecostalism speak so successfully with its continuous allusions to the 'powers of darkness'? What can the importance of the image of the Devil and the imaginary space woven around him teach us about certain African views of modernity – and, if one agrees with Appiah's (1992: 107) proposition that modernity can only be understood if both Western and non-Western perspectives are also taken into account, about modernity as such?

In order to find answers to these questions it is useful to take as a starting point Taussig's discussion (1995) of the devil contracts which stood central in his famous *The Devil and Commodity Fetishism* (1980) and which became subject to much animated anthropological debate (e.g. Crain 1991, Edelman 1994, Parry 1989). Rather than emphasising the dimension of critique of the capitalist economy, as he did in his book, Taussig (1995: 390) now insists that stories about the satanic should not be committed

> to the servile operation of getting them to say something that could be said otherwise – for example, to see them instrumentally, as things to achieve some other thing, such as equality, limits to individualism, morality tales against greed, prodigality, and capitalist logic.

Inspired by Bataille, he argues that the image of the Devil and the stories around him do not simply refer to morally bad ideas and practices, but thrive on a twofold movement of prohibition and transgression of which the Devil is the arch-figure.

I fully agree with Taussig that any explanation of the emergence of imaginary spaces, such as the one standing central in this essay, in instrumentalist terms is highly reductionist. The essence of the attraction of such a space certainly is not the articulation of a clear-cut critique of the capitalist economy in the name of a pre-capitalist, 'traditional' ethics, which is remarkably similar to Marxist critique. Rather than being a repository of pre-Christian thinking and ethics, it appears that this imaginary space evolves as part and parcel of people's encounter with Western Christianity and modernity. Therefore the form this space takes is closely connected to the ways in which Christian discourse, and also the discourses of 'civilisation' and 'modernisation' of which it forms part, establishes social, economic and moral systems on the basis of a politics of exclusion and repression – systems inscribed in the Order of the real, the good and the useful. Yet in the very moment of excluding and repressing matters which run counter to the new Order – such as extended family ethics and the worship it entails, but also selfish pleasure in money and consumption – these matters start a life of their own under the auspices of the Devil, and are recast as modernity's demons. Rather than staying behind at the rubbish-heap of 'progress', these demons keep on haunting people by appearing in dreams or in any situation in which a person experiences the incapacity to keep control over his/her life or submit to the prevailing Order. These demons are the shadows which come into being through the bright light of modernity and through Pentecostal discourse they are firmly established as the 'powers of darkness'.

This demonic upsurge, of course, appears to be a general feature of modernity. Not only have authors noted the rise of beliefs in demons in periods of transition from a pre-capitalist to a capitalist economy (for example, Crain 1991; Edelman 1994; Geschiere 1994, 1997; Lan 1985; Luig 1993, 1994; Pels 1992; Shaw 1996; Thoden van Velzen and Van Wetering 1988; White 1993); it appears that modernity as such cannot be thought simply in terms of disenchantment. As the Romanticist criticism of the Enlightenment claimed, rationality itself has its dark side and may give birth to monsters that threaten the claims of Enlightenment discourse (e.g. Peukert's 1989 exegesis of Max Weber, and Thoden van Velzen and van Wetering, chapter one of this volume). It is certainly time for social scientists to develop an understanding of modernity beyond the paradigms of modernisation and rationalisation, an understanding which can not only accommodate the emergence of imaginary spaces such as the one described here, but also Western obsessions with horror films and transgressive theatre (see Verrips 1996, and chapter seven of this volume). Once this view is accepted, it appears that any distinction between Western and non-Western modernity in terms of the presence of demons becomes obsolete (see Comaroff and Comaroff 1993; Geschiere 1997) and that there are no grounds for postulating an ontological difference between the West and the Rest. Having said this, let us now return to Africa.

By entering – or perhaps, by being drawn into – the Christian imaginary space, Pentecostalists in Ghana are enabled to experience 'the unspeakable mystique of the excessive, the abrogation of the useful, and the sensuous no less than logical intimacy binding overabundance to transgression in a forwards and backwards movement that is difficult to put in words' (Taussig 1995: 395). Indeed, much more difficult to put in words than in images. What I mean to say is that by confronting the images of the Devil and consorts, Pentecostalists face the dark side of modernity and get the chance mimetically to eschew the strict control they are to submit to in their daily lives. In this sense, obsession with evil certainly is a product of Christianity, rather than a survival of pre-Christian, pre-modern practice. Pentecostalism offers a virtual space – a dreamland located at the bottom of the ocean – to fantasise about its forbidden pleasures which defy any rational, utilitarian stance and thus offers room for the dramatic, mimetic enactment of people's wildest dreams in which they lose themselves in their desires. It thus provides a space in which they can celebrate the colourful come-backs of the repressed and engage in the negation of the powers of good which are to form the basis of ideal Christian belief and practice. This space, in other words, forms the stage for collectively shared fantasies (Thoden van Velzen 1995), which thrive on contradictions and dramatise them excessively.

Pentecostalism, however, does not only enable people to dramatise the negation of Order. At the same time, it is involved in the assertion of the ultimate power of God over the Devil, and thus in a complex dialectics of the negation of negation. In this sense, Pentecostalist discourse clearly goes further than the local rumours about Devil contracts described by Taussig. Here we encounter a politics of the fantastic, which attempts to confine popular collective fantasies to a particular space and to keep its demons under control. Pentecostalism does not only permit transgression into a virtual realm of abundance and excess, but also assures people that it is possible to become wealthy and consume without losing themselves to satanic powers, that is, to do well in the mundane order of everyday life. It is this doubleness which accounts for the tremendous attraction of Pentecostalism, whose power stems from the capacity to mediate between order and destruction, rules and transgressions, repression and lust, control and temptation, that is, between God and the Devil and hence the dazzling contradictions imbued in modern life without, however, ceasing to assert that Satan will eventually be defeated.

Yet the assurance that it is possible 'to manage life' and 'be delivered from the powers of darkness' is more a promise than a reality. For in actual practice, the evil spirits in Pentecostalism's imaginary space are attributed with tremendous power. Clearly, Pentecostalism is unable fully to control the demons it invokes by calling on divine power, and can't help but focus on their supposed machinations. In this way a tremendous amount of time and energy is devoted to the powers of evil which cannot easily be trapped in a simple dialectics of Otherness. Rather than subsuming them under divine power, they are its permanent companions. In the same way as in people's experience modernity appears to go hand in hand with enchantment, being *born again* entails the encounter with demons. In this sense, the Pentecostal message neatly links up with experiences of modernity: it takes its enchantedness as a point of departure and at the same time claims that it is possible to 'disenchant' the life world of *born again* Christians through the power of prayer. Yet at least for the time being, the image of the Devil is still dearly needed in order to be able to embody, in ways similar to that of the witch, 'all the contradictions of the experience of modernity itself, of its inescapable entice-ments, its self-consuming passions, its discriminatory tactics, its devastating social costs' (Comaroff and Comaroff 1993: xxix). Actually, the Devil is the image around which Pentecostalist prac-tice evolves, passionate mottos such as 'You Devil, go away from me' notwithstanding.

Notes

1. In this essay I attempt to synthesise a number of issues which I previously dis-cussed in separate publications. It is based on historical research in the archives of the Norddeutsche Mission in Bremen and ethnographic research in Peki, Ghana. For stimulating comments I wish to thank Jojada Verrips and the edi-tors of this volume.
2. By 'Pentecostalist churches' I refer not only to internationally spread Pente-costal churches of American and European origin, such as the Church of Pen-tecost or the Assemblies of God, but to all churches in the Pentecostal spectrum, including the so-called 'charismatic' churches (for further clarifica-tion see below).
3. The historical documents considered are the *Monatsblatt der Norddeutschen Mis-sionsgesellschaft* (MB), a German-written monthly periodical for the supporters of the mission; missionary ethnography produced for an academic audience, espe-cially students of comparative religion; unpublished documents written for the mission board by missionaries and Ewe mission workers in either German, Eng-lish or Ewe which are kept in the NMG-archives in Bremen. Moreover, during my research among the Peki Ewe I received much information through oral history. In making use of these sources one has to take into account that they were produced for different audiences and were to serve different aims. Although the archival documents reflect the asymmetrical power relations in which the missionaries and the Ewe were involved, they need not be dismissed as mere distortions of pre-mis-sionary culture or Ewe ideas and practices regarding conversion. By reading them 'from below' and against the background of oral history, it is possible to get a glimpse of the Ewe point of view (see Meyer 1995a: 102ff).
4. Until the end of the nineteenth century, when Western tropical medicine took a big step forward through the discovery of quinine as prophylaxis, the mis-sionaries' medical ideas were not superior to those of the Ewe, and less well adapted to tropical circumstances (Fischer 1991).
5. Christianity certainly cannot be held responsible for the fact that people wanted to be wealthy as such. Prayers for health and wealth formed an important part of Ewe religion and the wish to prosper and to possess Western trade goods instigated Ewe in the nineteenth century to participate in new religious cults. The decisive difference between these cults and Christianity lay in their differ-ent attitude towards the distribution of riches.
6. NMG-Archive, Staatsarchiv Bremen, Stab 7, 1025–2/27, *Halbjahresbericht von Peter Alomenu*, Dzake, 21 July 1915.

7. Rich people feared being bewitched by envious relatives with whom they failed to share in non-Christian society (e.g. Spieth 1906: 300).

8. Unfortunately he did not pay much attention to the phenomenon. In the book *Die Ewe Stämme* he presented a report about *adze* among the Ho people (1906: 544–45) and short statements about *adze* by other informants (ibid.: 682, 724, 832, 850, 906). In his book on the Ewe religion he devoted three pages to this phenomenon (1911: 299 ff). According to Spieth, the Ewe's concept and practice of witchcraft originated from the Yoruba.

9. The suffix *tɔ* expresses a possessive relationship between the noun preceding it and the object or person referred to. The term *adzetɔ*, which is usually translated as 'witch', thus literally describes a person as 'owner of *adze*'. Another expression employed by my own informants was 'he or she *has* witchcraft'. The Ewe expression was *adze le asi*, that is, witchcraft is in his/her hand (the Ewe express active ownership by saying that something is in somebody's hand).

10. According to many reports the *dzotɔwo* were the most respected in town. The *trɔ* priests and even the chiefs 'by and by almost became their subordinates' (Stab 7, 1025–58/8: 126). For references, see for example Stab 7, 1025–56/8: 56, 106, 124, 127.

11. See Stab 7,1025–56/8: 230, 256–57, 321.

12. Whereas Debrunner (1961), Field (1960) and Ward (1956) suggested that, due to modern economic changes, witchcraft accusations and suspicions were on the increase, Goody (1957) stated that they were also a feature of pre-colonial society. Although I agree with his argument that African pre-colonial societies and religions should not be conceptualised as static, I would nevertheless maintain that the incorporation of Ghana into a global economy brought about new problems that were to be dealt with in new ways. In pre-colonial times, the tension between individualism and family affiliation was never as marked as in colonial and post-colonial society (see McCaskie 1981: 136–37).

13. Elsewhere, I have discussed the issue of 'backsliding' in some detail (1996) and shown that the return to Ewe religion has to be explained against the background of the fact that the politics and economy of colonial society were partly out of tune with the new Christian religion. Though Christianity offered an avenue towards 'civilisation', it did not bring about the actual transformation of traditional society in such a way that people would be able to live up to their individualism. In economic, social and symbolical respects they were still related to the extended family.

14. This voyeuristic fascination with the satanic is of course not limited to Ewe Christianity: witness the following quote by the German Pietist theologian Christoph Blumhardt (1842–1919): 'What stupid people the Christians often are: When they are to talk of heaven, they do not know of anything to say, and when they are to talk of the Devil, they all know something' (1972: 115–16; original in German, my translation).

15. On the other hand, many converts found it difficult to become fully separated from their extended families with whom they remained linked at least by the collective ownership of land. Many cases of so-called backsliding occurred in which Christians sought help from their ancestors or family gods and returned to live in the midst of their families (Meyer 1996).

16. This council was founded in 1929, and it comprised the African Methodist Episcopal Zion Church, the English Church Mission, the Ewe Presbyterian

Church, the Presbyterian Church of Gold Coast and the Wesleyan Methodist Church. In 1934 the Salvation Army also became a member.

17. Because of their use of candles, incense and other object, spiritual churches have come to be vehemently attacked by Pentecostalist churches, who claim that Christian are to rely on the Word alone. Pentecostalists regard spiritual churches as potentially occult and led by 'false prophets'. In reaction to these assaults, a number of spiritual churches, among them *Agbelengor* (Meyer 1999: Chapter 5), have done away with objects and have reformed themselves along Pentecostalist lines.

18. Of course, there have been particular forms of *dzo* aimed at making one's business flourish (see also note 5), but it worked at the cost of a relative's life, as is the case with *adzegã*.

19. There was one *Mami Water* priestess in Peki. I learned that she was born of Christian parents, who had both been born into the EPC and later switched to the Apostolic Church. Since her childhood, the priestess had had dreams about living at the bottom of the sea. Once she dreamt she was approached by a white man who kissed her. At first she sought deliverance in a spiritual church, but gradually she realised that she herself belonged to these spirits and became initiated as a priestess. She told me that she had travelled to the bottom of the sea several times, where she saw many shops and riches. The people living there were all white and among them there was no death, sickness or poverty. According to her, *Mami Water* spirits can help people get healing, children and money through their earthly priests and priestesses. When I interviewed her on 22 May 1992, the priestess had not yet been able to assemble sufficient funds with which to establish her shrine, but she intended to do so in the near future.

20. For instance, when I asked Kenneth Bonsu, a twenty-seven year old member of the EPC 'of Ghana', whether I was right to assume that people in Peki consider *adze* to be the main agent of *Abosam* – the Devil – he answered: 'Well, *adze* of course is an agent, but I don't think it is the main agent. I would rather think those spirits from the sea [that is, *Mami Water* spirits] are the main agents.'

References

Appiah, K. A.,1992, *In My Father's House: Africa in the Philosophy of Culture*. New York and Oxford: Oxford University Press.

Baeta, R. and Sedode, T., 1911, *Reste heidnischer Anschauungen in den Christenge-meinden Togo: Zwei Aufsätze von Lehrern der Norddeutschen Mission*. Bremen: Verlag der Norddeutschen Missionsgesellschaft.

Blumhardt, C., 1932, *Report on Common Beliefs with Regard to Witchcraft*. Accra: Scottish Mission Depot.

Blumhardt, C., 1972, *Worte des evangelischen Pfarrers und Landtagsabgeordneten Christoph Blumhardt*. Wuppertal: Jugenddienst Verlag.

Christian Council of the Gold Coast, 1932, *Report on Common Beliefs with Regard to Witchcraft*. Accra: Scottish Mission Depot.

Comaroff, J. and Comaroff, J., eds, 1993, *Modernity and Its Malcontents: Ritual and Power in Postcolonial Africa*. Chicago: The University of Chicago Press.

Crain, M. M., 1991, 'Poetics and Politics in the Ecuadorean Andes: Women's Narratives of Death and Devil Possession', *American Ethnologist*, 18 (1): 67–89.

Debrunner, H., 1961, *Witchcraft in Ghana: A Study on the Belief in Destructive Witches and its Effects on the Akan Tribes*. Accra: Presbyterian Book Depot.

Drewal, H. J., 1988, 'Performing the Other: Mami Wata Worship in Africa', *The Drama Review*, 32 (2): 160–85.

Edelman, M., 1994, 'Landlords and the Devil: Class, Ethnic, and Gender Dimensions of Central American Peasant Narratives', *Current Anthropology*, 91 (1): 58–93.

Eni, E., 1988, *Delivered from the Powers of Darkness*. Ibadan: Scripture Union, 2nd ed.

Fabian, J., 1978, 'Popular Culture in Africa: Findings and Conjectures', *Africa*, 48 (4): 315–34.

Field, M. J., 1960, *Search for Security: An Ethno-Psychiatric Study of Rural Ghana*. London: Faber and Faber.

Fischer, F. H., 1991, *Der Missionsarzt Rudolf Fisch und die Anfänge medizinischer Arbeit der Basler Mission an der Goldküste (Ghana)*. Herzogenrath: Verlag Murken-Altrogge.

Geschiere, P. (with Fisiy, C.), 1994, 'Domesticating Personal Violence: Witchcraft, Courts and Confessions in Cameroon', *Africa*, 64 (3): 321–41.

Geschiere, P., 1997, *The Modernity of Witchcraft: Politics and the Occult in Postcolonial Africa*. Charlottesville and London: University Press of Virginia.

Gifford, P., 1994, 'Ghana's Charismatic Churches', *Journal of Religion in Africa*, 64 (3): 241–65.

Goody, J., 1957, 'Anomie in Ashanti?', *Africa*, 27 (1): 356–63.

Jules-Rosette, B., 1994, 'The Future of African Theologies – Situating New Religious Movements in an Epistemological Setting', *Social Compass* 41 (1): 49–65.

Lan, D., 1985, *Guns and Rain: Guerrillas and Spirit Mediums in Zimbabwe*. London: James Currey.

Luig, U., 1993, 'Besessenheitskulte als historische Charta: Die Verarbeitung europäischer Einflüsse in sambianischen Besessenheitskulten', *Paideuma*, 39: 343–54.

Luig, U., 1994, Constructing Local Worlds: Spirit Possession in the Gwembe Valley, Zambia. Paper for the Tenth Satterthwaite Colloquium on African Ritual and Religion, 16–19 April 1994.

Maier, D. J. E., 1983, *Priests and Power: The Case of the Dente Shrine in Nineteenth-Century Ghana*. Bloomington: Indiana University Press.

Marshall (-Fratani), R., 1991, 'Power in the Name of Jesus', *Review of African Political Economy*, 52: 21–38.

Marshall (-Fratani), R., 1993, "'Power in the Name of Jesus': Social Transformation and Pentecostalism in Western Nigeria 'Revisited'", in Ranger, T. and Vaughan, O., eds, *Legitimacy and the State in Twentieth Century Africa*. Basingstoke: Macmillan.

Marshall (-Fratani), R., 1998, 'Mediating the Global and the Local in Nigerian Pentecostalism', *Journal of Religion in Africa*, XXVIII (3): 278–315.

McCaskie, T. C., 1981, 'Anti-Witchcraft Cults in Asante: An Essay in the Social History of an African People', *History in Africa*, 8: 125–54.

Meyer, B., 1992, "'If You Are a Devil You Are a Witch and, if You Are a Witch You Are a Devil': The Integration of 'Pagan' Ideas into the Conceptual Universe of Ewe Christians in Southeastern Ghana', *The Journal of Religion in Africa*, 22 (2): 98–132.

Meyer, B., 1995a, *Translating the Devil. An African Appropriation of Pietist Protestantism. The Case of the Peki Ewe, 1847–1992.* University of Amsterdam: Dissertation.

Meyer, B., 1995b, ''Delivered from the Powers of Darkness': Confessions about Satanic Riches in Christian Ghana', *Africa,* 65 (2): 236–55.

Meyer, B., 1996, 'Modernity and Enchantment: The Image of the Devil in Popular African Christianity', in van der Veer, P., ed., *Conversion to Modernities: The Globalization of Christianity.* London and New York: Routledge.

Meyer, B., 1998a, ''Make a Complete Break with the Past': Memory and Post-Colonial Modernity in Ghanaian Pentecostalist Discourse', *Journal of Religion in Africa,* 28(3): 316–349.

Meyer, B., 1998b, 'Commodities and the Power of Prayer: Pentecostalist Attitudes Towards Consumption in Contemporary Ghana', in Meyer, B. and Geschiere, P., eds., *Globalization and Identity: Dialectics of Flow and Closure. Development and Change,* 29 (4): 751–77.

Meyer, B., 1999, *Translating the Devil: Religion and Modernity Among the Ewe in Ghana.* Edinburgh: Edinburgh University Press.

Monatsblatt der Norddeutschen Mission, Hamburg 1840ff/Bremen 1851ff.

Parry, J., 1989, 'On the Moral Perils of Exchange', in Parry, J. and Bloch, M., eds, *Money and the Morality of Exchange.* Cambridge: Cambridge University Press.

Pels, P., 1992, 'Mumiani: The White Vampire. A Neo-diffusionist Analysis of Rumour', *Etnofoor,* 5 (1/2): 165–87.

Peukert, D., 1989, *Max Weber's Diagnose der Moderne.* Göttingen: Vandenhoeck u. Ruprecht.

Shaw, R., 1996, 'The Politician and the Diviner: Divination and the Consumption of Power in Sierra Leone', *Journal of Religion in Africa,* 26 (1): 30–55.

Spieth, J., 1906, *Die Ewe-Stämme: Material zur Kunde des Ewe-Volkes in Deutsch-Togo.* Berlin: Dietrich Reimer.

Spieth, J., 1908, *Wie kommt die Bekehrung eines Heiden zustande?* Bremen: Verlag der Norddeutschen Missionsgesellschaft.

Spieth, J., 1911, *Die Religion der Eweer in Süd-Togo.* Leipzig: Dietersche Verlagsbuchhandlung.

Staatsarchiv Bremen 7, 1026–56/8.

Taussig, M. T., 1980, *The Devil and Commodity Fetishism in South America.* Chapel Hill: The University of North Carolina Press.

Taussig, M., 1995, 'The Sun Gives Without Receiving: An Old Story', *Comparative Studies in Society and History,* 37 (2): 368–98.

Thoden van Velzen, H. U. E., 1995, 'Revenants that Cannot be Shaken: Collective Fantasies in a Maroon Society', *American Anthropologist,* 97 (4): 722–32.

Thoden van Velzen, H. U. E. and van Wetering, W., 1988, *The Great Father and the Danger: Religious Cults, Material Forces, and Collective Fantasies in the World of the Surinamese Maroons.* Dordrecht: Foris Publications.

Van Dijk, R., 1992, *Young Malawian Puritans. Young Puritan Preachers in a Present-day African Urban Environment.* Utrecht: ISOR.

Van Dijk, R., 1997, 'From Camp to Encompassment: Discourses of Transsubjectivity in the Ghanaian Pentecostal Diaspora', *Journal of Religion in Africa,* 27 (2): 135–60.

Ward, B., 1956, 'Some Observations on Religious Cults in Ashanti', *Africa,* 26 (1): 41–61.

Wendl, T., 1991, *Mami Wata oder ein Kult zwischen den Kulturen*. Münster: Lit Verlag.

White, L., 1993, 'Cars out of Place: Vampires, Technology, and Labour in East and Central Africa', *Representations*, 43 (Summer): 27–50.

Wicker, K. O'B., n.d., 'Mami Water in African Religion and Spirituality', in Olupona, J. K., and Long, C. H., eds, *African Spirituality*. Crossroad Press: forthcoming.

Verrips, J., 1996, 'The Consumption of Touching Images: Reflections on Mimetic 'Wildness' in the West', *Ethnologia Europaea*, 1996: 51–64.

5

Modernity, Crisis and the Rise of Charismatic Catholicism in the Maltese Islands

Nadia Theuma

University of Malta

a phenomenon centred on belief in the direct inspiration of the Holy Spirit in the lives of the individuals, personal and emotional piety, and the formation of closely knit groups of people who have similar experience (Hitchock 1991)

Introduction

The first Charismatic Renewal Movement (CRM) meeting ever to be organised in Malta took place in 1975. From this one public meeting the Charismatic expression has expanded to a number of localities in the Maltese Islands. This paper is based on research carried out in four different localities in Malta and Gozo between 1994 and 1995. At this time there were sixty-six prayer groups and communities in the Maltese Islands (according to the Charismatic Annual Conference publication, 1995), with an affiliation of 5,000 members.[1]

In recent years there has been an increased revival of Protestant and Pentecostal Movements globally, but especially in developing countries (Martin 1991 and Meyer, chapter four of this volume). In such contexts, 'development' and 'modernisation' would appear to go hand in hand with the assumption that the kinds of changes they involve lead inevitably to a rationalist world-view. However, contrary to the expectation that modernisation leads to disenchantment with the world, involvement with modernity seems to actually encourage people to resort to religious movements. Developing countries are often struggling with economic problems, social change and at times ethnic conflicts. Beckford (1986) has commented that such 'rapid social change' is one of the factors which leads to the rise of religious movements.

Religion, Social Change and Modernity in the Maltese Islands

A former British colony, the Maltese Islands (Malta, Gozo and Commino) lie nearly at the centre of the Mediterranean. With a total area of 343 km^2 and a population of 378,000 they are the most densely populated country in Europe. The Maltese Islands are Roman Catholic, with nearly 99 per cent of the population baptised in this Church. Religion and religious activity were and to a certain extent still are the fulcrum of Maltese life (Boissevain 1993). Following Independence in 1964, the Maltese Islands went through a process of socio-economic development. The effects of this development were not felt until much later when urbanisation, media and tourism left their marks on the traditional Maltese lifestyle (Vassallo 1979).

Increased affluence, information technology and an increased awareness that the Maltese Islands are not as isolated from external pressure, caused a section of the population to question the practicability and utility of Roman Catholicism as it was practised. This had diverse effects on the population. In some instances there was disenchantment with the traditional Church. Recent studies published by the Maltese Church show that there is a decline in church attendance, while fewer young people are opting for religious life (Abela 1992, Tonna 1993). In other instances, the changes gave rise to new religious expressions, such as the CRM.

Such movements are seen by the Church as a threat to established modes of religious expression. In this chapter I argue that the Charismatic Movement, through its use of prayer, song and the reading and interpretation of the Bible, gives a more 'spontaneous' or individualistic feel to religious expression that contrasts with the more ritualised forms of the established Church. In doing so, it provides a new vocabulary to consider, deal with and rationalise the existential problems of life in late twentieth-century Malta.

The Rise of the Charismatic Renewal Movement in the Maltese Islands

At the time when the CRM was establishing its roots in Maltese society, Malta was going through major socio-economic changes brought about by new political styles and swift economic development. This rapidly changing environment seems to have provided the necessary conditions for the CRM to flourish.

By the mid 1970s an extensive building boom led to an intensive urbanisation process resulting in the widespread movement of people from the area around Grand Harbour to developments further inland. This population movement was coupled with an increased demand for owner-occupied property which led to the further uprooting of people. Young couples were faced with a new situation in which they were separated from the close family circle, having set up homes in areas where they had no relatives or previous contacts. This new housing pattern gave rise to new residential areas within or next to traditional villages. These new 'communities' did not belong to the traditional social pattern and the existent social fabric was not ready to incorporate these new elements. New religious movements such as the CRM thrived in these new communities, initially attracting young people, and later families.

The first Charismatic meeting was held in May 1975. That year the International Charismatic Movement was holding its annual meeting in Rome.[2] One of the leaders of the local Movement felt that it would be a good idea to invite a foreign speaker to give an introductory meeting. After having obtained permission from the local ecclesiastical authorities, the meeting was held at a local church school. The meeting was publicised in the local press and had as its main speakers two leading foreign Charismatics. The Movement then spread to a number of parish-based groups, but its expansion from one parish to the next was slow. Despite being predominantly a lay movement, in order to thrive and grow in villages and towns the CRM needed the support of the local clerical authorities. This was not always forthcoming and in areas such as Gozo, which is more traditional than Malta, the Movement could thrive only if a priest was leading the group (Theuma 1997).

Structure of the Charismatic Renewal Movement

The CRM is a loose organisation of sixty-six individual prayer groups and communities co-ordinated by a body called the National Service Committee (NSC). Each group or community is run independently, with its own leadership team. This team – called the Service Team – is responsible for the group's activities and religious growth, which is maintained by weekly prayer meetings and cell group meetings. On a social level the Service Team organises picnics and other outings which serve to further enhance community spirit. The Service Team maintains contact with the NSC through meetings arranged by the latter.

The National Service Committee is responsible for providing means of adhesion for the national Charismatic community. One of its main activities is the three-day Annual Charismatic conference which is held on the first weekend after Easter Sunday. This three-day event involves teaching, celebration of mass, healing sessions and social activities. Since the first conference held in 1978 this event has always been well attended; advanced booking is recommended, and usually the conference is fully booked before the closing date. It is a priority of every Charismatic to be at this conference to attest the validity of their religious expression as well as celebrate community spirit.[3]

The NSC organises teaching seminars for group and community leaders and is responsible for the publication of a monthly newsletter and other reading material. The National Service Team also serves as the main link between the individual groups and provides the necessary help when needed.

The initial links forged with the International Charismatic Community are still present. With the NSC as its formal representative, the CRM maintains formal links with the central body in Rome. International speakers are invited on a yearly basis to address the annual Charismatic conference, and besides this, representatives of the Maltese Charismatic community meet once a year with their international counterparts to evaluate the year's work.

Gender and Socio-Economic Background, and Charismatic Catholicism Affiliation

Traditionally in the Mediterranean, religion treats men and women differently to varying degrees (Christian 1989; Boissevain 1993; Du

Boulay 1986; and Davis 1984). Charismatic movements in the wider sense of the word try to do away with such gender differentiation (Galanter 1989; Scott 1994). Maltese Charismatic groups maintain an ideology whereby membership is neither gender- nor age-specific: 'all are welcome, whether priest, religious, man or woman, old and young' (President, NSC). Since there are no membership lists, statistical analysis can be problematic, but an indication of the gender and age composition of the CRM can be gauged through the analysis of the annual conference application forms. The data discussed here are of the 1995 Annual Conference and cover less than one half of the Charismatic population. One could argue that this is indicative of the Charismatic population provided it is realised that the conference tends to attract the more active Charismatics.

Table 1: Composition of the Charismatic Renewal Movement by Gender

Category	Number	% of the total (n = 2139)
Women	1394	65.2%
Men	745	34.8%

Source: Conference Publication, April, 1995

Table 2: Composition of the Charismatic Renewal Movement by Category

Category	Number	% of the total (n = 2139)
Clerics	25	1.2
Nuns	11	0.5
Attending with spouse (couples)	1042	48.7
Attending on their own (men)	199	9.3
Attending on their own (women)	862	40.3
Children*	331	

* children are not included as a percentage of the total as although they accompany their parents to the conference, they do not participate in the actual activities.

Source: Conference Publication, April, 1995

The data show that twice as many women as men registered at the conference. It is significant though that the majority of men who attended the conference are married and accompany their wives and children. This tends to highlight the fact that men attend as part of a family rather than on their own. The attendance of the family as a whole unit in both prayer groups and Conference is encouraged by the very ethics of the Movement. Although clerical and religious people are a very small minority, the Movement seems to be more popular with clerics than nuns.

People tend to resort to religious movements at particular stages in life. This is also true of the Charismatic groups as shown by reference to the 1995 Annual Conference data and a survey I conducted among Charismatics.

Table 3: Composition of the Charismatic Movement by Age

Age (in years)	Number	% of total (n = 2139)
up to 25	214	10.0%
26–35	245	11.4%
36–45	631	29.5%
46–55	476	22.3%
56–65	292	13.6%
65 +	100	4.7%
not declared	181	8.5%

Source: Conference Publication, April 1995

The above table indicates that nearly 52 per cent fall within the 36 – 55 year age brackets. From the survey carried out it transpires that the average Charismatic is married with an average age of 43 years. In discussing age and affiliation one has to be careful. It is not enough to look at the average age of a Charismatic at present, but one has to look also at the age at which these people *became* Charismatics. From the survey conducted, the age at which one is likely to become a charismatic is 32 years. In contemporary Western society, this age is defined as early adulthood. Psychologists argue that this stage can be quite stressful as it is a time when major life decisions are made – marriage, setting up a family and the consolidation of a career. In a context in which family and work tend to take priority over other values (Abela 1994: 4–5), the uncertainties associated with this time of life could be said to precipitate anxieties that lead people to the CRM.

Charismatics could be defined as 'middle class' (Hargrove 1989: 327), although class is a problematic indicator, especially in Malta where the middle class includes people coming from very diverse backgrounds. The Movement's members come from a wide range of backgrounds – manual to professional workers, though the latter are in a small majority. People in leading positions, both in individual groups and communities as well as in the National Service Team, tend to have had more schooling (at times even tertiary education) than the rest of the group.

So far I have argued that social changes were the catalyst in the establishment and diffusion of the CRM. It has also been mentioned that local groups arose as a reaction to the established hierarchy and prevalent religious mentality. Yet analysis of age and socio-economic background tend to suggest that women are still in a majority and that there is some form of hierarchy within the group based on educational background.

Age and socio-economic structure can give an indication of the general structure of the Movement. Yet not all people who are in their early adult years or those who come from a middle-class background join the Charismatic Movement. The following section will discuss some case studies of how people come to join.

Joining the Movement

Fieldwork has shown that people have a multitude of reasons and motives for joining, which can be simplified and classified into two – active and passive. Passive recruitment implies joining the Movement for no particular reason other than being attracted to the idea of 'belonging to a movement'. People who join in this fashion may or may not become fully converted to the Movement's teachings. I met three couples and four single persons who entered the Movement in this manner. The couples heard of the Movement through evangelisation, a process that was very popular during its early days. It consists of a series of talks spread over a week carried out in parishes. One particular couple was invited by the parish priest. Since they had refused the invitation several times before, they thought that it would be a good idea to go so that they could say (if invited again) that they had been to a meeting! They liked the group of people, and since they were new to the locality with few friends, they decided to stay. Today both husband and wife are committed Charismatics. Not all of those who join the Movement stay in. Chris, a young single man, wanted to join a Charismatic Movement because he was lonely and at the time he was going through emotional problems. Initially he liked the idea of having friends, but the religious element and the fundamentalist approach to life promoted by the Movement were too much for him to take.

The majority of Charismatic people went through an active affiliation process. They saw the Movement as a means of 'assistance', social or religious. This trend is common to both sexes, yet there are subtle differences in the way men and women were affiliated. Miceli (1995) points out that in Malta women are the main recipients of social assistance. This is because women need help during their childbearing years and since women tend to outlive their male counterparts, they need social assistance later in their lives. Life histories of female Charismatics reveal that in their majority they joined the Movement because of psycho-social needs.

Marija is a 54 year old woman, and a mother of two young men. She joined the Movement in 1978. At that time her husband was threatened at work because of his political beliefs. This situation proved to be strenuous for the whole family. Marija felt that the normal religious measures were not having the desired effects – if anything, she was growing angrier at God for permitting such a situation. It was some time later that Marija heard of Sister Anne, a nun who was organising prayer groups. Determined to try anything to improve her family's situation, she attended her first meeting. Another informant, Josephine, turned to the same women's group, again because of her husband who was heavily involved in politics. Apart from this, he had not attended mass for several years. Worried about him and the effects this might have on her two adolescent children, Josephine decided to look for help. She found help and assistance from Sister Anne and her group. Today, both these women and their husbands are deeply involved in the Movement.

In another locality six women, all members of a Charismatic community, introduced a weekly morning meeting specifically for women. The main reason for setting up this group was to help women who had 'problems' at home. The fact that certain personal problems are never discussed with kin, even though mothers and sisters might be a telephone call away, has created a niche for this group. As Hall (1992) points out, religious groups are often the first instance where one can acquire assistance. Religious groups offer the right context for women to address their problems through prayers and communal support. Pauline, one of the leaders of this group, remarked that these women 'are bursting to unburden their problems to someone apart from their husbands or kin'. This is similar to Kennedy's (1986) discussion of women's friendships in Crete. As with the Cretan women who need friendship to get on in life, the Maltese Charismatic Movement provides an adequate medium for women to establish friendships and, later on, spiritual kin groups. Through religion, a body of sisterhood is formed: 'it is through knowing God, through prayers that we can learn to unburden ourselves and get closer to one another' (a female informant).

In Malta, social life for the married woman is still limited, especially in rural areas. Though an increasing number of women work, the trend in Malta is to stop working once children are born. Work is not resumed until children are of schooling age, if not later (Abela 1994: 24–30; Borg and Spiteri 1994). A substantial number of women are bound to their home life and very often find themselves in crisis over their private life. One of my informants said that her first year of marriage was extremely difficult. She did not like her husband's occupation (car mechanic) and this proved to be a recurrent problem in her marriage. Through the support given by other prayer group members, she was able to come to terms with her problem. Not only this, but she was able to share the problem with her husband.

In most of the couples I interviewed, the women joined first, followed sometime later by their husbands. Recruitment usually occurs on a one-to-one basis, through evangelisation. The one-to-one method is more effective among people of the same gender, such as a woman inviting her friend along or two youths attending together, but when it comes to husbands it is an altogether different story; 'men are by nature resistant to religion', one of my female informants commented. Thus a wife's eagerness for her husband to join is usually met with protests. Yet a number of husbands end up joining. In order to entice their husbands, women make use of unobtrusive pressures. One such case is Doris who initially started to attend the prayer group together with a friend. She used to try to involve her husband Tony, a dockyard worker, in her goings on:

> He used to tell me, why should I come? I used to prepare his food before attending the meeting. On returning home I used to tell him what we had discussed and also mention the names of those present, especially men from our village whom he knew. You know, men who have acquired a bad name . . . In the meantime I started to change, character-wise, feeling more realised as a person. Maybe this could have induced Tony to come along, one Sunday, to a meeting.

When I asked her why she persisted so much, she answered that her husband deep down was a good man, and if others had reformed he could as well.

This is but one example. Similar incidents suggest that women consciously employ certain strategies to involve their husbands, although they would not say so in front of their spouses. The fact that the majority[4] of husbands finally join is explained in terms of incessant praying: 'a woman should support her husband by means of prayer and sacrifice'. Women are motivated by two main factors to urge their husbands to join in. First, women are encouraged by the presence of other men in the prayer group. Secondly, and perhaps more importantly, they are encouraged by the Movement's teachings to involve their husbands. Asking why it is so imperative for the Movement I was told that it is through sharing the experience of spiritual growth with one's spouse that a relationship between God and the Charismatic can be fruitful. Maximum benefit is attained when both spouses are involved.

The inclusion of couples was a later development of the Movement, which started off as a single person's group attracting students (Aquilina 1985, Baldacchino 1995, and Poloma 1992). Once the Movement branched out into the various localities and parishes, however, it attracted a different audience, mainly couples. This had an impact on how people started to perceive religious participation. Rather than the formation of single-sex groups as was the case with other religious organisations, like the M.U.S.E.U.M. society – the local society for Catholic doctrine – and the Legion of Mary, religious participation meant the involvement of the whole family. Thus, although the Movement brought a fresh outlook in religion, it also reinforced existing social norms, by promoting the 'sacredness' of the family.

A substantial number of men joined in as a result of their spouses' involvement. As outlined in the example of Tony above, some joined the Movement because they sensed that their wives' involvement was beneficial. Others had heard of the Movement, were not impressed by its 'exaggerated' outward behaviour, but were eventually convinced and ended up joining.

It seems that single men came from a different background from those who joined as a result of their spouse's involvement. Not all men joined as married men, which includes members of the National Service Team (*Tigdid*, May 1995). In looking at the life histories of these individuals two factors emerge as important. The first is that they had a higher educational background, in some cases including tertiary education. The second is that these men were looking for a religious expression which was new and challenging.

> It was a time of spiritual metamorphosis. I was looking for something with deeper meaning. I was not happy with what the Church was offering (not that it was bad) . . . I had a hollow feeling . . . I wanted to try something new, something exciting. (Peter, National Service Committee)

Gender Differences and Group Dynamics

I will now discuss how people perceive their religious experience. If social changes occurring in wider society led this Movement to challenge implicitly the traditional mentality of church hierarchy, one expects that this would also have brought about a change in the way people deal with and perceive their religious experience. These experienced are heavily influenced by gender. Once a person becomes involved with the group, s/he is supposed to experience a change for the better. In looking at these changes and how Charismatics recount them, I discovered that men and women use different tones and expressions. Men express themselves with more fervour and, surprisingly, tend to be more emotional than women when speaking about their religious experiences. Joe, one of the elders in one of the locations studied, describes his life as having changed completely:

> I was always keen to know the truth; [before becoming a Charismatic] I read the Bible for its historical sake. Today, I read the Bible because it is the word of God. My life has changed completely, I am more determined and the energy I used to invest in politics I am investing in the Movement. This experience has become my life experience, God has taken control of my life.

Women, on the other hand, are somehow less passionate in their views. During the time of fieldwork Edwina had been involved with the Movement for four years. She spoke about her experience in the following way:

> My life has changed . . . I am more calm . . . I tolerate people more. Today I realise how proud I was. God has filled me with courage.

Given their traditional religious role, I would argue that women are already familiar with religious experience, thus their contact with the Movement serves to consolidate their beliefs rather than to replace them with new ones. Josephine commented that the Movement helped her to *affirm* what she knew already. On the other hand, the male Charismatic is either apprehensive of the Movement or is looking for a new experience. Once he is convinced of the Movement and converts, the spiritual experience becomes a personal event which is expressed as such. A female informant summed up this difference in the following way: 'it is normal that religion appeals more to a woman but once a man is involved, there is no turning back'. O'Neill (1990) argues that men and women communicate their religious experience differently because of their gender identities. Since men are associated with leadership, their speech is generally more powerful, while that of females reflects their submissive role. In the CRM context one might identify the male emphasis on personal experience in these terms. Powerful, emotional experiences become associated with authority and leadership. This is born out in the examples outlined below. In the first, Doris and Tony express their views of how they felt when they were converted:

Tony: I felt so elated, I wonder whether I will ever feel the same, there was so much happiness . . . We were asked to forgive, it was not easy but I had to. Once I committed myself to Jesus, there was no turning back . . . Once I discovered God's love I was not going to let go easily.

Doris: It was a wonderful meeting, so different from the usual religious practice. For the first time I felt I could relate to God . . .

Tony is clearly more effusive in his description of the experience of conversion, whereas Doris is more diffident. Yet this is not a hard and fast rule. There were other couples whose experience was recounted using very similar terms and tones. For example, Benny and Maria described conversion as follows:

Benny: We were going through difficult times. It was then that we turned to God . . . We saw the way and held on to it. Things did not change, but our perspectives changed.

Marija: My priorities changed . . . I started putting a pinch of love in everything I did.

Thus not only are there gender differences but couples tend to differ as well. The first couple is traditional in their views regarding gender roles in society. This was very evident from the way the couple handled the interview. Tony was the person who answered my question, even though I involved Doris as much as him. Another factor worth noting is that Doris is still in the 'nursing' stage as the couple have a six-year-old daughter. The fact that a woman is still nurturing a child is presented by the Charismatics as a reason for not participating fully in the groups' activities: *home duties surpass any other obligations*. On the other hand, Marija and Benny are less traditional in their views of gender roles. They are grandparents, that is, past their reproductive stages. Since Benny has retired from work the couple have more spare time which can be dedicated to spiritual and group matters. Whereas Tony and Doris are group members, Benny and Marija occupy important positions within the group, running the Healing Ministry, and form part of the Service Team of their locality.

Given that the differences in expression of religious experience are linked to established gender identities, where these identities are challenged, or persons are disengaged from social expectations, these differences are reduced. For example, in couples where both spouses work, similar tones and expressions are used when talking about religious experiences. Social rank or authority within the group can also have an effect, as in the case of Benny and Marija, for whom the social expectation of reproduction has also been removed, thus making her and Benny's similar description of religious experience doubly explicable. These variations of rank and social expectation are issues that O'Neill does not mention.

Power relations are another aspect of the Charismatic Movement. One of the main achievements of the CRM is that authority in interpreting the Holy Scripture is no longer the domain of the clergy but it becomes available to the lay person. In principle, men and women are equal both in their religious standing and in their rights to leadership. However, there is still a marked gender hierarchy.

Most of the important positions are occupied by men. In the National Service Committee nine out of the eleven members are men. In three of the localities under study, women form part of the leading core-group and run a number of cell groups. Despite this, general female participation in the prayer group is low. As Falk (1995) suggests, it is common that certain women disappear after some time within the Movement, leaving their husbands as, at times, prominent members. If both men and women are involved with the running of the group, men are still pushed forward as the 'figureheads' of the group. The fact that this phenomenon is also seen in other Charismatic and Pentecostal groups (Csordas 1995, Scott 1994) shows that the Movement's teaching and the behaviour of its members do not tally. Why is this so?

In discussing the issue of male versus female involvement in the group, an ex-leader (male) pointed out that the group involves women in all spheres; there are members of the Service Team who are women, as well as cell group leaders. Yet there are few women who can be regarded as teachers. According to this ex-leader, women still prefer to be led – they are still bound to a traditional pattern. This perspective was not only shared by men but also a number of female informants who were of the same idea. One female informant commented:

> I really like it when I see men running the group. I am happy to see men participating with such fervour in these religious groups. I must admit I feel more comfortable when there are men in charge of the group.

These perceptions may be the result of three factors. The first is that women do not have enough confidence in themselves to lead a group. This is the implication of the fact that, in their majority, women prefer to see men run the group because these are *the* expected roles. Secondly, a substantial number of women are still bringing up children. Thus they cannot dedicate a lot of time to the group since their first duties are towards home and children. Yet the fuller participation of women beyond reproductive age suggests a possible symbolic linkage of reproductive sexual activity and spiritual pollution. Women who are free from reproductive activity might be seen as 'cleaner'.

Third, despite the claims made by its members, the Movement reinforces social norms. Women leaders are a minority in the Maltese Islands and Charismatic groups are no different. Women leaders are perceived to put off male members. This notion is based on fact, as groups whose leadership is predominately made up of females end up being female prayer groups rather than mixed or couple-based groups.

Forms of Charismatic Language

'Specialised Language': Charismatic Jargon

The language style of a Charismatic is very distinctive and it immediately strikes a non-Charismatic as odd. This particular language is not only used during prayer meetings, but is also incorporated within Charismatics' daily life so that mundane conversations are interspersed with Charismatic language characteristics. In conversations a Charismatic refers to one's Christian name, uses phrases such as 'praise God', 'God willing' and Bible quotations to emphasise a point, even outside the context of a prayer group, and ends a conversation by saying 'peace be with you' (*il-paci mieghek*) or 'God bless you'.[5]

Upon conversion Charismatics adopt a new religious perspective that affects their attitude towards life experiences. This leads them to interpret life events in a different manner. Language use reflects this change in perspective. For example, following a village celebration to commemorate the vestment of altar boys (*vestizzjoni*), I accompanied the family with whom I was staying at the time to a small party, *festin*. I joined Pauline and her friends who were members of the two village prayer groups. The topics of conversation were children, their children's teachers and the celebration. Conversation then revolved around a woman called Martha who was in hospital until recently. Her friends (*ahwa,* sisters) asked her after her health. She commented that she was not feeling very well. Her friends expressed their support and promised her their prayers. Pauline sensed the gravity of Martha's illness and by way of sympathising she said, *Ma nafx x'nista' nghidlek aktar oht, kultant taf x'nghid, forsi ikun irridek titqaddes* ('I do not have anything else to add, dear sister. Who knows, perhaps this is your special calling').

Although this use of language is not limited to Charismatics it is of interest because it forms the crucial element in a Charismatic's identity. The frequency of these phrases is quite high in Charismatic language use and a non-Charismatic cannot fail to notice it. The above phrases and other similar ones become incorporated within the psyche of the Charismatic so much so that a person seems to be transformed. Events that could have natural explanations become events over which humans no longer have control.

Another important aspect of the use of these phrases is the element of belief. By utilising such phrases Charismatics are making inferences about God and 'his ways', which are not always clear. The general image of God is one of absolute kindness – God is kind (*Il-hniena t'Alla kbira*), God is gentle (*kemm hu helu il- Mulej*). Yet there are times when people find themselves in situations for which there is no empirical explanation. In such situations Charismatics argue that God's ways are unknown. In such circumstances, the Charismatic makes use of a 'fatalistic' terminology. According to Charismatic notions, God's obscurity is intended to test human faith.

In adopting this somewhat fatalistic approach, Charismatics nullify human abilities to cope with daily problems thus 'giving God his due merits'. In this light humans are rendered 'mere clay in His hands'. Thus Charismatics reveal an anomaly. On the one hand they are firm believers in God's power - they make use of such powers to heal and pray. Yet on the other hand they are willing to accept all life's pitfalls without ever questioning why.

Prayer

Charismatic prayer differs from traditional prayer on two counts. First, Charismatic prayer is 'spontaneous'. By spontaneity one understands that prayer can take the form of words, song, scripture reading or silence. Unlike formal prayers, which are learnt, Charismatic prayer experiments with style and format. There are no overt rules stipulated for prayer. Second, Charismatic prayer expresses thanksgiving to God, rather than request for intervention. Whereas the latter is often one-sided, with the devotee asking for something of the divine, Charismatic prayer is seen as a relationship, whereby both the believer and the Divine can converse. This relationship is developed through the media used and through silence, where one 'listens to God's word'.

Charismatics not only have a distinct way of praying, they also go against the established norm of prayer. From the accepted popular view of Catholic instruction we learn that one speaks *to* God whereas Charismatics speak *with* God. Such a manner of prayer gives the Charismatic individual a winning edge on the rest of the Christian community since one no longer needs a medium (human or otherwise) through whom one can converse with God, but this is done directly without any intermediaries. Charismatics speak of entering God's presence (*nidhol fil-presenza tal-Mulej*) or communicating with God (*nitkellem mal-Mulej*). As Bruner (1986) notes, the way people talk about their own experience, in this case behaviour, indicates the person's attitudes and thoughts. It is important to note that the *Madonna*, Our Lady, a key figure in the Maltese religious context, does *not* have a very high profile among Charismatics, consequently her name does not feature a lot in Charismatic prayers. Initially this was a cause of unrest among Charismatic members. Today Charismatics accept the idea that Charismatic prayer is more 'Jesus- oriented' than traditional popular prayer.

Although Charismatics define prayer as spontaneous, this does not come naturally to a new Charismatic especially since Charismatic prayer is quite unorthodox in nature and style. Yet on the other hand prayer is the key to Charismatic life. The leaders of the community highlight the importance of getting the maximum out of prayer, thus making it imperative for a Charismatic to learn the proper formulae of prayer. For this aim Service Teams organise teachings dedicated solely to the importance and manner of prayer. What is interesting is that if one is to follow the pattern set up by the leaders of the community, then prayer is no longer spontaneous but becomes structured. When I pointed this contradiction out to one of the elders he commented 'that guidance is important, therefore one needs to be told how to go about praying. Spontaneity comes in during the actual prayer where one is free to say what one feels'. This gives 'spontaneity' a distinct interpretation - not often encountered in its everyday sense.

Personal prayer is perhaps the most spontaneous form of prayer. This form of prayer, referred to as 'Quiet Time',[6] is important as this is the time when the Charismatic encounters the Divine. Usually, each household has a physical space where they can hold Quiet Time and where each member of the family, can encounter God - *jiltaqa' mal-Mulej* - individually. The 'Quiet Time' is a time where one is at ease with God:

> When I enter God's presence I feel comfortable, as if I am with a loved person, I feel secure and happy . . . I bow before His presence and I surrender (*nintelaq f'idejH*). There is a Psalm that says just that: *il-Mulej ihaddnek mieghu; idu idawwarhom it-tnejn mieghek* [God embraces you]. There is no set pattern of how I pray, if I have something troubling me I just unburden myself, or I read the Scriptures or any other reading that inspires me. There are times when I do not say anything. I wait for God and listen to Him talking to me. (A male Charismatic)

It was impossible for me to participate in a 'Quiet Time' as I felt I would be intruding. The nearest I got was family prayer. Many Charismatic families hold a family prayer time,[7] where the family gets together for a few minutes of prayer and meditation. During my stay with the family of Pauline and Joseph, I was asked to participate in this gathering somewhat passively at first. It was during Advent and we gathered around the crib of Baby Jesus. Mark and Anne, the family's children, took it in turn to light the advent wreath. Then, Joseph gave the day's reading from a Charismatic daily meditation book, *The WORD Amongst Us*. The children read the scripture and following this each member of the family recited a personal prayer. The parents' prayers were elaborate – a combination of formal prayer, Charismatic teachings and personal reflections. They were interspersed with colloquial phrases.

A particular form of Charismatic prayer is *glossolalia*, a synonym for the gift of tongues which means either *to pray in tongues* or the *power to speak in tongues*. There is a distinction between the two variants. Praying in tongues is best described as a series of unintelligible utterances (*tneghid*). These utterances are defined by Charismatics as the human soul crying out in joy as it encounters God. One informant compared these utterances to a baby's chatter, which is unintelligible to all except the mother and child, who are bound together by the maternal bond. Likewise, praying in tongues is unintelligible to all but God. On the other hand 'speaking in tongues' can be defined as prophecy, whereby under the influence of the Holy Spirit, a person speaks in a foreign tongue which is unknown to the self, but can be understood or interpreted by another member of the congregation, who in turn 'translates' the message to the rest of the community or congregation. The occurrence, of the latter form of *glossolalia*, is quite rare.[8] On the contrary, all Charismatics 'pray in tongues', that is the first form of *glossolalia*.

A Charismatic experiences *glossolalia* whilst in prayer or during Prayer Meetings, which involve a direct invocation of the Holy Spirit. It is particularly significant when experienced at this level because it unites the whole community. After praise, the person leading the session invokes the Holy Spirit to descend upon the congregation: *huti ejjew nitolbu il-qawwa ta' l-Ispirtu biex timlina lkoll* (Brothers, Sisters, let us pray for the Holy Spirit to fill us). Then the congregation starts singing hymns that hail or describe the powers of the Holy Spirit.[9] After singing the song twice or three times in succession, the congregation starts uttering words such as *ashshereja, ashshereja* (special terms used in Charismatic prayer). Subsequently, Charismatics break into lilting but incomprehensible songs. They enter into a state of trance and with their eyes closed and outstretched arms, they start making slow swaying movements with their bodies. The duration of this trance varies from one session to another depending on the group's feeling. Once the congregation comes out of the trance, the general atmosphere is much lighter. The congregation starts reciting a litany of praises such 'God you are Great', 'You are Love'. This is interpreted as being the work of the Holy Spirit who unleashes the soul to praise God.

At this stage the prayer group manifests itself through praise and through the uniting force of the Holy Spirit, which descends on the congregation. It is felt by all those present as a deep sense of community. This intensity of feeling at that particular moment can be explained by examining the structure of the meeting and the role of the leader in conducting the session. I will look at these issues in turn.

Just after the invocation, a sense of chaos overcomes the congregation. Charismatics start praying out loud or cite readings from the Scripture on the basis that they are inspired by the Holy Spirit. Very often there is more than one person praying at a given time and at this euphoric moment, a pandemonium can ensue. To avoid this, the leaders or elders, try to redirect the session and focus the congregation on the theme of the day. This can be interpreted as an attempt to keep order and to redirect those who get side-tracked. Yet, by doing so, the leaders are *structuring* the meeting and consequently hindering spontaneity. This leads me on to my second point, the role of the leader in the prayer meeting. It is only through and by means of the leader that the Holy Spirit is invoked. It is the leader who sets the pace of the session. It is the leader or leading persons through whom God communicates with the congregation. It seems clear, therefore, that by adopting this style the leaders and the elders are emphasising their leading positions.

Leaders and the Communication of Truth

The members of the Service Team of each prayer group or community are considered to be the spiritual leaders. Although there are more men in such positions, female spiritual leaders have a strong position and are respected by all the group members. Spiritual leadership is exercised during the prayer meetings where for the first part of the meeting intense prayer and praise are delivered. The animator of the session is said to be under direct influence of the Holy Spirit.

This perception of spiritual leadership leaves much space for the individual flair of the persons concerned. Some spiritual leaders firmly believe that a certain amount of preparation, thought and reading goes into any particular prayer session while others, as the one quoted below, adopt the notion of 'inspiration' literally.

> I do not prepare the talk beforehand, I just prepare the theme, then I ask God so that I will be his vessel. It is amazing how words start pouring out [once the Holy Spirit fills you]. (A male diviner, spiritual leader)

The notion of inspiration gives the diviner the authority to speak on behalf of the Divine. Thus during the prayer and praise session, the animator uses phrases such as *qed inhoss il-Mulej jighdilna* ('I sense God is telling us'), *il-Mulej jixtieq jara*, ('God would like us to'). There are instances where the inspiration of the speaker is heightened to such an extent that he or she talks 'in the Spirit'. This term implies that the speaker is actually the mouth of the Divine and he or she is only present in body – God uses the speaker's voice to get across to the community.[10] A speech is judged as being in the Spirit if the speaker talks incessantly without ever consulting notes, and there is a visible change in the speaker's nature. The speech is different in content and occasionally in context from the original one intended and prepared by the speaker. It is emotional in its delivery and 'it reveals truth'. The speech not only affects the congregation but also transforms the speaker. The Holy Spirit 'seizes' (Danforth 1989: 103) and inhabits the human body, *il-Mulej hakimni*, for the duration of the speech. Afterwards, when the speaker has finished, he or she feels a sense of overwhelming peace.

These qualities highlight the role of the leader. Being a leader in a Charismatic community means that one is also a servant of the rest of the community. Since the leaders become a direct link between the Divine and the rest of the congregation, they assume a much more powerful position as they divulge truth statements. In Charismatic terminology this implies that the leader is deciphering God's message. Yet Charismatics interpret this role in terms of 'God uses me' – *Alla juzani* – suggesting almost a tormented soul. The role of the leader becomes more ambiguous than ever.

Authority through Language – Language used as a sign of Authority

One aspect of language use in religious contexts is its performative role of authority. In looking at family conversations during meals, Tannen (1987) identified instances where parental authority was established merely by calling the children's name (or the spouse's) before making important statements. This pattern of authority is prevalent in the Charismatic context as well. Generally, members refer to one another as brothers and sisters, but this is not always the case. One instance where this rule is put aside is when new members start attending the prayer meeting. Initially they are referred to by their first names, implying that these new members are not formal members of the in-group. Eventually new members become 'brothers' or 'sisters'. During the initial stages of my field-work Charismatics used to call me by my first name. Later on, when my status as an observer and researcher was clarified, Charismatics referred to me as sister when discussing group matters, but when I required clarification pertaining to the Movement, then my first name was used before clarification was divulged. This shows that instances of teaching require formal first-name addressing. This occurs as well during cell group meetings and during group workshops. Persons who just a few minutes earlier refer to one another as brother or sister, in a cell group context refer to one another by their respective first names. This marks a hierarchy. The persons participating in the group are no longer equal, as the leaders have more knowledge and experience than the other members of the group. This tends to suggest that in such instances a hierarchy based on knowledge is established. A new relationship, very similar to that between teacher and student (leader and group member) or parent and child (spiritual leader and spiritual siblings during Baptism in the Spirit seminars), is established.

A particular trait of authority and leadership among Charismatics is the use of Bible excerpts in conversation. These are used by the persons engaging in conversation to illustrate particular points. There are a number of contexts where this form of speech is used. When used in mundane conversation between Charismatics of equal status[11] Bible quotations imply that the interlocutor is just highlighting his or her point. Usage of Bible excerpts is more common among Charismatics of different standing within the hierarchy of the group. One such context is teachings. The person delivering the teaching gets the message through by basing his or her talk on the Bible. This means that the Bible is being used as a source of knowledge. In another situation, where a leader or an elder and members are interacting, Bible quotations have a double meaning. They both show authority on the subject and assert one's leading position.

Discussion

Charismatic Catholicism as practised in the Maltese Islands suggests that Charismatics are in a way reacting against 'ecclesiastical authority'. Yet as shown above, Charismatic converts readily accept leader/member and male/female hierarchy. The reason for this may be that Charismatics do not define the Movement as one that liberates members from an existing oppressive system but as one that liberates the self from misconceptions about the Divine and its powers. This can be explained by the following two examples.

Following her marriage, Pauline got into a housework routine which left her with very little spare time for herself and others. Once she joined the Movement she found time for others and was able to manage her life better. She commented that this was possible because the teachings of the Movement helped her readdress her attitude towards the 'housewife's role' – there was more to life than just cleaning and tending the house, although these were important tasks for a good housewife and mother. Pauline was not the only Charismatic housewife who experienced this transformation. One can say that for these women the re-structuring of their lives is a form of liberation not from mundane tasks, but a liberation from activity which was in itself self-defeating.

For men, the liberating factor of the Movement is perceived in another dimension. In providing leadership positions, men are given the opportunity to acquire importance and thus redefine personal identity. By means of the Charismatic Movement, men have found a niche where they can assume important positions. Not all men become leaders, but all men say that the Movement has given them another liberating force – the ability to speak about the value of truth and speaking in favour of religion – an increasingly anomalous practice in the Northern Mediterranean:

> Today I can say that I am a family man. If it were not for the Movement, today I would probably be at the local club drinking and playing cards. The Movement has taught me how to appreciate [family] life once more. (Tony)

> I am no longer ashamed of praising the Lord's name and if I hear someone blaspheming, I ask him to shut up. (Mike)

Having obtained religious liberation Charismatics do not object to the hierarchies mentioned above but at times they ensure that these hierarchies are adhered to for the Movement's sake. This dual dimension of the Movement is clear from the use of language among Charismatics, and is reflected in the egalitarian intra-group religious dynamics and the hierarchical intra-group role differences.

Conclusion

The Charismatic Renewal Movement in the Maltese Islands arose at a time of social and economic change. Rather than moving away from religion, part of the Maltese population has resorted to a new religious expression which empowered converts to deal with the changes that were taking place in the wider society.

The Movement has revolutionised the idea of religion, thus making it accessible to the lay person and giving women the opportunity to participate more. Charismatic men and Charismatic women are seen as spiritual equals who are judged by God according to the same standards. This notion is adopted by the Movement's prayer groups and members who attest that they are equal. Yet, in reality, there is a marked distinction in status. Men occupy the posts that count most; women, although freer to express their views, are still enmeshed in an ideology of traditional behaviour promoted and reinforced by the Movement itself.

Charismatic converts come from diverse socio-economic backgrounds and are of different ages. However, one could argue that although the Movement does not attract any particular group (see Hargrove 1989), there is the tendency that people join the Movement at times of life-crisis, as demonstrated by the various examples above.

Its attractiveness lies in the central message of the Charismatic expression – the concept of spiritual kinship. This is attained during the early stages of one's conversion, and further enhanced when converts are 'baptised in the Spirit'. In a situation where there was increased mobility, uprooting and the setting up of new families away from blood relatives, the CRM provided the ideal situation for the forming of groups based on sisterhood and brotherhood and at the same time for strengthening the ideals central to Roman Catholicism – the family. This group of spiritual kin not only lent support and assistance when needed but also provided the right medium for people to repent for the sins of their past lives (Theuma 1997).

Spiritual kinship is not only manifested in individual Charismatic groups but also expressed at local, national, and global levels. The Annual Charismatic conference helps to gel further a group which at a first glance may appear to be loosely associated. The role of the National Service Team further enhances this role. Maintaining links with the International Charismatic community demonstrates that the CRM is not an isolated group reacting to the chaos brought about by modernity and globalisation, but it is transcending that very thing by linking and keeping in contact with the numerous 'sisters' and 'brothers' worldwide. The use of Charismatic language consolidates this link, acting as a kind of *lingua franca* for the expression of Charismatic religiosity.

Notes

1. The accuracy of this figure is debatable, but is the quoted membership given by a number of group leaders.
2. This meeting was crucial for the International Charismatic Movement as for the first time ever the Pope allowed a lay movement to celebrate mass on the main altar at St. Peter's.
3. One informant tried to explain the importance he attached to this conference by stating that those three days are the first days of vacation leave he applies for every year.
4. Some other men are happy to see their wives attending the weekly meetings but prefer to stay out of it.
5. These phrases are expressed in either English or Maltese, depending on the person's preference. The latter phrase is expressed in English, regardless of one's usual language medium.
6. There is no equivalent for this phrase in Maltese. All Charismatics, notwithstanding their language preference, refer to it as such. However, there is a parallel in Maltese when one says '*hallini kwiet*' (leave me in peace). This phrase implies that one needs to be left for a few minutes on one's own, generally to think or to relax.
7. This is very similar to a Catholic practice popular up to some time ago where families gathered to recite the Rosary before or after supper. Some Charismatic parents with adolescent children no longer require that their children be present for family Quiet Time. One parent specifically said that he never involved his children as he did not want to force them into anything.
8. During the course my fieldwork I came across two informants who said they have participated in a session where someone spoke in tongues. One informant described it as an utterance which was later interpreted as a prophecy. The other informant came across this form of prayer while participating in a prayer meeting during his stay in America. 'A member of the group stood up and started talking in a tongue which later was identified as Turkish. The interlocutor was not familiar with this language. After his outburst, a deadly silence fell, we all knew this was a prophecy of some sort. Then a young woman stood up and gave an interpretation of the prophecy.'
9. At this instance, hymns like the following are sung: 'Come, come, Spirit of God; come make your dwelling place; within my heart; Come and refresh my soul; with waters of life; Come sweet Spirit of God.'
10. This state is very similar to that of a Spirit Medium, who uses his/her body as a vehicle for spirits to communicate with the living and vice versa.
11. Equal status means that two persons have approximately the same position in the group, for example, two members or two leaders, or that they have been involved with the Movement for roughly the same time.

References

Abela, A. M., 1992, *Changing Youth Culture in Malta*. Malta: Jesuit Publications.

Abela, A. M., 1994, *Shifting Family Values in Malta*. Malta: Media Centre.

Aquilina, J., 1985, *Dun Gorg Preca: Fundatur tat-Tigdid Karizmatiku f' Malta?* Malta: Ufficju Tigdid Karizmatiku Kattoloku.

Baldacchino, N.,1995, *Hajja, Qawwa u Glorja*. Malta: Ufficju Tigdid Karizmatiku Kattoloku.

Beckford, J. A., ed.,1986, *New Religious Movements and Rapid Social Change*. London: Sage.

Boissevain, J.,1993, S*aints and Fireworks: Religion and Politics in Rural Malta*. Valletta: Progress Press, 2nd ed.

Borg, N. and Spiteri, L., 1994, *The Influence of Education on Maltese Women*. Unpublished B. Ed. (Hons) Dissertation, University of Malta.

Bruner, E. M., 1986, 'Experience and its Expression', in Turner, V. W., and Bruner, E. W., eds, *The Anthropology of Experience*. Chicago: University of Illinois Press.

Christian, W. Jr., 1989, *Person and God in a Spanish Valley*. Princeton: Princeton University Press, new revised ed.

Csordas, T. J., 1995, 'Oxymorons and Short-Circuit in the Re-Enchantment of the World', *Etnofoor*, 8 (1): 5–26.

Danforth, L., 1989, *Firewalking and Religious Healing: The Anastenaria of Greece and the American Firewalking Movement*. Princeton: Princeton University Press.

Davis, J., 1984, 'The Sexual Division of Religious Labour in the Mediterranean', in Wolf, E. R., ed., *Religion, Power and Protest in Local Communities: The Northern Shore of the Mediterranean*. Berlin: Mouton.

Du Boulay, J., 1986, 'Women - Images of their Nature and Destiny in Rural Greece', in Dubisch, J., ed., *Gender and Power in Rural Greece*. Princeton: Princeton University Press.

Falk, N., 1995, 'Introduction', in Haddad, Y. Y., and Findly, E. B., eds, *Women, Religion and Social Change*. New York: State University.

Galanter, M., 1989, *Cults: Faith, Healing and Coersion*. Oxford: Oxford University Press.

Hall, C. M., 1992, *Women and Empowerment: Strategies for Increasing Autonomy*. USA: Hemisphere Publishing Corporation.

Hargrove, B., 1989, *The Sociology of Religion*. New York: Harlan Davidson, Inc.

Hitchcock, J., 1991, 'Catholic Activist Conservatism in the U.S.', in Marty, M. E., and Appleby, R. S., eds, *Fundamentalisms Observed?* Chicago and London: University of Chicago Press.

Kristu: il-Bidu u t-Tmiem Official Publication of the Annual Charismatic Conference, Malta, 21–23 April, 1995.

Kennedy, R., 1986, 'Women's Friendships on Crete: A Psychological Perspective', in Dubisch, J., ed., *Gender and Power in Rural Greece*. Princeton: Princeton University Press.

Martin, D., 1991, *Tongues of Fire: The Explosion of Protestantism in Latin America*. Oxford: Blackwell.

Miceli, P., 1995, 'The Invisibility and Visibility of Women', in Sultana, R., and Baldacchino, G., eds, *Maltese Society: A Sociological Inquiry*. Malta: Mireva.

O'Neill, M., 1990, *Women Speaking, Women Listening: Women in Iterreligious Dialogue*. New York: Orbis.

Poloma, M., 1992, *The Charismatic Movement: Is there a New Pentecost?* Boston: G.K. Halland Co.

Scott, S. L., 1994, ''They Don't Have to Live by the Old Traditions': Saintly Men, Sinner Women and the Appalachian Pentecostal Revival' *American Ethnologist,* 21 (2): 227–44.

Tannen, D., 1987, 'Remarks on Discourse and Power', in Kedar, L., ed., *Power Through Discourse.* USA: Ablex Publishing Corporation.

Tigdid, 10 (4); Valletta, Malta: Charismatic Renewal Movement.

Theuma, N., 1997, '*As the Spirit Guides Us': The Charismatic Renewal Movement in Malta.* Unpublished M.Phil Dissertation, University of Malta.

Tonna, B., 1993, *Malta Trends 1993: The Signs of the Times.* Malta: Discern.

Vassallo, M., 1979, *From Lordship to Stewardship Religion and Social Change in Malta.* The Hague: Mouton.

6

Good, Evil and Godhood: Mormon Morality in the Material World

Hildi J. Mitchell

University of Sussex

We don't spend a lot of time talking about or dreaming about the millennium to come; we've always been a practical people dealing with the issues of life. (Gordon B. Hinckley, President of the Church of Jesus Christ of Latter-day Saints, *Time* magazine, August 4, 1997: 55)

Introduction[1]

The Church of Jesus Christ of Latter-day Saints (known also as the Mormon Church) has been seen as *the* American religion (Bloom 1992). Born into the religious fervour of nineteenth-century America, and matured on the American frontier, it has become synonymous with Utah and the American Mid-West. During the presidency of Ezra Taft Benson (1985–1994), it was often openly anti-communist and pro-American (Quinn 1997: 66–115). The wealth of the Church, the extravagance of its temples, and the business-like appearance of its missionaries and representatives, also combine to create an image of a largely capitalist church, concerned with the accumulation of wealth. This is, however, only part of the picture.

Anthropology has long asserted that the separation of the economic sphere from other aspects of social life is an arbitrary distinction and a construction of a particular Western viewpoint

(Parry and Bloch 1989: 1–5). Since Mormons are in some senses 'Western', it might be tempting to assume that the distinction *does* apply here. But this is to ignore not only the fact that Mormonism, while born out of a particular moment in Western history, has in fact developed at many times in opposition to it (Mauss 1994, Bloom 1992: 88), but also anthropological insights which note a significant link between economic transactions and the reproduction of a social and ideological order.

Parry and Bloch argue that, while it is often assumed that a particular view of economics gives rise to a particular world-view, in fact, the opposite is frequently true – with an existing world-view shaping ways of representing economic activity (1989: 17–19). This chapter draws on this observation to suggest that Mormon materialism makes sense within a particular Mormon world-view – that Mormon cosmology and Mormon activity are closely intertwined. Further, it argues that the connectedness of spirits, mortals and gods, apparent in Mormon history, theology and everyday discourse, informs a Mormon cosmology in which materialism plays a central and *positive* role. Unlike Catholicism, for example, Mormonism sees the body and the world as a source of good, even as the source of godhood. As mortal Mormons strive to become gods through participation in ritual activity and in the practical building of the *Kingdom of God* on earth, they participate in a moral economy in which spirits, mortals and gods all play their part.

Actions in the earthly realm are able to effect changes in the spirit world. The infamous Mormon practice of *baptism for the dead,*[2] like other Mormon rituals, depends upon such a scheme. In such a cosmology, where the building of the *Kingdom of God*[3] is simultaneously a religious and a politico-economic enterprise, and where mortals, spirits and gods interact freely, worldly activity comes to occupy a central position. Spiritual salvation depends upon earthly actions. Not only is ritual action by humans in earthly temples essential for their own salvation and that of their dead ancestors, but everyday engagement with the world informs a temporal moral economy affecting eternal religious outcomes.

This chapter first explores the historical and theological foundations of a Mormon cosmology that informs a Mormon sense of the nature of humanity and earthly and heavenly relations. This is then related to Mormon economic practice and worldly activity – both historically and in contemporary everyday life. Together, these illuminate the way in which 'the totality of transactions form a general pattern which is part of the reproduction of social and ide-ological systems concerned with a timescale far longer than the individual human life' (Parry and Bloch 1989: 2), or the ways in which Mormon temporal earthly action is related to the reproduc-tion of an eternal social and cosmic order.

Spirits, Mortals and Gods in Mormon History and Theology

Mormonism is a materialist religion. The influence of Hellenistic and Roman philosophical thought leads traditional Christian the-ology to hold that the ultimate 'real' is the idea, or the spirit, rather than matter itself. Mormonism, in contrast, accepts even God as a material being, having 'body, parts and passions' (Doctrine and Covenants, henceforth D&C 131: 7[4]). For Mormons, devils, mortals and gods are all made of the same essence, they are simply at dif-ferent stages along a continuum of *eternal_progression*. The worlds they inhabit are closely connected, both in theological and practi-cal ways.

In the spring of 1820, a young man named Joseph Smith was visited by God the Father and by his son Jesus Christ, or so he records in his account of the *first vision* which appears in Mormon Scripture (*Joseph Smith History* Chapter 1). The two heavenly per-sonages spoke to Joseph and advised him that the true church of God was not on the earth, and that he would be instrumental in restoring it. The appearance of God and Jesus to Joseph Smith in the *first vision* serves as a symbol of God's renewal of communi-cation with humanity. After thousands of years of apostasy, he responds to a young man's earnest seeking for truth with the infor-mation that the truth is not on the earth but that it will now be restored, which requires further communication from heavenly beings, both spirit and embodied (see Fig. 1). The appearance of God and Jesus in human form has the further function of clarify-ing the nature of God and the make-up of the Godhead. God appears to Joseph Smith in the form of a man who is separate from His son, Jesus Christ. This idea of God as human was a revolu-tionary idea at the time of the *first vision* and is further developed in Mormon theology (Mullen 1967: 21). God is considered to be of the same essence as man, having once been mortal (Harris and Butt 1925: 9), and he is considered to maintain a loving, caring, guiding relationship with his mortal children, through continuous

Figure 1: *Different Kinds of Beings*

Kind of Being	Action of Spirit to Request to Shake Hands	Kind of Body	Good or Evil?
Pre-mortal *spirit*	Refuses	Yet to have a body	Good
Spirit follower of Satan	Tries, but fails	No body	Evil
Post-mortal (not resurrected) *spirit*	Refuses	Has had a body	Good
Resurrected being	Shakes hands	Transformed body	Good

revelation (Mullen 1967: 20–21, Harris and Butt 1925: 10–13). This relationship is re-established for the current *dispensation* – phase of existence – in the events of the *first vision*.

Having established the nature of God, the *first vision* also establishes the existence of evil. The story tells how, prior to God's appearance, Joseph was seized by a dark force, such that he feared his imminent destruction. This establishes a motif which has been reworked throughout Mormon history, of Satan working to prevent the re-establishment of truth upon the earth. In the *first vision*, as in other versions of this motif, Satan recognises righteousness and potential developments for the Lord's work and attempts to thwart it. Satan appears as a powerful but disembodied force, thus prefiguring the development of a Mormon theology in which both spirits and bodies play important roles.

Within contemporary Mormonism, bodies and the material world are not only important, but essential for salvation. They are therefore essentially good. Although everyone has a spirit, disembodied spirits are more ambiguous. They are insufficient for godhood, since both God and exalted humans are in possession of 'bodies, parts and passions'. Sometimes they are unequivocally evil. Spirits and beings of several different types can visit a person (see Fig. 1), and even Mormon children know how to tell the difference between them. You simply ask the being to shake hands with you. If s/he refuses, it is a good spirit, because only embodied spirits *can* shake hands and a good spirit would not attempt to deceive. If s/he attempts to shake hands, but can't, it is an evil spirit.

Although I have never met anyone who says they have actually asked a spirit to shake hands with them in this manner, it is a generally accepted procedure. The history of the Church is replete with stories of visits by both good and evil spirits. Indeed, the very *restoration* of the gospel through Joseph Smith depended on heavenly visitations. But even the founder of the Church must have had some means of distinguishing good from evil. All the types of being appear to the living to be embodied, but only the person who has died and been resurrected actually is. The other types – disembodied spirits – may be visually indistinguishable. It is only through touch that one can tell the difference between a good spirit and an evil one. This division of spirits into good and evil relates to broader moral assumptions about the nature of good and evil, and is key in understanding the nature of humanity for Mormons.

Parkin (1985) suggests that there are two possible *foci* for the understanding of evil – evil as a negative aspect of a moral system, and evil as a metaphysical property. These two are deeply connected. The metaphysical evil is implicit in moral evaluation. As Parkin argues, it shows 'how people distinguish human from non-human and evaluate states, acts, conditions and consequences in the light of this distinction' (3). Ideas about what constitutes moral behaviour are tied up with ideas about what it means to be human. Such a connection is especially clear for Mormons, for whom the distinctions between human and non-human are so closely tied up with worldly existence and *activity*. Transition to godhood requires participation in mortality – including being physically embodied and dealing with material concerns. This is an essential feature of Mormon life – action and behaviour become extremely important.

According to popular Mormon theology, in the pre-mortal world, a meeting was held, during which Jesus, one of the spirit children, was chosen to be the saviour of the world. In the process of reaching this decision, however, Satan (Lucifer), another of the spirit children of God, was thrown out of heaven because he challenged God. He had wanted to be the saviour, and to force all the other spirits to be obedient and thus return to God. This was against God's plan, since he wanted all the children to choose for themselves, and Satan was ejected from heaven, taking with him one third of the spirits – who had chosen to follow him rather than God (D&C 29, Abraham 3[5]). These spirits, by leaving the presence of God at this time, forfeited their right to a mortal existence. They were condemned to exist only as spirits, never having a body and therefore never having the opportunity to live on earth, to prove themselves and ultimately return to God.[6] Evil here is characterised as the absence of choice, or *free agency*. Satan's sin was to want to force God's children to be good and thus return to him. God's plan, on the other hand, was to allow his children to choose this for themselves. The concept of *free agency* requires that mortals make their own choices, based on faith, about whether they will do what is required to return to God. This involves keeping the command-ments, but also participating bodily in rituals which are only pos-sible whilst inhabiting the earthly sphere.

This is an essential feature of evil for Mormons. It consists of thwarting God's plans and of restricting His children's *free agency*. It is considered to be a force, which, like good, exists in the uni-verse, independent of either God or Satan. God and Satan, are, for Mormons, subject to the same universal laws as mortals, obser-vance of which effects good outcomes, while disobedience results in evil (see Hobart 1985, Parkin 1985: 9, 17, 21). Although it is developed further in theology, what concerns most Mormons is the way in which this is experienced as everyday morality. Satan can, for example, tempt us to do evil, but the very act of giving in to such temptation is an abdication of *free agency* and responsibility for one's own actions. Evil is both a metaphysical power, 'embod-ied' in Satan and his followers, and a feature of what made those beings evil – the rejection of the morally good principle of *free agency*. Since they cannot achieve exaltation and a return to God's presence, Satan and his angels are characterised as tormented and jealous – wishing to take the faithful spirit children with them to eternal damnation. They therefore constantly try to either posses the bodies of mortals or to influence mortals to do bad, thus ensur-ing that they will fail to keep their second estate and return to God.

Mormon theology does allow for a hell, in which there is 'weep-ing and wailing and gnashing of teeth' (Alma 40). Hell is known as *outer darkness* which will be inhabited by the *sons of perdition*, or followers of Satan. They will dwell in 'darkness', away from the light associated with God and the kingdoms of heaven. The main element of *outer darkness* is that those who end up there will have no body (much like Satan's followers at the present time) and no chance of ever progressing beyond this state. The torment of hell is therefore understood as a lack of progression towards godhood because of lack of a body. Dis-embodiment is, for Mormons, the ultimate punishment. Even in heaven, bodies symbolise degrees of exaltation. Those who reach the *celestial kingdom* (see Fig. 2) will have *celestial* and perfect bodies, while those who reach lower degrees will be penalised by not having all their bodily functions, primarily, they will lack the ability to procreate. The *plan of salva-tion* (Fig. 2) is a diagrammatic representation of this Mormon cos-mos, depicting the pre-mortal and post-mortal worlds, and the centrally placed mortal experience. It also clearly shows the place of the disembodied *sons of perdition*.

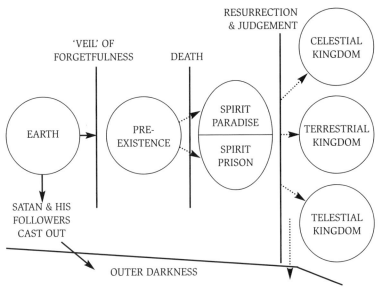

Figure 2: The Plan of Salvation[7]

In contrast to the ambiguous or evil nature of spirits, bodies are seen as essentially good. An influential essay by an early Mormon leader, Orson Pratt, entitled 'Absurdities of Immaterialism' denounced any theology which was not materialist. This, like other doctrines of the early Church, contrasted with prevailing Idealist notions of the purity of the spiritual or conceptual. Mormon doctrine in this area, while undergoing some development since Pratt's essay, has always concerned itself with engagement with the material world, which it has seen as a source of progress and good, not as a source of evil:

> At the most basic level, Mormon cosmology is the story of humankind's increasing immersion in matter for the sake of progress and growth ... We live on earth, not as exiles from a more perfect realm of spirit and crystal, but rather as initiates into a new, and higher, stage of existence: the realm of element, of matter, of bodies. (Peters 1993: 47–52)

The main purpose of life, for Mormons, is to become like God, who was once also mortal, as is expressed in the popular Mormon couplet, 'As man is, God once was; As God is, man will be'. This is at the basis of Mormon theology,[8] and informs the Mormon understanding of the world. It is generally accepted that God created, in the sense that he organised into their present form, spiritual beings out of *intelligences* which already existed, and which were time-less, eternal and co-existent with God himself. In this sense then, humans are spirit children of God, and are of the same essence as him. Through *eternal progression*, humans can develop this godlike essence until they become gods themselves. This progression is based upon a Mormon theology which holds that there was a pre-mortal existence, in which mortals, as spirits, existed in the presence of God, and that, through (and only through) our actions in this earthly existence, we can return to live with God as exalted beings.

This life is not simply a test, it is a time for important and necessary work to be done. The most important actions one must undertake while living in a body on earth are the ritual actions which form the Mormon salvation ordinances. *All* persons who wish to gain the highest glory in the next life, and return to live with God, eventually to become gods themselves, must do the following:

- be baptised by immersion for the remission of sins and as a member of the Church of Jesus Christ of Latter-day Saints.
- be confirmed a member of the Church of Jesus Christ of Latter-day Saints.
- be *washed and anointed*.
- receive the *endowment*.
- enter into a *celestial marriage*.

These are not simply *rites de passage*, marking transformation of life stages and progression through social statuses, although they do operate as such markers. They are necessary salvation ordinances, and can only be performed on earth. None can be done in the spirit realm. For this reason, Mormons practice *baptism for the dead*, in which dead relatives, who are thought to have been being taught the gospel in the Spirit World since their death (see Fig. 2), are baptised by proxy. Although baptism and confirmation for the living may take place anywhere, as long as they are done by the proper priesthood authority, baptism and confirmation for the dead can only be done in Mormon temples. The other rituals can also only be performed (for the living as well as the dead) in temples.

Temples not only provide a place for the performance of rituals essential for spiritual progression. They also serve as a metaphorical link between the spiritual and material realms. The temple is constructed as a representation of the Mormon cosmos, having different rooms representing different parts of the spirit realm. During the *endowment* ritual, participants move to different parts of the temple representing different stages in the development of humanity. It is common for people performing proxy ordinances for relatives or friends whom they knew to claim that they felt their presence during the ordinances. This seems fitting since the temple is the closest place one can be to God on this earth and iconographically represents this connection. The temple is sacred because only good Mormons can enter it, and it is thus unspotted by the unclean-ness of the unrighteous. However, it is not kept apart from things of the material world. Indeed, the decoration of such a sacred space with elaborate and costly fittings and ornaments indicates that the Mormon God finds gold, crystal and fine fabrics to be a source of pleasure and good.

Spirits, Mortals and Gods in Everyday Discourse

This relationship between gods, mortals and spirits, and consequent understandings of good and evil, can be illuminated by examining discourse and action within the Mormon community. Although, as I have suggested, these ideas can be developed theologically, most Mormons act as their own theologians (Davies 1987), and the lay nature of the Mormon clergy means that individual experience and interpretation plays a more significant part in the religious life of most members than any scholarly argument. I have already indicated the significance of visions and heavenly messengers in the restoration process, which set up what Armand Mauss has called (1994: 3):

> the other-worldly heritage of Mormonism, the spiritual and prophetic elements, the enduring ideals and remarkable doctrines revealed through the prophet Joseph Smith and passed down as part of a unique and authentic Mormon heritage.

This 'other worldly heritage', which played so large a part in the origins and history of Mormonism, is still taken for granted today. The same loving God who appeared to Joseph Smith continues to guide his children through continuing revelation to the leaders of The Church of Jesus Christ of Latter-day Saints. The highest leaders are all sustained by the Church membership as 'Prophet, Seer and Revelator', and are thought to have frequent and straightforward communication with God. One Mormon woman recalled her family asking an unusual question about Church policy. She had been a teenager at the time and had expected that the Prophet (as Church members usually respectfully and affectionately refer to their President) would 'just have a word with Jesus, and find out what to do.' Her disappointment when an answer was not speedily forthcoming is another story, but her expectation is typical of many members, and there is certainly a strong belief that the Prophet and his close colleagues are visited by God and Jesus, especially in the Salt Lake Temple.

The Devil too makes an appearance in everyday discourse, and, according to my friends and informants, in everyday experience. The Devil is often invoked to explain situations of bad fortune. During a recent attempt by Manchester Stake to expand their Institute programme, the Devil, or the *Adversary*, as he is often named on such occasions, was blamed for the difficulties encountered. Institute is the Church's religious education programme for young adults, particularly students. Due to the high concentration of students in the Manchester area, the Church Education System and the local Institute leaders were trying to expand the programme in line with the North American model, and provide pastoral care as well as religious instruction. To fulfil this aim, they were looking for a building to let, close to the University area of the city. Several times it looked as if a suitable property had been found, but these all fell through. The Institute director, however, was undeterred in her enthusiasm for the project. She told me:

> I know we are doing the right thing here and that we will succeed. I know it because the Adversary is working so hard to stop us. He knows that we are doing the Lord's work and that we will be reaching out to so many people, and that's why he's putting it into the hearts of these people [property owners and landlords] to change their minds about the buildings. But we have to just be stronger and not be beaten, because we're doing the right thing.

Such an attitude to misfortune is typical when the misfortune can be associated with a broader conflict between the forces of good and evil. My own ambiguous status as an anthropologist – simultaneously insider and outsider – itself invited comment along these lines. At one point during the fieldwork, I was told that the personal difficulties I was having were the result of the conflict between good and evil which was being raged as God and Satan fought over my soul. It was suggested that this would be resolved, and peace in my personal life restored, if I would just become a good Mormon.

Personal involvement with the Devil and, more particularly, his evil spirit angels, can, however, be even more intimate than that. Stories about possession by such spirits abound and their circulation indicates that they represent a reality which is considered acceptable within the mainstream Church. They therefore tell us much about the way in which this reality is conceived. It draws, I have already suggested, on a history and a theology rich with examples of the importance of bodies and the connectedness of spirits, gods and mortals.

I was told the following story by Will, a young man in his mid-twenties. One evening, when he was at college, having recently returned from his mission,[9] he was visited by a young woman friend, who was being beaten up by her husband. She had come to his house to ask him for a blessing.[10] He had tried to give her a blessing, but, as he put his hands upon her head and prepared to speak, she 'turned into a different person'. He told me that she was possessed by an evil spirit. She looked different, her eyes, face, expression and voice had changed, and he couldn't give her the blessing. The spirit would not leave the woman's body, even when he commanded the spirit to leave in the name of the priesthood. This would normally be expected to make the spirit leave. Worried, Will then phoned his brother-in-law, but the phone kept going dead. He tried commanding the spirits to leave the phone, after which his sister phoned back to say that the telephone extension his brother-in-law had been using had 'fried'. It was melted and useless. He then tried to reason with the spirit. Addressing her as a female, he told her that she would not be happy staying here, and that she should go to the spirit world, where she could be taught the gospel and perhaps have the opportunities she wanted. If she wouldn't go on her own, then she would be made to go. The spirit still did not leave. Will then *raised his arm to the square* in a sacred symbol of the priesthood, taught in the temple, and commanded her to go. At this point, the young woman fell to the floor, unconscious. When she regained consciousness, she was herself once again.

Another story was told to me by Pat, a woman in her early fifties. Her husband, Mick, suffered with depression, and, at one point, had been in bed for several days, unable to get up, or even to speak to her. Although she recognised that this was often a feature of his condition, she told me that on this particular occasion, she had been convinced that he was possessed by an evil spirit. She said she felt an 'evil presence' in the room, and was extremely frightened. Her husband, although a priesthood holder, was, in his depressed and possessed state, unable to do anything, so she took matters into her own hands. As an *endowed* woman, who had entered into the priesthood covenant of *celestial marriage*, she felt that she shared in the priesthood of her husband,[11] so she *raised her arm to the square* and commanded the spirit to leave her husband. She told me that she immediately felt the presence leave the room and said that her husband was much improved and she was able to make him get out of bed and go downstairs with her.

Both these stories tell us about the cosmology of spirits and mortals in Mormonism, about the metaphysical and moral manifestations of good and evil and about the ways in which these powers are used in earthly endeavour. In Will's experience, he assumed the spirit to be female, which fits with a recent Mormon statement that gender is eternal (*The Family: A Proclamation to the World*, 1995), and suggests that spirits possess bodies of the same gender as themselves. He also assumed the spirit to be one which had the potential to be saved – suggesting to her that she go to the spirit world to be taught (see Fig. 2). Pat's spiritual encounter was with a more malevolent being. She felt frightened and was aware of evil in the room. This would probably indicate the presence of an irredeemable angel of Satan. However, in neither story does the possessed or the spirit actually play a significant role. I was not told of any demands made by the spirit, nor of any lasting effects on the possessed, or of any particular reason that the possession took place, although we might assume that both possessed individuals were in situations of some distress and suffering. Parkin suggests that:

> In the association of evil with human suffering, and the negation of happiness, our attempt to understand other people's ideas of evil draws us into their theories of human nature. (Parkin 1985:6)

Certainly, here, possession by a disembodied spirit comes at a time of stress for the possessed person. However, more significant is the fact that in both these cases, as with every other case I have heard, it is the exorcisor who has the key role, and, in both these cases, s/he is also the narrator, a fact which differs from most accounts of spirit possession (Boddy 1994).

These stories therefore can be seen to serve as reaffirmation of the place of the priesthood, and the moral superiority of mortals over spirits – being, as they are, part-way to godhood. This demonstrates, ultimately, the superiority of body over non-body.

Although it may be tempting to assert that possession by spirits can be seen as a form of communication by oppressed groups about social concerns, as some recent studies have done (for example, Ong 1987, Comaroff 1985), such an approach cannot stand up in the Mormon case. The stress on the authority of the priesthood, and of the superiority of righteous mortals, who have participated in the essential rituals of Mormonism on their way to godhood, suggests, instead, that spirit possession is used to uphold the moral order of Mormonism. Even Pat, who, as a woman, was practising an unorthodox and potentially challenging use of the priesthood, was conforming. Her story was told privately, indeed, she confided that she would not tell such a story in Church, but it conformed, if not with current orthodoxy, then at least with historical precedent (Madsen 1992). Stories of possession by spirits are here part of the 'cultural template' (see Parry and Bloch 1989: 19) through which other kinds of worldly activity are viewed – not an obscure form of comment on them.

This Mormon practical theology, in which spirits, mortals and gods inhabit positions along a 'spiritual continuum' (Davies 1987: 86) provides a cultural template for Mormon worldly action. The history of Mormonism can be rendered in economic terms (see, for example, Arrington 1958), and its contemporary nature can be characterised in terms of its high-profile materialism (*Time*, August 4, 1997), but the true significance of its orientation to economic activity is revealed only when viewed through the cultural template outlined above. As Parkin notes, conceptions of metaphysical evil illuminate understandings of humanity (Parkin 1985: 3). Further, understandings of humanity, and its place in the cosmos, also inform practical action in the here and now. Such action may be viewed as reproducing the metaphysical and human order on a much larger, eternal scale (see Parry and Bloch 1989: 1–4). The second part of the chapter will explore how this has occurred in the Mormon case, as economic history has been played out within a moral and religious idiom, producing a *moral* economy.

In the Beginning: Motifs from the Book of Mormon

The Book of Mormon tells the story of the ancient inhabitants of the Americas (generally believed by Mormons to be the ancestors of Native Americans) who left Jerusalem around 600 BCE and were led by God to the *promised land* of America. It is a history of these people and of God's dealings with them. Mormons believe that the *Kingdom of God* on earth existed among these people – in other words, that the Church was in existence at that time. Church members in the modern *dispensation* can therefore learn about how they should behave and organise themselves from reading this history, much as Christians of other denominations look to the New Testament.[12]

Thomas O'Dea, in his influential 1950's study of Mormonism, argued that, 'The Book of Mormon is concerned fundamentally with the problem of good and evil' (O'Dea 1957: 26). He identifies two theories of evil at work in the Book of Mormon. In the second book of Nephi, there is a philosophical explanation of the problem of evil and the necessity of opposition in all things. However, throughout the rest of the book, another theory is assumed, that evil is the result of pride and worldliness which arise in situations of economic success. 'It's fundamental theme,' says O'Dea, 'combines the concomitance of righteousness and prosperity of the later Calvinism with the call to repentance and humility of revivalistic Christianity' (O'Dea 1957: 27). This can be seen in a key motif in the Book of Mormon – that of a cycle of righteousness, prosperity, wickedness and destruction (Fig. 3). This cycle is repeated in varying forms throughout the book, as the successive populations of ancient America prosper and decline in turn, eventually destroying an entire people. O'Dea suggests that the cycle (1957: 27):

> begins with virtue and prosperity and leads to pride and iniquity, to social divisions and arrogance, to sin and decadence, and thence to the Lord's chastisement. This, if it does not end in destruction, is followed by repentance and the reinstatement of righteousness, which leads to prosperity and a recapitulation of the theme.

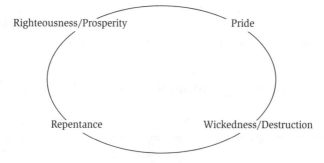

Figure 3: The Book of Mormon Cycle of Pride/Destruction

This emphasis on pride, rather than rapacity, as sinful or evil contrasts with the historical development of Christianity, in which during the eleventh and twelfth centuries, avarice came to supplant arrogance as the vice *par excellence* (Parry and Bloch 1989: 18). Contrary to the argument presented by MacFarlane that monetary economies supplant the idea of real evil and blur the distinction between right and wrong (MacFarlane 1985), Parry and Bloch suggest that the increasing attention paid to trade and commerce during these centuries resulted in greater concern with the moral perils of money (Parry and Bloch 1989: 17–19). The fact that Mormons remain preoccupied with pride illustrates the way in which their cosmology informs their view of economics. Monetary economy is simply one aspect of worldly action within a total frame of being. Pride remains more sinful that avarice because economics are an inevitable – and positive – feature of human material existence.

Mormon theology and ancient history combine, since the Book of Mormon is officially held to be an historical document. Together, they set up a moral code grounded in worldly action, which mirrors and supports the importance of earthly activity – both ritual and economic – in the process of eternal progression. The effects of this can be seen both in the history of the Church, and in contemporary action and discourse.

History and the Application of Gospel Principles

The Book of Mormon contains an account of the *Kingdom of God* on earth in ancient times. The restoration of the gospel through Joseph Smith also entailed a rebuilding of this kingdom, which was to be a political and economic structure, as well as a religious organisation. 'In its highest reaches, Mormon theology desired to bring about a heaven on this earth' (McNiff 1972: vii), but it was a very practical heaven. One of the ambitions of Joseph Smith and his successor Brigham Young was to create an independent Mormon community - a direct application of their interpretation of scripture regarding the *Kingdom of God*. Such moves were considered threatening by other inhabitants of places where Mormons settled, and were a prime reason they were so continually persecuted (the introduction of polygamy simply added fuel to an already smouldering fire). Eventually Salt Lake City, Utah, was established as the Mormon home, but even here the Mormons never achieved complete isolation. They were always affected by the inherited non-Mormon background of their converts, by the use of Salt Lake City as a stop-over for prospectors on their way to California in the late 1840s and by their economic 'entanglements' with Eastern business – particularly the railroad companies. What physical isolation they did have came to an end with the arrival of the railroad in 1869 (McNiff 1972: 23). However, in the attempt to create this heaven on earth, this Zion, this separate *Kingdom of God*, the Mormons pursued several economic policies which bear the print of their unique theology.

These policies were attractive to many who heard the news of the new religion as far away as Britain and Scandinavia. The hard-working, ambitious working classes who joined the new church (Taylor 1965, Lively 1989, Bartholemew 1995: 3–6,Harrison 1989: 14) were attracted in part because of its emphasis on practical efforts and preparation for the second coming. Unlike many other millenarianist movements, Mormonism provided a practical plan whereby members could do something now. The Perpetual Emigration Fund[13] provided support for new members to emigrate to America, which offered them both a potential liberation from their lowly position in British society, and a chance to be involved in a very practical building of Zion in preparation for the second coming. Mormonism encouraged and fostered the values already held by its converts. Self-help, and reliance first on the family and then on the local Church community was formalised in the Church's welfare programme.

The main economic and religious principle (it is important to note that it was both) instituted by the nineteenth-century Church was the Law of Consecration which actually took several forms and exists today in a revised form in the temple ceremony. The original Law of Consecration was announced in 1831 and required members of the Church to dedicate everything they possessed to the use and benefit of the *Kingdom of God* (Arrington 1958: 145). This law did not work very well as many members were unwilling to make such a sacrifice, and it was replaced by the law of tithing in 1836 (McNiff 1972: 39). The Church revived the Law of Consecration in 1854. Those who wished to comply with what was characterised as a law of God were asked to deed all their property to the Church ('conse-crate'). They would then have returned to them as a 'stewardship' whatever they needed to meet the needs of their family.

According to Arrington, the Law of Consecration, together with other economic policies such as the Perpetual Emigration Fund and the co-operative movement of the late 1860's, contemplated a comprehensive re-organisation of society (Arrington 1958: 323). In an article in the *Deseret News* on June 2 1869, Brigham Young (Church President from 1847 to 1877, following the death of Joseph Smith in 1844) argued that this movement 'is only a stepping stone to what is called the order of Enoch, but which is in reality the order of Heaven' (ibid.).

The *United Order of Enoch*, or *United Order*[14] as it was known, was born in St. George, southern Utah, in 1874, following a depression which affected even the Mormon economy, still 'entangled' as it was in 'economic alliance' with the East. It was based upon similar principles to the Law of Consecration, and church members were expected to contribute time, labour, property and money to the order. The order was a spiritual as well as an economic 'union'. There was a long list of behavioural rules which participants were expected to observe. (Arrington 1958: 328–29). One of the main achievements of the *United Order* was the building of temples – combining in a practical way the spiritual and economic elements of the order. However, the order was short-lived and was replaced by less demanding co-operative enterprises under the presidency of John Taylor (1880–87).

Reasons for the failure of the *United Order* included disputes over need, cultural difference between members (many Scandinavian converts did not even speak English), the growing non-Mormon population of Utah and the fact that increasing numbers had not known Joseph Smith or experienced the earlier persecutions and hardships. In other words, that there was insufficient unity among the members to live this kind of order. 'Human nature' was also blamed, and there was a problem of people having pre-existing debts, particularly to the Perpetual Emigration Fund (Sandberg 1996, Roberts 1930: 488). The main problem, however, was seen as being the *saints'*[15] unrighteousness. This was officially the reason for the failure of the *United Order* – the failure of what was considered a spiritual law was framed in terms of spiritual shortcomings. In the official history of the Church, B. H. Roberts records (1930:489):

> It cannot be a matter of surprise that the faith of all the members was not equal to the sacrifice of their earthly possessions to an adventure of this description, for 'sacrifice' it indeed was.

It is a significant point to make that whatever the material reasons for the failure of the *United Order*, the faithful tended to prefer a spiritual explanation – the *saints* were not worthy to live the higher law of God (a similar argument was made regarding polygamy). It is the same with the reasons for the institution of the *United Order*. While economic historians like Arrington identify factors such as heavy investment in immigration, colonisation, public works and industry and repeated agricultural failures as contributing to Church fiscal policy, it is more popularly (and officially) perceived as a movement to engender a closer spiritual and moral union between the *saints* and their God (Roberts 1930: 485), and, importantly, as a commandment of God.

Church Economy in the Contemporary World

While the *United Order* experiment failed and the Law of Consecration was redefined as a higher law which would be entered into at some future, unspecified date, the Church had greater temporal success with the law of tithing, introduced in 1836. This was a ten per cent levy on the income or 'increase' of Church members. In the early days, tithing was paid in many forms – the Church had several farms on which herds of cattle, horses and sheep, which had been received as tithing, were kept (Arrington 1958: 134–37), but it is now paid in money. Tithing was not compulsory until the Twentieth Century. It now forms part of the requirements for being admitted to the Temple, and therefore participating in the ritual practices necessary to ensure salvation. Tithing officially goes towards chapel and temple building programmes, but, despite its practical uses, the most important thing as far as Church members are concerned is that it is a commandment from God. Like the *United Order* and the Law of Consecration, tithing is defined as essentially a spiritual law with spiritual blessings attached to it, not merely as a temporal requirement.

Contemporary non-Mormon commentators often draw attention to tithing, and stress the Church's massive wealth. Until the 1950s, the Church was often heavily in debt. Since then, however, it has substantially turned around its economic situation. This has been achieved in part by embracing world capitalism, rather than rejecting it, as other millennial communities have. The Church has used the international markets to good effect, creating wealth through shrewd investment. The tithing still figures highly in Mormon finances, a fact emphasised by non-Mormon commentators. *Time* magazine, on August 4, 1997, after receiving 'unusual co-operation from the Latter-day Saint hierarchy', who provided financial figures and information about Church businesses, estimated that the Church's current annual income totals $5.9 billion (*Time* 1997: 53) and that income from tithing makes up $5.3 billion of that figure. The total assets of the Church were estimated to be a minimum of $30 billion.[16] Unsurprisingly, perhaps, the cover headline for this article was 'Mormons Inc.' This image of a 'corporate church' is related not only to its massive wealth and investment programme, but also its approach to church organisation. The business model is invoked at many levels. Official policy urges young Mormon men to dress conservatively and in a 'businesslike' fashion; white shirts, dark suits, short hair, clean shaven. It tends to recruit its leaders from the ranks of successful businessmen, and many Mormon businessmen explicitly credit their success to values they learned at Church. Mormons clearly do not see capitalism and the world of goods and commodities as a source of evil. Indeed, it has become an essentially *American* church, implicitly and sometimes explicitly anti-communist and pro-capitalist (Bloom 1992).

However, this obscures an important fact. Mormon ideology stresses that the finances and assets of the Church, like the finances and assets dedicated under the *United Order*, are for the purpose of doing God's work. *Time's* listing of Mormon assets includes farms, property, meeting houses, temples, radio and television stations, newspapers and colleges. However, Mormons see all these as being for the purposes of preaching the gospel, perfecting the *saints* or redeeming the dead. Any commercial use or financial gain is tied in to these religious goals, so that although their economic policy suggests a profoundly capitalist materialism, this is also a spirituality. All material goods and commodities are to be used in ways commanded by God. People must acknowledge the hand of God in allowing them to prosper and must dedicate what they have (time and money) to building the kingdom. In this way they recognise the proper order of things and a correct sense of the relationship between God and humans – the spiritual and the material worlds. In her analysis of the contemporary Church's economic practices of tithing and welfare, Dunn shows that the way in which these practices are narrated as 'gifts' rather than economic transactions serves to foster a moral community among Church members (Dunn 1996). However, such activity not only reproduces the Church community, it also produces a sense of a wider community of gods, spirits and mortals which provides context for the concept of *eternal progression*.

Again we can look to everyday experience and discourse for

elaboration of the spiritual nature of tithing. Many members have stories in which they recount blessings they received as a direct result of tithing. Pat recalls a time when her four children were small, and they were living on her husband's modest wage while he worked for better qualifications. She frequently ran out of money to buy groceries, but always paid her tithing. One day, returning from the local shops worried that she did not have enough food to feed her family that week, she was stopped by a neighbour she had never seen before, and was never to see again. This neighbour offered her a large bag of tomatoes from her garden, which Pat was able to use to supplement her family's meagre diet. This neighbourly act of kindness is explained by Pat as being a direct result of her obedience to the law of tithing. Stories like Pat's are, however, recounted not simply to show the temporal rewards gained by paying tithing, but primarily as 'faith-promoting' testimonies of God's pleasure and love when we obey his commandments. There is a common belief that if one lives in accordance with God's laws one will never really suffer. God will provide for his children – who prove their faith by freely giving back to him just a small part of the bounty he provides. Note again the importance of *free agency* for Mormons.

This is not to say that Mormon economic practice is without controversy. In many ways, it seems that the individualistic aspect of Mormonism has triumphed over its communalism. The Church as a whole does make significant contributions to humanitarian aid programmes in many parts of the world, and many individual members or groups of members do valuable charity work. But often when the subject of welfare is considered, it is in relation to looking after one's own – encouraging members to be self-sufficient within their families and wards (the Church's equivalent of the parish). The association of righteousness and wealth in the Book of Mormon is often interpreted by Mormons as implying an individualistic, materialistic and capitalist world view. Emphasis on wealth as a reward for righteous living often overshadows the idea that wealth can provide a way of living and doing good things.

This individualism and materialism is criticised in some Mormon circles. One Mormon, writing in *Sunstone*, a liberal Mormon publication, summed up the problem this way:

> Does not true godliness consist partly in the taming of one's longings for the lofty and infinite long enough to do what one can to bring about the salvation and exaltation of particular people? Is not this world of

material things and embodied spirits designed as an education in the things of eternity? Maybe an attitude adjustment of the rich would be one step in the right direction toward the more serious issue: how to care for the poor of the earth. (Peters 1993: 47–52)

Such questioning of the legitimacy of these central notions of morality and worldly action may be rare within Mormonism, but it is significant. Underneath Mormonism's apparent unity lies a diversity which most Mormons do not recognise (Dolgin 1974). The common Mormon notion of the Church as a single body of faith, which is both consistent and consensual, does not hold up to empirical investigation (Knowlton 1994: 4) There *are* critiques of Mormon economics. For example in America, recent concern that Mormon tithing dollars were being contributed to fight the same-sex marriage campaign in Alaska led to the formation of an informal Internet fundraising group, donating money to fight for the legalisation of same-sex marriage,[17] and to individuals withholding tithing payments from the Church. Such divergent views and critiques of the central tenets of Mormonism tend to be associated with small groups of intellectuals and liberals. As such they cannot be taken as a general dissatisfaction with Mormon practice, and indeed what is striking is that they do not tend to criticise the cultural template underlying Mormon action. They may disagree about particular policies or practices but they conform to the central assumptions behind those policies. When feminist and homosexual Mormons withheld their tithing donations in protest at the Church's involvement in right-wing Alaskan politics, they made alternative arrangements – paying their tithing dollars to non-Church charities, or banking them until Church policy changed.[18] The concept of tithing, based upon, and upholding, a sense of the eternal continuum between spirits, mortals and gods, was not at issue. Rather, they critiqued the *use* of the tithing by the Church.

Conclusion

Mormon theology defines matter and spirit in such a way that the traditional philosophical distinction between them is dissolved. Joseph Smith, the movement's founder, argued that spirit was itself a purified form of matter. This definition can be seen in the Mormon conception of the make-up of Gods and humans. Gods and humans are of the same essence, they just exist at different stages of a continuum of development. Similarly, the worlds of spirits and mortals are so closely connected that they exist within the same frame. Actions in each world affect outcomes in the other, and one moves through them in line with one's progression along the development of spirit to mortal to God. The *Kingdom of God*, a religious or spiritual entity, is, in this cosmology, simultaneously a practical and material kingdom, and efforts to build this kingdom on the earthly plane necessarily involve political and economic activity.

Mormon economics is at a basic level a *moral* – as opposed to immoral – economy in which engagement with the material world is essential to make mortals more God-like. Any debates about correct use of economic means share the basic assumption that humanity may progress towards Godhood through righteous living in a material world. Debates about what constitutes righteous living in terms of this material world are debates about morality which are informed by the cultural template offered by Mormon cosmology.

Notes

1. The doctoral research upon which this chapter is based was supported by a DENI Quota award from 1995 to 1998. I am grateful to the participants in the Social Anthropology post-graduate seminar group at Queen's University of Belfast and to Elizabeth Tonkin, Jon Mitchell and Paul Clough for comments on earlier drafts of this chapter.
2. *Baptism for the dead* is performed in Mormon temples. It has attracted a great deal of attention, due in part to the Church's vast genealogical efforts at seeking out details of dead relatives to baptise, and in part to imaginative attempts by non-members to comprehend what is involved in the practice.
3. Terms in italics are those which have a particular Mormon usage, in addition to any wider usage with which readers may be familiar. They could be called 'indigenous terms'.
4. The Doctrine and Covenants is a Mormon book of scripture, commonly abbreviated as D&C.
5. Abraham is a book in the Church scripture The Pearl of Great Price.
6. There is some evidence (especially in the temple endowment) which can be interpreted to indicate that Brigham Young espoused the idea that both Satan and Adam had had bodies at one time – but this has not entered mainstream Mormon theology (Kirkland 1986: 11).
7. The format of this diagram is familiar to all Mormons and a similar diagram is used by missionaries in teaching *investigators*, people interested in the Church.
8. This has, however, been the subject of some recent controversy in America, when the current Church President, Gordon B. Hinckley, refused to confirm to reporters on two occasions that this was official Mormon doctrine, which might be explained in terms of an attempt at assimilation into mainstream American society (see Mauss 1994). News of this controversy has not reached English Mormons to any significant extent.

9. As part of the Mormon lifecycle it is common for young men and women in their late teens to leave their families for a two-year period of missionary activity. This is known by all Mormons as 'their mission'.

10. Mormon priesthood holders give *blessings* to heal and for reassurance, as well as part of rituals such as naming children and confirmation. They are a special kind of prayer, backed up with the authority and power of the priesthood.

11. This view is held by some women, and is backed up by historical evidence. However, it is not without controversy, and contemporary women would not normally admit in public that they have used the priesthood to bless or administer. See Madsen 1992.

12. Mormons also link themselves to the early Christian Church.

13. The Perpetual Emigration Fund (PEF) gave loans of financial assistance to members wishing to emigrate to Salt Lake City. These loans were then paid back, ensuring the fund was continuous.

14. There were actually several *united orders* set up throughout Utah, which ran on variations of the standard concept.

15. *Saints* is used to refer to Church members, as in *The Church of Jesus Christ of Latter-day Saints*.

16. The Church, in its semi-annual General Conference, always states that the Church financial records have been audited and have been found satisfactory. However, they do not release financial records.

17. This group, known as MORMON AID, was nominated for a 1998 Human Rights Award presented at Lamb of God Metropolitan Community Church, Alaska, on January 17, 1999.

18. Information based on personal electronic communications with individuals involved.

References

Arrington, L. J., 1958, *Great Basin Kingdom: An Economic History of the Latter-day Saints 1830–1900.* Cambridge, Mass: Harvard University Press.

Bartholemew, R., 1995, *Audacious Women: Early British Mormon Immigrants.* Salt Lake City: Signature Books.

Bloom, H., 1992 , *The American Religion: The Emergence of the Post-Christian Nation.* New York, London: Touchstone, Simon and Schuster.

Boddy, J., 1994, 'Spirit Possession Revisited: Beyond Instrumentality', *Annual Review of Anthropology,* 23: 407–34.

Comaroff, J., 1985, *Body of Power, Spirit of Resistance.* Chicago: Chicago University Press.

Davies, D. J., 1987, *Mormon Spirituality: Latter-day Saints in Wales and Zion.* University of Nottingham: Nottingham Series in Theology.

Dolgin, J. L., 1974, 'Latter-day Sense and Substance', in Zaretsy, I. I., and Leone, M. P., eds., *Religious Movements in Contemporary America.* New Jersey: Princeton University Press.

Dunn, E., 1996, 'Money, Morality and Modes of Civil Society among American Mormons', in Hann, C. and Dunn, E., eds, *Civil Society: Challenging Western Models.* London and New York: Routledge.

Harris, F. S. and Butt, N. I., 1925, *The Fruits of Mormonism.* New York: MacMillan.

Harrison, J. F. C., 1989, 'The Popular History of Early Victorian Britain: A Mormon

Contribution', in Jensen, R. L., and Thorpe, M. R., eds, *Mormons in Early Victorian Britain*. Salt Lake City: University of Utah Press.

Hobart, M., 1985, 'Is God Evil?', in Parkin, D., ed., *The Anthropology of Evil*. Oxford: Basil Blackwell.

Kirkland, B., 1986, 'Of Gods, Mortals and Devils: As Satan Is, Man May Yet Become', *Sunstone*, 10 (12): 6–12.

Knowlton, D., 1994, 'The Unspeakable and Intellectual Politics In Mormonism', unpublished paper, presented at 1992 *Sunstone* Symposium, Salt Lake City, Utah, under the title, 'Secrecy, Deceit, and the Sacred in Mormonism'.

Lively, R. J., 1989, 'Some Sociological Reflections on the Nineteenth-Century British Mission', in Jensen, R. L., and Thorpe, M. R., eds, 1989, *Mormons in Early Victorian Britain*. Salt Lake City: University of Utah Press.

McNiff, W. J., 1972, *Heaven on Earth: A Planned Mormon Society.* Philadelphia: Porcupine Press Inc.

MacFarlane, A., 1985, 'The Root of All Evil', in Parkin, D., 1985, ed., *The Anthropology of Evil*. Oxford: Basil Blackwell.

Madsen, C. C., 1992, 'Mormon Women and the Temple: Toward a New Understanding', in Beecher, M. U., and Anderson, L. F., eds, *Sisters in Spirit: Mormon Women in Historical and Cultural Perspective.* Urbana and Chicago: University of Illinois Press.

Mauss, A. L., 1994, *The Angel and the Beehive: The Mormon Struggle With Assimilation.* Urbana and Chicago: University of Illinois Press.

Mullen, R., 1967, *The Mormons.* London: W. H. Allen.

O'Dea, T. F., 1957, *The Mormons.* Chicago, London: University of Chicago Press.

Ong, A., 1987, *Spirits of Resistance and Capitalist Discipline: Factory Women in Malaysia,* Albany: State University Press.

Parkin, D., ed., 1985, *The Anthropology of Evil*. Oxford: Basil Blackwell.

Parry, J., and Bloch, M., eds, 1989, *Money and the Morality of Exchange.* Cambridge: Cambridge University Press.

Peters, J. D., 1993, 'Reflections on Mormon Materialism', *Sunstone*, 16 (4) (issue 90).

Quinn, D. M., 1997, *The Mormon Hierarchy: Extensions of Power.* Salt Lake City: Signature Books.

Roberts, B. H., 1930, *A Comprehensive History of the Church of Jesus Christ of Latter-day Saints: Century 1 in Six Volumes.* Salt Lake City: Deseret News Press, Vol. 5.

Sandberg, K. C., 1996, 'Getting Up a History of Monroe: The Long Shadow of the United Order', *Sunstone,* December.

Taylor, P. A. M., 1965, *Expectations Westward: The Mormons and the Emigration of their British Converts in the Nineteenth Century.* Edinburgh and London: Oliver and Boyd.

Time Magazine, August 4, 1997, 'The Empire of the Mormons'.

Church Scriptures and Sources cited:

The Doctrine and Covenants (D&C) Copyright 1981 by the Corporation of the President of The Church of Jesus Christ of Latter-day Saints Salt Lake City, Utah.

The Book of Mormon Copyright 1981 by the Corporation of the President of The Church of Jesus Christ of Latter-day Saints Salt Lake City, Utah.

The Pearl of Great Price Copyright 1981 by the Corporation of the President of The Church of Jesus Christ of Latter-day Saints Salt Lake City, Utah.

The Family: A Proclamation to the World given by Church President, Gordon B. Hinckley, on September 23, 1995.

7

The State and the Empire of Evil

Jojada Verrips

University of Amsterdam

Introduction[1]

In the beginning of 1995 a Dutch member of Parliament asked the Under-secretary of Health, Welfare and Sports whether she knew about the existence of the videofilm *Faces of Death*, whether she thought that that film could be harmful to young kids, whether she was informed about the easiness with which the film could be rented, and whether she thought that that product should be banned by the government as in England and Germany. The first three questions the liberal under-secretary answered in the affirmative and about the fourth she said that a general prohibition of videonasties would be difficult, but that she would ask the Secretary of Justice to find out whether the paragraph in the Criminal Act concerning the prohibition of the offer of pornographic images to youngsters under sixteen could be expanded to the offer of videonasties.[2] In September it was announced that government officials were working on an Act to make it impossible for adolescents under sixteen to get access to videofilms with a lot of extreme (sexual) violence. Evidently the authorities were of the opinion that the self-censorship of the producers and importers of videonasties, which they had accepted till then, was not sufficient any longer to limit the access for youngsters to hard core and ugly violence. Since the Member of Parliament phrased his questions with regard to violent videomovies in 1995, several Dutch politicians not only regularly aired their worry about their accessibility, but also worked on the design and introduction of all kinds of rules and regulations to seriously restrict it.[3]

At about the same time when there was a lot of turmoil in the Dutch political arena and, as a consequence, in the media about the bad influence of hyper-violent (video)movies and one could hear people demand a ban on their easy accessibility everywhere, the American Republican politician Robert Dole accused the multimedia producer Time Warner of bringing on the market violent rap songs (of groups like Snoop Doggy Dog, Dr Dre and Gorefest) and films (such as, for instance, *Natural Born Killers* by Oliver Stone).[4] Dole, who strongly opposes a law against the distribution of firearms, branded the company 'a preacher of Evil' and made it perfectly clear that in his opinion the point had been reached at which popular culture seriously threatened the character of the American nation.[5] Shortly after his vehement Philippic even the Democrats showed their approval by putting forward a bill to establish a board of censors for TV. 'Programs with a lot of violence or indecent sex should be coded. A so-called v-chip in the TV should make it possible for parents to block these unwanted programs upon their wish' (Miller 1994: 250; *NRC Handelsblad,* 8 June 1995; Kunkel 1997).[6]

As a consequence of the Bulger affair at the end of 1993[7] and the heated public discussions about the devastating influence of violent movies on children entailed by it, the House of Commons in England decided to tighten up the criteria for the classification of videofilms in the Criminal Justice and Public Order Act 1994. It now reads as follows:

> The designated authority shall in making any determination as to the suitability of a videowork, have special regard . . . to any harm that may be caused to potential viewers or, through their behaviour, to society by the manner in which the film deals with a) criminal behaviour, b) illegal drugs, c) violent behaviour or incidents, d) horrific behaviour or incidents or e) human sexual activity.[8]

Although campaigns by certain groups of the population (i.e. religious ones) against the harmful content of films, and for the introduction of local and national regulations to prevent their uncensored showing are as old as the medium itself, it seems that the pressure upon the state (at least in a number of West-European societies) to take measures against (video)films with too many naked and/or destructed bodies has been increasing since the early 1970s. This increasing pressure seems to be a direct consequence of the fact that on the one hand ever more of this kind of films are made (indeed an indication of a growing demand) and on the other the fact that the people who campaign against these products apparently do not trust the social control and corrective power of such institutions as the churches and religious denominations any longer. Evidently the state has the duty not only to formulate the rules and regulations (in the form of acts and laws) with respect to what other people should or should not see/show in the area of sex and/or violence, but also to control their strict observance. It often seems as if these campaigners for the institution of strong censorship have the intention of re-Christianising society through the state, or at least blocking the secularisation process and the shocking erosion of crucial (Christian) norms that goes with it. In this connection it is striking that several politicians are prepared to form a coalition with those who think that certain films are not only able to corrupt (young) individuals but in the last instance whole societies. This increasing trend to call upon the state to act as the guardian of social morals with respect to a very important part of Western public culture and the inclination of many a politician to deal seriously with this demand by introducing bills in order to muzzle it, is a very intriguing phenomenon that begs many questions, some of which I address in this chapter.

In the first place there is the question of why certain people (in different Western societies) are so afraid of the immoral impact of films that they want them to be cut or even banned by the state. The issue whether art in the broadest sense of the word has a positive or a negative effect upon people is a very old one, but in no case it crops up in such a persistent way as with regard to movies – performances congealed on celluloid which, in principle, do not differ much from theatrical performances. A clear answer to this question is hard to give, if one does not pay attention to the kind of people who contend that films can morally corrupt, but if one does, one very soon discovers, as I demonstrate below, that these people measure with two rods. Furthermore there is the interesting question, which the advocates of censorship and the politicians who support them seem to avoid, as to why nowadays there is such an increasing demand for films full of rude violence and/or plain sex. Put differently, to what kind of fundamental desires of their consumers do these films speak? Directly related to this is the question of what role this kind of movie plays in a secularising (Western) world and whether this role is affected by cutting out passages deemed to have harmful effects upon consumers. Before I try to answer these questions, I will make a few short remarks about the genre of movies in which the unashamed showing of gruesome violence and plain sex seems to be an end in itself, and against which people like Bob Dole campaign because they fear that they will split asunder society's moral fabric.

Films and Censorship

It is broadly agreed upon that the emergence of unbridled violence in movies took a turning – or maybe it is better to say starting – point with the production of the film *Bonnie and Clyde*. As Rick Trader Witcombe in his book *Savage Cinema* remarks (1975: 59):

> What has really happened in the last decade is that filmmakers have become less tolerant with the old cinematic metaphors representing violence. Now, if a character's head is blown off by a shotgun, they want to show us just how terrible an event that is. A watershed in the change from indirect to direct methods of presentation was the release of *Bonnie and Clyde* in 1967.

In the beginning of the 1970s similar violent movies came out such as *Straw Dogs* (1971) and *A Clockwork Orange* (1971), both notorious for their rape scenes which triggered, for instance in England, sharp debates and stimulated certain people to demand that the (local and national) authorities forbid their public display in cinemas.[9] Another film evoking heated feelings, this time because it unashamedly showed anal sex, was *Last Tango in Paris* (1972) by Bertolucci. This movie was even forbidden in Italy and led to an imprisonment of three months for its maker. Recently there has been a lot of discussion with regard to the movie by Oliver Stone *Natural Born Killers*, in which a young couple unscrupulously kill more than fifty persons (see Harbord 1997). Other examples of recent films in which extreme manifestations of physical violence and/or unabashed sex are shown are *C'est Arrivé Près de Chez Vous, Reservoir Dogs, Pulp Fiction, Henry, Portrait of a Serial Killer,* and *Funny Games.*

Besides these mainstream movies, all sorts of ugly, gross, and gory violence upon the (human) body occurs in the horror-genre and especially in the so-called splatter or slasher movies. As Noel

Carroll puts it in his fascinating book *The Philosophy of Horror* (1990: 211):

> One particular dimension of this violence is the extreme gross fury visited upon the human body as it is burst, blown up, broken, and ripped apart; as it disintegrates or metamorphoses; as it is dismembered and dissected; as it is devoured from the inside out.[10]

These splatter or slasher movies have expanded in video format since the VCR became popular at the end of the 1970s.[11] In these kinds of movies the 'art' of showing monstrous violence and the degradation of the human body to pure flesh has risen to such heights that one wonders whether it will still be possible to think out new variants.

It is especially products in the horror genre that campaigners would like to see submitted to more and more legal restrictions, controlled and sanctioned by the state. Indeed, it seems that their moral campaigns or crusades (see Starker 1989: 182) are not without results, for in an increasing number of countries the rules regarding their distribution are becoming tougher. Since I cannot deal here in detail with the development of film censorship in all Western countries, I will confine myself to a few remarks on developments in England.[12]

Since 1908 it has been possible for British local authorities to refuse a license for showing a movie in an inflammatory environment. Soon, however, these authorities used the act, which made such a refusal possible, to forbid the display of movies they deemed to be of an immodest character. For that reason the film industry, afraid as it was to lose money, decided in 1912 to start self-censorship through a self-designated body, the British Board of Film Censors (BBFC). In doing so the industry hoped to get rid of the interference of municipal councils with their business. Yet they were mistaken, for the local authorities continued taking their own decisions. Thereupon the industry attempted to convince the national authorities to establish a national board of censors in order to get rid of the exacting local officials. This effort was in vain, for in the early 1920s the decision was taken, for instance in London, that a permit would only be given to show a film if the certificates of the BBFC were accepted. From that moment onward 'a body responsible only to the industry carried out the actual censorship, but its certificates were given legal validation and impressed on the public by local authority licensing powers' (Wistrich 1978: 18). Only as late as 1952 were local authorities forced by law (The Cinematographic Act of 1952) 'to censor films for children'. However, they were not obliged to do so for adults. The municipal councils could replace a BBFC decision by one of their own and they were allowed to give licenses for the showing of films without a BBFC-certificate. This power of the local authorities was of crucial importance for the system, because without it the certificates of the BBFC would have been absolutely arbitrary and no cinema-owner would have been obliged to acknowledge them. Some filmmakers have even profited from this situation in order to get a license for a film which was censored or banned elsewhere. The Greater London Council, which used to have a rather liberal reputation, was often approached to that end. Up until 1975 it was difficult in Great Britain to start legal action against films. Because Parliament assumed that films were censored by a particular control system (that of the BBFC) they were not included in the Obscene Publications Act of 1959 and the Theatres Act of 1968. This situation changed in 1975 after several failed attempts to prohibit the showing of particular films via the Obscene Publications Act (for instance, *Last Tango in Paris*). Since then the laws have been regularly adapted and made stricter in order to be able to do something against the distribution and showing of (video)films deemed to be harmful to particular viewers.

In the US a similar kind of development occurred, for there the film industry also took the initiative to start self-censorship rather early (see Black 1994; Miller 1994; Paul 1994).[13] However, this did not alter the fact that state authorities, referring to different laws, regularly decided to prohibit the showing of particular films. Only in the last decades has there been an increasing interference of the federal authorities in the distribution and showing of (video)films. In several (Western) countries a similar trend can be observed – just at a time when the control of distribution and consumption of audio-visual products becomes more and more difficult, due to rapid technological developments and the commercialisation of the sector.[14] What one tries to prevent in particular, through legal regulations, is the easy accessibility of gruesome movies for minors whose 'innocence could be spoilt.'

It is an interesting development, for one evidently does not any longer regard the Church as the foremost guardian of morals and fighter against the empire of evil, as was the custom in the Western world for ages, but rather the state. It is increasingly expected that the state should wage war against what one deems to be the diabolical and demonic in the Western world. The state is to assume the role of exorcist of the forces of evil, who took possession of the body social.

Who and Why?

In the foregoing I remarked that the question as to why one fears the morally disrupting effects of movies to such a large extent cannot be answered adequately if one neglects the groups that complain about them and advocate the introduction of powerful (legal) measures with respect to their consumption. Here I want to pay attention to two groups: a) orthodox Christians who fight for the maintenance of Christian norms and values and against the increasing secularisation of their society and b) conservative members of what I would like to call the bourgeois elite who already since the rise of the working-class in the nineteenth century have had problems with its lifestyle and taste regarding fashion, music, sports and – since they appeared for the first time – movies. Since films, at least in the beginning, were often shown at fairs, the bourgeois elite soon associated them with lower-class amusement, which sharply contrasted with the kind of arts and theatre that they themselves used to frequent. But let me first concentrate here on orthodox Christians.

Orthodox Christians (such as politically right-wing and religiously fundamentalist Calvinists, Pietists, Methodists, and Catholics) have often been against going to the cinema, because generally speaking they deemed movies to be nothing less than picture-books of the devil through which one would be tempted to change the narrow for the broad path full of evil.[15] For a long time, however, it was not necessary really to campaign against it, for one could easily avoid cinema shows and there was no direct intrusion of the medium into the private lifesphere. This drastically changed in the 1960s with the introduction of TV. From then on more and more films perceived to be morally corrupting were broadcast by people who dominated this medium and who believed less, or not at all, in the relevance of keeping up particular Christian norms.[16]

In this connection it is interesting and illuminating to look at what Morrison and Tracey (1978) have written about the National Viewers and Listeners Association (NVLA), founded in England in 1965. According to them the NVLA, which forcefully campaigned against the showing of movies such as *A Clockwork Orange* and *Last Tango in Paris* in the 1970s, was an organisation of right-wing

Christians who wanted to immediately stop the expansion of the secularisation process going on in their society and the rapid decay of the Christian norms and values it implied.[17] When they were not only confronted with the emergence of a disorienting modernist spirit within the churches they belonged to and the schools their children used to frequent, but also with the penetration of their homes by that spirit via films shown on TV, they joined forces with the ladies Mary Whitehouse and Norah Buckland who had started a crusade against that kind of 'decay'. Where possible they tried to stop it through lawsuits and, if these failed, to have the laws changed and adapted to their desires. A year after the NVLA had started its moral campaign one of its leading figures, Dr Sturdy, said the following:

> I have always looked upon the television campaign as a gateway to a much bigger campaign through which we would mobilise all the forces of good in the country in a mighty uprising to overthrow the forces of evil. It so happens that television was the inspired target on which to make a concentrated attack, but as one MP pointed out, it is the mouthpiece of the forces of secularism, humanism, liberalism, impuritanism and communism, etc. We are in fact tackling one of the main citadels of evil in the country (cited in Morrison and Tracey 1978: 53).

However, in a formal sense the NVLA was not in favour of (a sharper) censorship on the basis of new laws, because the organisation emphasised the functioning of the individual conscience. As Morrison and Tracey have shown, the NVLA was not so much after the conversion of a particular group or class, but aspired to arrest the secularisation process in British society as a whole and to set in motion a re-Christianisation process instead:

> N.V.L.A. stands in opposition not to a group or a class but to a total social order; instead of secular values, it wants Christian values. However, radical as it may be, its radicalism is both reactionary and conservative. It is reactionary in the sense that it objects to on-going social trends, and conservative in that it makes appeals to the past for support of its values. Its conservative rhetoric stems in part from its class composition but much of its conservatism derives from the dislike of a world which no longer embodies, in any meaningful sense, religious values. (Morrison and Tracey 1978: 46)[18]

This brings me to the second social group which can make a lot of fuss about the corrupting nature of particular pictures: conservative members of the bourgeois elite. In this case, however, there is a clear-cut opposition to a particular group or class, namely the working class which – according to these conservatives – nowadays is the most important consumer of videofilms (Barker and Petley 1997: 5). In the same vein, earlier members of this elite used to regard the working-class as the most important consumer of films (Wistrich 1978: 9) – films which the bourgeois elite in the meantime has learned to accept as art, albeit in particular cases.[19] Since the rise of the (urban) mass of labourers, the conservative part of the bourgeois elite, as I already remarked, has been irritated by its different life style and patterns of taste and has developed the idea that it should do something civilising about it in order to prevent society and culture from falling apart in the very near future (see Starker 1989: 168 ff.). When today's conservative members of the bourgeois elite worry about the putative pernicious content and influence of videonasties, which indeed very often are consumed in lower class circles,[20] and are in favour of taking (legal) measures against these products, we are confronted with the upsurge of an old fear in a new shape, of possible societal disintegration threatening to start from these milieus.[21] In this case it is not so much a matter of launching a moral transformation process for society as a whole, as in the case of the orthodox Christians campaigning against 'evil' films, but rather for particular strata which are thought to have always had popular – read: bad – taste and therefore represent a kind of spectre for the future. Nevertheless it can be observed that the two groups, that is orthodox Christians and conservative members of the bourgeois elite, join forces in their campaign against the kind of moral decadence and decay as it is supposed to be shown in a particular type of movie and which in their view can easily lead towards socially disturbing, immoral, and even criminal behaviour.[22] That is exactly what happens right now in the Netherlands.[23]

In this connection it is important to realise that both groups use double standards. The orthodox Christians overlook the fact that the source of their moral inspiration, the Bible, overflows with stories which could easily function as scenarios for horror movies. The Bible teems with sex and violence, naked and destructed bodies, *Eros* and *Thanatos*. The same can be observed with regard to literature, plays, ballets, operas as well as films which are consumed by the bourgeois elite but which, according to that elite, nevertheless bear witness to good, even legitimate, taste. One is confronted here with the making of questionable distinctions.

It is interesting to note here that, with the acceptance of the

Theatres Act in England in 1968, theatre plays suddenly became more or less immune to possible censorship, because the age-old office of the Lord Chamberlain, since Elizabethan days responsible for censoring these plays, was abolished. Since then it has become impossible to start private legal prosecutions, because only the Lord Chamberlain was is entitled to take measures regarding plays and shows. According to Wistrich, who was once Chairman of the Film Viewing Board of the Greater London Council, '[I]t had become safe to emancipate the theatre because its patrons were "well educated" and largely adult' (1978: 8). However, the cinema had not yet reached a similar respectable status at that time and films therefore remained a target for moral campaigners, among other reasons because, as Wistrich has rightly remarked (9–10):

> precisely those who are in positions of authority and influence are least likely to patronise the cinema. Cinemas frequently remain in the respectable consciousness as doubtful social venues and by implication films are a doubtful form of entertainment . . . Controls which would be seen as intolerable for any other medium of communication or entertainment are accepted and the pressure for even stricter controls is pervasive.

In order to illustrate her point she gives several examples of censorship applied to films (such as *O Calcutta*, *Emmanuelle*, and *The Story of O*) and not to the books, plays, and shows on which they were based. Obviously people are afraid of the pictures, because '[T]hey substitute the possibility of chaos, disturbance and revolution for stability and order' (7). It would be worthwhile to conduct an in-depth study of the seemingly different treatment and moral evaluation of different audio-visual products, such as plays and shows on the one hand and (video)films on the other. Though both are consumed through the same 'distance senses' (of seeing and hearing), their effects in the minds and bodies of their consumers are deemed to be totally different. People who advocate a stronger censorship of films in one way or another think that film images can 'bewitch' or possess human beings, especially those with weaker minds and stronger – thus more dangerous for the body social – bodies. In this connection it is striking that the proponents of decency laws regarding fictional violence in films seem not to have much trouble with the commercialisation and commodification of particular kinds of 'real-life violence', nor with the real-life violence inflicted in the name of commerce. As Pinedo puts it (1997: 108):

Critics who take aim, at film violence, from mainstream politicians like Bob Dole to the rightwing American Family Association, are loathe to criticise the larger context of capitalism's profit-driven, anything-goes stance and reserve their venom for the Hollywood establishment whose support for a liberal social agenda is anathema to conservatives.

To what needs do the films speak?

It is not easy to answer the question of why people take the trouble to visit the cinema in order to see movies with much crude violence and sex, or why they rent such films from videoshops to watch them in the privacy of their home. Although much has been written about the content and supposedly negative influence of horror films and videonasties, only little serious research has been conducted on its consumers, the reasons why they watch these products and the effects the films have on them. Yet there are plenty of suppositions and hypotheses. According to James Twitchell (1985) there is every indication that the audience, at least in the US, is mainly adolescent. This is also the impression of Carol J. Clover, who writes (1992: 6):

> To the question of who watches such films, there is no neat answer ... Still, what formal surveys and informal accounts there are bear out with remarkable consistency Stephen King's presumption that adolescent males hold pride of place.

I shall soon return to the significance of this statement (see Dronkers 1993; Weaver and Tamborini 1996) for an understanding of the role of these films. But first I want to touch on a number of general facets of the tremendous popularity of films abounding with destroyed and naked bodies and address the question as to why they are so fascinating.

I contend that one of the reasons for their fascination lies in the fact that they trespass existing taboos with regard to sex and violence or the beginning and the end of life (Starker 1989: 179). Here it is important to realise that the 'civilised' always presupposes the 'uncivilised' or 'wild' and that stronger demands to affect regulation and self-control go hand in hand with a conscious or unconscious desire for the contrary, that is, an unbridled expression of primary impulses – an abolition of 'the lid on the *id*.' In this respect films are a splendid mimetic means to meet that need. For, by showing the 'uncivilised' processes by which the intact (naked) body transforms into a terribly destroyed body, they offer the possibility to somehow undo, by way of the eye, the imprisonment of the concrete touch in Western societies (see Verrips 1996).[24] This is exactly what happens in popular horror films and videonasties, yet it is ignored by orthodox Christians and the bourgeois elite. Their calls for censorship occur despite the fact that the bourgeois elite has no difficulty at all with the consumption of literature, operas and plays in which the very same gruesome trespasses occur as in the films which they consider to be dangerous for social morality,[25] and despite the fact that the Christians have a wealth of myths in which these trespasses also figure regularly. These groups do not raise the question of how far these accepted genres stimulate socially undesirable behaviour. Yet there are indications that these art forms may be equally disastrous and disorienting as the films against which the groups campaign ... and also to an equally scanky extent.[26] The latter has been indicated with regard to films by a number of researchers (see, for example, Randall 1997: 438; Wistrich 1978; Tudor 1989; Carroll 1990; Van der Burg & Van den Heuvel 1991: 42; Krasniewicz 1992; Buckley 1993: 177–78; Harbord 1997: 156; Barker & Petley 1997; Boomkens 1997: 17). Except for a few incidental cases of negative influencing, the kind of large-scale moral disruption that the opponents of the genre regard as an inevitable consequence of (regularly) watching gruesome and horrific (video)movies, has never been observed.

This is not as amazing as it sounds, for if one conducts a serious study of the content and meaning of these products, which are supposed to have a very negative effect upon their (youthful) consumers, one cannot help but conclude that they are nothing else than modern myths,[27] which just as the classical myths and the myths of so-called primitive peoples contain speculations about inherent and latent possibilities, and in which extreme positions are 'imagined in order to show that they are untenable' (Lévi-Strauss 1967: 30; see also Twitchell 1985: 85).[28] Twitchell observes that (sexually) violent horror films are consumed especially by adolescents, and advocates the idea already launched by Evans (1975), that this consumption can best be interpreted as a modern *rite de passage*.[29] According to Twitchell it is ridiculous that anthropologists paid a lot of attention to *rites de passage* and the myths associated with them everywhere in the world except in their own societies. I think that he is right and that it is rewarding to approach the consumption of horror films and videonasties from this angle. As he has tersely remarked, they are products which play out the 'do's' and 'don'ts' of (adolescent) sexuality – or lay down the rules of socialisation and extrapolate a hidden code of sexual behaviour. This is exactly the thing adolescents are looking for, since they are often going through a confusing phase in their lives. In a later publication (1989) Twitchell deals not only with the outrageous violence in modern horror films, but also in pulp fiction, comics, TV drama, music videos and arcade games. He elaborates his ideas on the basis of Victor Turner's work on the *sacra*, and how *initiandi* are made familiar with them during initiation ceremonies. However, Twitchell fails to do this very systematically, neglecting, for example, Turner's classic article on liminality, 'Betwixt and Between: The Liminal Period in Rites de Passage' (in Turner 1970). Here, Turner deals at length with three characteristic features of the *sacra*, which also strike a chord in relation to horror films – particularly their disproportion, their monstrousness and their mystery. The whole ensemble of disproportional, monstrous, and mysterious *sacra* that is given to the *initiandi*, forms a symbolic framework for the whole system of values and beliefs that exists in a particular society and by which that society continues to exist (see Stewart 1982: 40). Though there exists a clear-cut family resemblance between the mythical stories presented to youngsters during classical initiation rites and the modern myths consumed by adolescents in movie theatres and on TV, the context is rather different. Whereas in the first case direct control and supervision by adults is never lacking, this very often does not hold true in the latter. Moreover real *rites de passage* are highly structured phenomena, while the visits paid to movie theatres by young people bear a rather different character.[30] I will now illustrate the importance of hidden beliefs and social values in horror films on the basis of an example, the film *Fright Night*.[31]

Every now and then this film is shown on one of the many channels one can watch in the Netherlands. I once saw it announced in a TV-guide as follows: 'American movie made in 1985 by Tom Holland. When Jerry Dandridge – at first sight the ideal neighbour – invites you for a night-cap late in the evening, you have to realise one thing: he loves to drink his drinks warm and red and right from the carotid artery. With amongst others Chris Sarandon, Amanda Bearse and Roddy McDowell.' *Fright Night* is a horror movie of the most pure kind, in which the themes of vampirism and werewolfism are interwoven in a complex way. Very shortly formulated the film is about an adolescent boy, Charley Brewster, who feels himself threatened by his new neighbour, Jerry Dandridge, who, according to him, is not just an ordinary killer, but a vampire and a werewolf at the same time. To his dismay nobody seems to be prepared to share his view that the new neighbour is a totally strange person engaged in all sorts of shady and frightening acts. However, after some time he gets help from a certain Peter Vincent, who used to present a horrorshow on TV that Charley frequently watched. Incidentally, the name Peter Vincent is probably composed on the basis of the names of two great horror actors, Peter Cushing and Vincent Price. Together with this man Charley at last succeeds in disarming the terrifying and terrorising neighbour.

Before I can present the sociological scheme in this film and the hidden moral message it contains, it is necessary to specify which other persons next to Charley, Jerry Dandridge and Peter Vincent play a role in this movie. Respectively, these are the following: Charley's mother, who is either divorced or a widow (that remains unclear); Amy Peterson, Charley's girlfriend who desperately wants to have sex with him; Ed Thompson alias 'Evil,' Charley's friend who boasts to be afraid of nothing between heaven and earth; and Billy Cole, the friend and house-mate of Jerry Dandridge. The sociological scheme of the movie looks as follows. Jerry Dandridge is, as already said, a vampire and werewolf at the same time. He has the strange habit of killing prostitutes he invites to his house. After he has killed his regular female visitors, he disposes of their corpses with the help of his companion Billy Cole, who – though rather late in the film – turns out to be a vampire and werewolf as well. The first Dandridge victim in Charley's own network is 'Evil.' He appears not to be able to resist the charms this man undeniably has and transforms into a vampire-werewolf after Dandridge has bitten him in the neck. The second victim is Amy, for she gives in to his charms and is then seduced. We see how Dandridge bites her and blood flows. Though this evil character also desperately tries to make Charley his victim, he is not successful. First Peter Vincent manages to eliminate 'Evil,' then he and Charley succeed in doing the same with Billy Cole and Jerry Dandridge, but not without much effort, for every time the two think they have eliminated them for good they come alive again in a monstrous shape. Although Amy is bitten by Dandridge we remain unsure about the effects of that act – she might be infected by him, but it could be that she is not. In the final scene of the movie we see her lying in bed with Charley, just as in the opening scene.

What kind of moral message can one distil from this pattern of relationships and sequence of actions? In my view, we are confronted here with a message that pertains to the kind of sexual relationships that are acceptable and unacceptable or – in other words – to the ones which are dangerous and the ones which are not. Charley is still a virgin, just as his girlfriend Amy is. He is, so to speak, on the verge of experiencing his sexuality in relation with a girl. At that particular point in time there suddenly appears a beautiful but strange man in the house next door, a man who lives together with a friend, a man who has sexual affairs with prostitutes, and a man who likes to have relationships with young boys – such as 'Evil' and Charley – and girls – such as Amy. In other words through his neighbour Charley is respectively in a more or less hidden way confronted with a) homosexuality, b) prostitution, and c) bisexuality, as well as with the dangers that go together with them. Indeed, the ones who have sexual relationships with Dandridge have to pay for this with their lives – like the prostitutes – or are infected by him with the vampire-werewolf-virus and as a consequence become both dangerously ill and dangerous to others. What we seem to be confronted with is a metaphorical representation of sexually transmittable diseases in general, and AIDS in particular. The vampire-werewolf Jerry Dandridge stands for a carrier of the AIDS virus, who maintains multiple sexual contacts, and with whom one had therefore better have no relations at all. The main message of the movie thus seems to be this:

> Young boy and young girl, watch out for sexual contacts with strange men, because they may infect you with a sexually transmittable disease. Always fight against the temptation to give in to their efforts to seduce you.

Next to that message other more or less hidden, highly moralistic messages might be distilled from this film, but this will do for the moment.

Recently Louise Krasniewicz argued that films overflowing with extreme (sexual) violence, which are deemed by certain social groups to be an important source of the moral corruption of youth, in no way function like that, but instead should be seen as a moral gift from society to its adolescents – a gift which requires a counter-gift in the shape of socially acceptable (sexual) behaviour (1992: 45–46):

> the cinema is a gift whose enormously important social value rests in its role of providing not only guiding mythological stories but a social

obligation to respond positively to those tales . . . Our obligation in return for these horrible stories of broken taboos in the horror film is the total surveillance of our bodily activities so that not only will incest and bestiality not occur, but so that no activities that might incite or inspire others to these acts will be allowed to take place. In a continuing gift spiral, we obligate ourselves to increasing self-control through movie-viewing, and we therefore obligate the movie-industry to give us more and more tales of 'illicit sexuality' that will thankfully remind us of our weaknesses, our potential sins, and the thin line between real life and horror.

Just like Twitchell, Krasniewicz does not see horror films as a threat and danger to the societal order, as so many people do, but instead as an important educational instrument that contributes to the maintenance and continuation of that order. It is exactly this kind of conclusion I see myself forced to each time I start to decipher the hidden messages contained in gruesome (video)films. They appear to be indispensable means of civilisation which, instead of provoking socially undesirable outbursts of 'wildness,' function to prevent these disorderly effects, and the breakthrough of unbridled sexual and aggressive impulses which would establish hell on earth.[32] Apart from also being dramatic means to express all sorts of fears and anxieties, the films some people want to censor – and sometimes even ban – can best be seen as particular kinds of educational device which, by using the disproportional, the monstrous, and the mysterious, broadcast moral messages about how one can, and must, deal with aggressive and sexual passions and emotions.[33] On closer examination these much-resented films do not differ much from the fire-and-brimstone sermons with which so many Christians are raised. In a sense they are paintings of Hieronymus Bosch coming to life, or sixteenth- and seventeenth-century scenes of witchcraft in which bodily dismemberment and mutilation figure prominently (see Zika 1997: 97). They are modern myths, which provide new means of orientation in a secularising world. If I am right, then the people who campaign against the distribution and consumption of these modern myths, and request the authorities to take legal measures against them because they could corrupt individuals and, as a consequence, society, should be glad, instead of alarmed. After all, it does not seem to be true that evil is steadily in the advance and only to be stopped by introducing stricter legal rules and regulations. Politicians should realise that giving in to pressure groups striving to legally muzzle the kind of modern public culture I am dealing with here, would in fact boil down to a serious maiming of a new mythology which appears not to spoil its consumers but instead may help them to design a socially acceptable course in a world in which unifying and binding narratives such as those offered by Christianity seem to be losing their appeal and orienting function. Seen from this angle, it seems that a state or government which gives in to pressure groups and lets itself be forced into the role of the exorcist of cinematic evil causes in the last instance more moral harm than it banishes. Moreover its officials should remember what Dubin succinctly stated (1992: 9):

> while censors may be the enemy of art and other types of expression, time is usually the enemy of the censor. References to censorship generally freeze a moment in the ongoing struggle between proponents of license and restraint. These are *episodes*, not necessarily finales.

Conclusion

In this chapter I have emphasised the significance of the consumption of seemingly 'wild' and 'uncivilised' modern myths – horror films – for the prevention of the moral corruption of individuals (especially adolescents) and, as consequence, for the maintenance of stable societies. It is time for scholars who specialise in Europe and the US to begin systematically studying the ways in which the media, especially films, function as sources of a new mythology and therefore morality in which – as with a former morality – graphic portrayals or manifestations of 'evil' abound. Though it might sound absurd, the producers of contemporary horror movies show a family resemblance with medieval monks who were also – at least some of them – engaged in representing and (re)producing detailed horror stories in which evil figured prominently, with no other purpose than making clear that although it might be fascinating, it will not lead to any good in this world or the next. Just as the religious modes of production, distribution and consumption of evil imagery has been, and still is, big business, the (post)modern horror film industry is equally so. In commoditising old and new fantasies about good and especially evil it does not only deliver its share to the economy, but also to the maintenance as well as transformation of moral standards, without which Western societies really would be endangered. Transgressive fantasies in which (the D)evil plays a prominent role are not only important in helping people to cope with the consequences of capitalism, but also in the same way as advertisements and television commercials, they play an important role in keeping it going. Although the association of advertisements with transgressive films might seem to be farfetched, I think there are reasons to think otherwise. In the first place one is nowadays often confronted with rather horrific ads and commercials – for example the ones Benetton uses to promote its products. Secondly, apart from this kind of superficial resemblance, one can also observe a deeper similarity. As I have tried to show, 'the abject', which fascinates and abhors at the same time, is explicitly shown in transgressive films with the implicit purpose of stimulating audiences to refrain from it and stay on the right (social and economic) track. In advertisements, by contrast, 'the abject' is implicitly present in a genre aimed at explicitly signalling the (moral and economic) good life. In order to persuade potential consumers to buy their products, advertisers offer a very orderly, safe, civilised, clean, pure, healthy picture of persons and places. In short, they present a world devoid of the abject – a kind of paradise on earth which will come true as soon as the advertised products are bought and used (see Sibley 1995: 62 ff.). One could therefore maintain that the abject is used in both cases, though differently. In the one case it is graphically shown and in the other it is evidently implied in the exaggerated pure and civilised pictures or strikingly present through its salient absence. In both cases it serves the continuity of the capitalist societal order. It is striking that the use of the abject by implication – as in advertisements and television commercials – is widely accepted, whereas its explicit use, as in transgressive films, is almost automatically associated with possible societal distortions and disruption. It is high time that we, and especially politicians and state officials who are confronted with requests to introduce decency laws, realise once again that implicit and explicit representations of evil and the abject are often in the service of the (capitalist) order which they themselves strive to maintain.

Notes

1. For critical comments on this essay, which I once upon a time presented as a paper in Washington and at Malta, I am most grateful to many colleagues in and outside the Netherlands, especially Birgit Meyer who always knows how to keep me going. It is written as part of a larger project on the development of the anthropology of the 'wild [in the] West' (see also Verrips 1993).
2. A few years earlier the Minister of Justice, Hirsch Ballin, raised a storm by

threatening the owners of videoshops and TV-makers with criminal prosecution, if they would not immediately control themselves with regard to renting out and showing violent movies. During a debate in Parliament his colleague, the Minister of Welfare and Culture, subtly reminded him of the Cabinet's decision to replace the film censorship board by what was called 'conditioned self-regulation' (*NRC/Handelsblad*, 22 December 1993). For an historical overview of film censorship in the Netherlands see Van der Burg and Van den Heuvel (1991).

3. In 1996 and 1997 the Minister of Justice, at the time Mrs Winnie Sorgdrager, regularly threatened to take legal measures against people who made it too easy for young people to watch films full of sex and violence. In this threat she too was joined by several of her liberal colleagues in the Cabinet. At the same time authorities everywhere in the country undertook actions against phenomena which they labelled as obscene and considered to be offensive. In Amsterdam the municipal council took measures against the public offer of indecent post-cards and confronted the gay scene with a decency code with regard to its yearly parade. In Leeuwarden some local politicians tried to prevent a show of the British group Rockbitch, and in Groningen authorities wanted to remove a photo by Serrano (showing a man urinating in the mouth of a woman) from an exhibition in the municipal museum.

4. Earlier the American Minister of Justice, Reno, had formulated similar views and threatened with legal measures. In 1996 the ex-Minister of Education, Bennett, started a Dole-like campaign against the violent nature of rap songs and the companies distributing them.

5. 'However, there is an important footnote to Dole's apparent hostility toward Time Warner. His "shaming" of Time Warner came despite the fact, which Dole later revealed, that the company had contributed 23,000 dollar to his campaigns' (Croteau and Hoynes 1997: 83).

6. In March 1996 it was indeed decided that from 1997 onwards all TV-programs would be rated, and that programs with this rating would eventually be transmitted by a special signal which could only be received by a v-chip. Just before this decision was taken in America the European Parliament already decided that in the near future it would be forbidden within the EU to sell TV-sets without such a chip (*NRC Handelsblad*, 1 March 1997).

7. In 1993 a small boy, James Bulger, was killed in Liverpool by two children who, according to popular accounts, were inspired by the videofilm *Child's Play III* (see Barker and Petley 1997).

8. It concerns a tightening up of the Video Recordings Act 1984, partially as a consequence of the pressure by the supporters of the Festival of Light (a religious organisation) led by Mrs Mary Whitehouse. She had campaigned all over England and said everywhere that the consumption of videonasties would lead towards an unacceptable moral decay. Prominent politicians, for example Home Secretary Willie Whitelaw and Prime Minister Margaret Thatcher, took her side in her campaign against these pernicious products of the imagination. Whitelaw, as so many others, was convinced of the fact that videonasties formed an incentive to crime and that it therefore should be made very difficult to obtain them. A report on the pernicious influence of videonasties by Elizabeth Newson published in April 1994 played an important role in this development within the political arena (see Barker 1997). However, at the end of 1997 psychologists of the University of Birmingham published an official report in which the conclusions of the Newson report were attacked.

9. See Miller who relates the upsurge of sex and violence in films around this time to the dismantling of the Production Code in the US and its replacement by a ratings system in 1968 (1994: 210). According to Paul 'the elevation of the lower body' already started with rock 'n' roll in the 1950s and was worked out in movies in the 1960s: 'Movie theatres increasingly became the arena in which to celebrate the lower body' (1994: 46/7).

10. It is interesting to compare this with the following remark made by Drake Douglas in the preface of the unchanged reprint of his 1969 book *Horrors!*: 'these elements are all too common in the so-called horror films of today, and as a result, instead of our comfortable old classic monsters, we are inundated with horrendous slashers in goalie masks, axe wielders, and homicidal maniacs' (1989: 7). See Creed for an illuminating overview of how the body is represented in horror movies. She distinguishes 'twelve "faces" of the body-monstrous' (1995: 136 ff.). An important role in this development of representing the body in diverse transforming and disintegrating states is played by the rapid, technical evolution of the special effects branch. For some fans of the genre these effects are the sole source of their fascination (see Dronkers 1996).

11. According to insiders the first splatter movie which had a great influence was *Blood Feast*, produced in 1963. Another movie with a great impact on the genre was George Romero's *Night of the Living Dead*, made in 1968 (Dronkers 1996: 28).

12. For this overview I used the excellent study by Enid Wistrich (1978). See also Robertson (1985) and the British journal *Scapegoat: The Anti-Censorship Magazine*. The first issue (1995) contains a fascinating and highly informative overview of the results of a survey on film censorship in almost forty countries. England is mentioned as one of the countries in which film censorship is becoming stricter than it used to be in the recent past.

13. In 1994 a number of German TV-stations decided to start with self-censorship (Freiwillige Selbstkontrolle Fernsehen) in order to prevent the broadcasting of too much sex and violence. In Germany there already existed a board of film censors (Freiwillige Selbstkontrolle der Filmwirtschaft) which just as in the US and England was founded by the film industry itself and which decides which films can or cannot be shown as well as to whom. 'Public prosecutor's offices and courts can forbid the showing of films which contain celebrations of violence and hard pornography (with children, animals or violence)' (*Stern*, 20 April 1995). For the rise of a new wave of prudishness in Germany, see Stark (1996).

14. So far, for instance, all efforts to control effectively the presentation on digital highways, such as Internet, of so-called 'cybersmut' have failed. But, especially in the US, the battle between people who want decency laws on the one hand and their opponents – known as 'blue-ribbon-campaigners' – is still going on.

15. It is interesting to note that orthodox Christians had no objection to the visual representation of the broad or evil path that in the last instance led to a burning hell. The reason for this was rather simple: the evil or broad path had a clear counterpart in the good or small path leading to heaven. In the cinema the explicit showing of such a counterpart was evidently lacking. In the Christians' view, in the cinema one was only confronted with worldly temptations such as disgusting sex and violence, whose consumption would in the end lead to the total moral corruption of self and society. See Birgit Meyer (1995) for an

interesting description and analysis of a nineteenth-century lithograph of the broad and narrow paths.

16. In this paper I focus on right-wing Christians. Of course, I realise that in the whole Christian spectrum attitudes towards media differ. While Pentecostals, for instance, share the criticisms referred to in this essay, at the same time they appropriate the modern media and indulge in 'televangelism' with much success. For a study of the attitudes of different Christian denominations towards modern media in the United States see Stout and Buddenbaum (1996).

17. Compare, for instance, Black (1994) for a thorough description of the activities of Roman Catholics in the US during the period 1920–40, when the Legion of Decency was formed, and the Lord Quigley Code introduced to cover the making of 'motion and talking pictures'.

18. The NVLA is still active. In March 1998 the organisation, together with the action group Family and Youth Concern, campaigned against the showing of Adrian Lyne's film *Lolita* because it was supposed to celebrate paedophilia. According to the British Board of Film Classification the film could be shown, because it was not against any law.

19. This is a nice illustration of how a phenomenon which for a long time was considered an expression of a contemptible 'goût populaire' can become an expression of the 'goût légitime,' to use Pierre Bourdieu's terminology (1984). See also Paul (1994: 45).

20. The advance of the video cassette recorder (VCR) started as a lower class phenomenon. Robert Potts (*The Guardian*, 22 March 1996) wrote: 'Any new medium, especially with mass appeal and best understood by the young, attracts a desire for governmental control. The attitude underlying that control – that certain material is likely to induce or uncover criminal tendencies in the susceptible user – is that there are a sufficient number of weak-minded people in the country to require their protection from the occult influences and provocations of representations of sex and violence.'

21. See the seminal study by Irene Cieraad *De elitaire verbeelding van volk en massa* ('The elitist imagination of folk and mass') (1988). She shows how the bourgeois elite has been continuously inclined to see 'rural people' as a morally good social group which it placed back in time and to see the 'urban mass' of labourers as an immoral collection of people showing what kind of future lay ahead, if no civilising offensive was started.

22. My focus on two groups does not mean that there are no others, who sometimes join in. A third group which played and still plays an important role in the war against a gross representation of sex and violence in journals and on screen is that of particular radical feminists (but see Pinedo 1997). A fourth consists of social scientists (ranging from educationalists to anthropologists) who claim on the basis of research done that certain media, especially films, have ill effects on their consumers. The first attacks from this side were already formulated in the beginning of this century (see Starker 1989: 95 ff.). Since then the stream of scientific publications on the supposedly evil influence of films, especially on (working class) children, and the necessity of control, even censorship in one form or another, has never stopped flowing. Frequently the works of social scientists are used in the war orthodox Christians, conservative liberals, and feminists have waged against the corruption of society by the media. However, these works are also very often used in defending the position, as I do in this chapter, that the ill effects have to be doubted, which once

more underlines the fact that (social) science can function as a double-edged sword. See in this connection Dubin who proposes to see censorship 'as a *social process* whose initiation is not the exclusive domain of either the political right or the political left' (1992: 9).

23. It is remarkable that it seems as if women in both cases are more active than men where it concerns the waging of war against the showing and free distribution of evil movies and so-called videonasties. There might be a relation with the fact that women still have more to do with child education and that they figure prominently as the victims of (sexual) violence in these products.

24. Moreover, I would like to emphasise that the frequent appearance of the ill-treated naked and destructed body in all sorts of recreational genres, but especially in horror films, reflects a particular view of society (see Douglas 1982: 65): namely as an extremely fragile and vulnerable whole which can easily be raped, dislocated, and destroyed by a number of very 'uncivilised' 'caresses' and 'blows.' Of course, such a view is embedded in a particular context which only arises under certain societal circumstances, circumstances under which people fear for the maintenance of their own physical integrity. Reasoned in this way, it would be possible to relate the mimetical manifestations of excessive 'wildness' to fundamental uncertainties regarding social life in Western societies (Carroll 1990: 213).

25. See in this context the plays by the Austrian playwright Werner Schwab, the scandalising work *The Law of the Remains* by the American stage manager of Iranian origin Reza Abdoh, and the recent opera by Peter Greenaway and Louis Andriessen *Rosa, a Horse Drama*. In this opera there is, for example, much explicit presentation of cruelty and corporeality.

26. In Christian circles there exists, for instance, the inclination to explain murder and homicide not in terms of the presence of a biblically based worldview – after all the Bible is supposed to teach respect for other people's lives – but rather in terms of its absence. If one lacks such a world-view, many of them argue, one can lose one's self-control and kill somebody. Christians tend to deny that it is possible that the presence of a biblically-based world-view can also lead to deviant behaviour. If they do not do this, they tend to qualify these terrible acts ('reli-murders' as I would like to call them) as unchristian aberrations inspired by the Devil – worse than 'normal' murders. A pathological elaboration of Christian beliefs and, as a consequence, the killing of others does not occur frequently, but nevertheless with a certain persistency comparable to the frequency of violent behaviour inspired by films (see Verrips 1987, 1997).

27. The comparison of films with modern myths – and of movie houses with temples – is a rather old one. See, for instance, Delaye and Rivette (1964), Coleman and Johnson (1994), Drummond (1996), and Brottman (1996). Drummond deals with myth making about the relation of men and machines, animals, and the future in American popular movies, Brottman analyses Tobe Hooper's *The Texas Chainsaw Massacre* as an inverted fairytale 'on the premise that film genres serve the same function as myths within an institutionalised, mass-mediated popular culture' (1996: 7).

28. In his study on horror films, in which he emphasises that they do not stimulate people to become (sexually) violent, Carroll draws a parallel with contemporary post-modernism: 'What I would like to suggest is that the contemporary horror genre is the exoteric (popular) expression of the same feelings that are

expressed in the esoteric discussions of the intelligentsia with respect to post-modernism' (1990: 210). See also Pinedo (1997: 9–51).

29. See also Skal (1993: 275–76) and Zillmann and Gibson, who write: 'The horror film . . . may be viewed as a significant forum for the gender specific socialisation of fear and its mastery in modern times, a last vestige of ancient rites of passage' (1996: 25).

30. In this connection it is interesting to mention the theory Bloch developed with regard to the nature and especially the effect of *rites de passage*. According to him Van Gennep and Turner completely missed to notice the fact that the whole ritual process implied in these rites can ultimately 'be understood as the construction of a form of "rebounding violence" both at the public and at the experiential level' (1992: 6). For Bloch *rites de passage* are violent happenings which often turn *initiandi* (prey) into potentially violent persons (hunters), who can become rather aggressive to animals and people. I can imagine that opponents of horror films would be charmed by his rather exaggerated theory of rebounding violence.

31. This is a film which did not stir the emotions as much as, for example, *Child's Play*, but it is a similar product.

32. 'Much as the horror film is an exercise in terror, it is simultaneously an exercise in mastery, in which controlled loss substitutes for loss of control. It allows us to give free rein to culturally repressed feelings such as terror and rage. It constructs situations where these taboo feelings are sanctioned' (Pinedo 1997: 41).

33. But see Harbord who notes with respect to such films as *Natural Born Killers*: 'Mainstream Hollywood crime film narrative conforms less and less to a simple moral framework, and can therefore be disconcerting or frightening for audiences. This (unacknowledged) disconcertion may underlie some of the panic expressed about violent films' (1997: 156).

References

Barker, M., 1997, 'The Newson Report. A Case Study in "Common Sense"', in Barker, M. and Petley, J., eds, *Ill Effects: The Media/Violence Debate*. London and New York: Routledge: 12–32.

Barker, M. and Petley, J., eds, 1997, *Ill Effects: The Media/Violence Debate*. London and New York: Routledge.

Black, G. D., 1994, *Hollywood Censored: Morality Codes, Catholics, and The Movies*. Cambridge: Cambridge University Press.

Bloch, M., 1992, *Prey into Hunter. The Politics of Religious Experience*. Cambridge: Cambridge University Press.

Boomkens, R., 1997, 'Veiligheid, angst en geweld; enige gedachten over de geweldsfilm', *Justitiële Verkenningen*, 23 (3): 9–21.

Bourdieu, P., 1984, *Distinction: A Social Critique of the Judgement of Taste*. Trans. Richard Nice. London: Routledge.

Brottman, M., 1996, 'Once Upon A Time In Texas. *The Texas Chainsaw Massacre* As Inverted Fairytale', in Black, A., ed., *Necronomicon*. London: Creation Books, Book 1: 7–22.

Buckley, S., 1993, 'Censored', in Massumi, B., ed., *The Politics of Everyday Fear*. Minneapolis: University of Minnesota Press: 171–81.

Carroll, N., 1990, *The Philosophy of Horror or Paradoxes of the Heart*. New York and London: Routledge.

Cieraad, I., 1988, *De elitaire verbeelding van volk en massa: Een studie over cultuur*. Muiderberg: Coutinho.

Clover, C. J., 1992, *Men, Women, and Chain Saws: Gender in the Modern Horror Film*. Princeton: Princeton University Press.

Coleman, S. and Johnson, M., 1994, 'Comic Relief: Lévi-Strauss Meets the Wolf-Man: Horror Movies as Myths', *Cambridge Anthropology*, 17 (1): 89–99.

Creed, B., 1995, 'Horror and the Carnavalesque: The Body-monstrous', in Devereux, L. and Hilman, R., eds, *Fields of Vision. Essays in Fim Studies, Visual Anthropology, and Photography*. Berkeley: University of California Press: 127–60.

Croteau, D. and Hoynes, W., 1997, *Media/Society: Industries, Images, and Audiences*. Thousand Oakes: Pine Forge Press.

Delaye, M. and Rivette, J., 1964, 'Entretien avec Claude Lévi-Strauss', *Cahiers du Cinéma*, 156.

Douglas, D., 1989, *Horrors!* Woodstock, New York: Pantheon Books.

Douglas, M., 1982, *Natural Symbols: Explorations in Cosmology*. New York: Barrie.

Dronkers, W., 1993, 'The Face of Evil; A New Perspective on Modern Horror-films with Regard to Bataille', Paper Presented at the Conference 'Body Images', Amsterdam, 6–9 July.

Dronkers, W., 1996, 'Slacht-Offer: Horrorfilms, horrorfilm-consumptie en offer', MA Thesis in Cultural Anthropology, University of Amsterdam, 1996.

Drummond, L., 1996, *American Dreamtime: Cultural Analysis of Popular Movies, and Their Implications for a Science of Humanity*. Lanham: Rowman and Littlefield.

Dubin, S. C., 1992, *Arresting Images: Impolitic Art and Uncivil Actions*. London and New York: Routledge.

Evans, W., 1975, 'Monster Movies and Rites of Initiation', *Journal of Popular Film*, IV (2):

Harbord, V., 1997, 'Natural Born Killers: Violence, Film and Anxiety', in Sumner, C., ed., *Violence, Culture and Censure*. London: Taylor and Francis: 137–59.

Krasniewicz, L., 1992, 'Cinematic Gifts: The Moral and Social Exchange of Bodies in Horror Films', in Mascia-Lees, F. E., and Sharpe, P., eds, *Tattoo, Torture, Mutilation, and Adornment: The Denaturalization of the Body in Culture and Text*. Albany: State University of New York Press: 30–48.

Kunkel, D., 1997, 'Why Content, Not the Age of Viewers, Should Control What Children Watch on TV', *The Chronicle of Higher Education*, 31 January: 4–6.

Lévi-Strauss, C., 1967, 'The Story of Asdiwal', in Leach, E., ed., *The Structural Study of Myth and Totemism*. London: Tavistock: 1–49.

Meyer, B., 1995, 'Translating the Devil: An African Appropriation of Pietist Protestantism. The Case of the Peki Ewe in Southeastern Ghana, 1847–1992', Ph.D. diss., University of Amsterdam, 1995.

Miller, F., 1994, *Censored Hollywood: Sex, Sin, & Violence on Screen*. Atlanta: Turner Publishing.

Morrison, D. E., and Tracey, M., 1978, 'American Theory and British Practice: The Case of Mrs. Mary Whitehouse and the National Viewers and Listeners Association', in Dhavan, R. And Davies, C., eds, *Censorship and Obscenity*. London: Martin Robertson: 37–109.

Paul, W., 1994, *Laughing Screaming: Modern Hollywood Horror & Comedy*. New York: Columbia University Press.

Pinedo, I. C., 1997, *Recreational Terror: Women and the Pleasures of Horror Film Viewing*. Albany: The University of Wisconsin Press.

Randall, R. S., 1997, 'Censorship: From *The Miracle* to *Deep Throat*', in Ballo, T., ed., *The American Film Industry*. Madison: University of Wisconsin Press: 432–58.

Robertson, J. C., 1985, *The British Board of Film Censors: Film Censorship in Britain, 1896–1950*. London: Croom Helm.

Sibley, D., 1995, *Geographies of Exclusion: Society and Difference in the West*. London and New York: Routledge.

Skal, D. J., 1993, *The Monster Show: A Cultural History of Horror*. London: Plexus.

Stark, J., 1996, *No Sex: Die neue Prüderie in Deutschland. Moralapostel und Lustfeinde auf dem Vormarsch*. Reinbek bei Hamburg: Rowohlt Taschenbuch Verlag.

Starker, S., 1989, *Evil Influences: Crusades against the Mass Media*. New Brunswick and London: Transaction Publishers.

Stewart, S., 1982, 'The Epistemology of the Horror Story', *Journal of American Folklore*, 95 (375): 33–51.

Stout, D. A. and Buddenbaum, J. M., eds, 1996, *Religion and Mass Media: Audiences and Adaptations*. Thousand Oaks: Sage.

Tudor, A., 1989, *Monsters and Mad Scientists: A Cultural History of the Horror Movie*. Oxford: Blackwell.

Turner, V., 1970, *The Forest of Symbols: Aspects of Ndembu Ritual*. Ithaca and London: Cornell University Press.

Twitchell, J. B., 1985, *Dreadful Pleasures: An Anatomy of Modern Horror*. New York and Oxford: Oxford University Press.

Twitchell, J. B., 1989, *Preposterous Violence: Fables of Aggression in Modern Culture*. New York and Oxford: Oxford University Press.

Van der Burg, J., and Van den Heuvel, J. H. J., 1991, *Film en overheidsbeleid: Van censuur naar zelfregulering*. 's-Gravenhage: SDU vitgeverij.

Verrips, J., 1987, 'Slachtoffers van het geloof. Drie gevallen van doodslag in calvinistische kring', *Sociologisch Tijdschrift*, 14(3): 357–407.

Verrips, J., 1993, 'Op weg naar een antropologie van het wilde westen', *Etnofoor*, VI (2): 5–21.

Verrips, J., 1996, 'The Consumption of "Touching" Images: Reflections on Mimetic "Wildness" in the West', *Ethnologia Europaea*, 26(1): 51–64.

Verrips, J., 1997, 'Killing in the Name of the Lord: Cases and Reflections Regarding Reli-Criminality in the Western World', *Ethnologia Europaea*, 27 (1): 29–45.

Weaver, J. B. III, and Tamborini, R., eds, 1996, *Horror Films: Current Research on Audience Preferences and Reactions*. Mahwah, New Jersey: Lawrence Erlbaum Associates.

Wistrich, E., 1978, *"I don't Mind the Sex, it's the Violence": Film Censorship Explored*. London: Marion Boyars.

Witcombe, R. T., 1975, *Savage Cinema*. London: Lorrimer Publishing Limited.

Zika, C., 1997, 'Cannibalism and Witchcraft in Early Modern Europe: Reading the Visual Images', *History Workshop Journal*, 44: 77–107.

Zillmann, D. and Gibson, R., 1996, 'Evolution of the Horror Genre', in Weaver, J. B. III and Tamborini, R., eds, *Horror Films: Current Research on Audience Preferences and Reactions*. Mahwah, New Jersey: Lawrence Erlbaum Associates.

8

The Iconography of Evil in Maltese Art

Isabelle Borg

University of Malta

Introduction

The subject of evil in art engages curiosity and sometimes fear. In Malta, where the Catholic Church has a powerful cultural and social influence, it is natural that images of the Devil have been used as part of the visual language of communicating the Divine message. However, the evolution of an iconography of evil, in a broader sense than the representation of demons or the Devil – as the most specific personification of evil – is not limited to a religious culture, but finds its fullest expression in the secular art of the twentieth century. By its very nature, art produced in a private context will reveal more of the artist's conscious or unconscious motivations. Certainly, where religion has played a major role in the formation of the habits of the majority, even the most person-alised interpretation of evil will find its roots in the visual traditions fostered by the Church, which through the centuries has played patron to artists ranging from the most highly trained humanists to the least skilled vernacular artists who nevertheless have suc-ceeded in portraying the dialectic of good and evil locked in con-flict.

This is a study of examples in Maltese art showing evil within a recognisable code, for example the Devil struck down by the Madonna or St Michael. In some cases the defeat of the Devil directly illuminates aspects of the Church's history – against Luther and the Turks, the latter particularly relevant in illustrating Malta's position of stronghold of southern Europe in the Mediterranean (see Bradford 1974, Mitchell in chapter three of this volume). In some of the more recent examples the artist may use known symbolic representation to give a personalised message. The personification of evil in the female gender is a relatively recent phenomenon, with some relevance in nineteenth-century art, and only found in the work of artists working outside the Church's patronage. This chapter examines various examples of the Maltese depiction of evil, analysing them in relation to artistic influence as well as social developments, demonstrating their

Noel Galea-Bason, 1988, *Giullare per un dio – Playing jester to a god*

clear reflection of particular cultural patterns – most notably, the Baroque.

Malta is a society with a strong religious culture. The over-whelming majority of its inhabitants are baptised into the Roman Catholic Church, take their marriage vows in a religious ceremony, and are buried after a *messa praesente cadavere*. Most Maltese attend Mass on Sunday and many on weekdays, and a number belong to religious confraternities (Boissevain 1965: 15–26, Mitchell 1996). It is expected that in some way this religiosity should be reflected in its artistic images, especially those produced in connection with the practice of worship and veneration, and which formerly illustrated religious texts as a means of informing the illiterate. The Devil does not play any overly dramatic part in the iconography of religious art, and hardly at all in secular art. However, by looking closely at the instances where it has appeared, we may find clues to the way people use this image as a means of visualising a concept which is grotesque, frightening, and threatening to the stability brought by a religious routine. Much of the social 'character' of Malta is built on the notion of conflict and duality and it may be expected that in religious art the Devil should appear as an adversary to the power of good which will overcome.

Such religious imagery, created to serve a function rather than an aesthetic principle, will of necessity deal with a formula, and the image of the Devil will conform to the Western Christian symbol of evil incarnate, with its complex origins both in the Judaeo-Christian and Graeco-Roman traditions, deriving from Pan, and the Oriental manifestation of Cosmic Chaos (Stanford 1996). When appearing in secular art, the Devil does not lose its role as adversary. However, a distinction can be made between images of the Devil – the Enemy who actively promotes evil; those of the various demons which although evil spirits are without the focus on absolute power; and images of evil which may be read in broader cultural terms. Rather than limit any appearances of the Devil to a particular category, this discussion of the iconography of evil in Malta will attempt to offer an overview of its development. Early examples are limited to a religious context, whereas later, the movement of visual symbolism into contemporary secular culture is reflected, as a paradox presents itself: the Devil as an adversary to be overcome has an easy popular familiarity, detracting from its ability to inspire fear, but on the other hand is portrayed essentially within the iconography of conflict which the Maltese have inherited as part of the Baroque sensibility.

Earliest Images of the Devil

The earliest known images of the Devil in Malta are in the medieval chapel at Bir Miftuh, of medieval origins (Bautier Bresc 1976: 115). Dated to the last decades of the fifteenth century, the fresco shows no influence of classical idealisation in the figures, which have a strong similarity to the type of figures which illustrated medieval texts in Northern Europe. On the wall above the west door are the remains of a fresco showing a scene from the Last Judgement, popularly known as 'the side of the Damned'. The opposite wall, above the east door, shows an equivalent scene; 'the side of the Just'. This typically medieval arrangement of opposites must have drawn the attention of early congregations to the activities of the white demons with the souls of the Damned, represented as naked women, in an un-idealised, rather naïve style. The horned semi-bestial pale demons are not frightening in their depiction but in their actions as they drag the Damned to their punishment – one is heaved into a flaming cauldron, another being led by the neck to the same fate. The faces of these demons are drawn in a primitive manner with cat-like grins, and hardly appear threatening. In comparison, a Pan-like profile of darker colouring on a fragment of gesso corresponds more to what we recognise as a typical depiction of the Devil with its origins in classical sources.

Another early image, dated to the mid-fifteenth century, depicts St Margaret and the Dragon.[1] The legend of Margaret of Antioch – removed from the Church calendar in 1969 – states that the Christian virgin, refusing to marry the prefect of Antioch, was tortured and thrown into a dungeon, where Satan appeared in the form of a dragon and devoured her. The cross in her hand, shown clearly in the Maltese fresco, caused the dragon to burst open and the saint to emerge unharmed. As is the case in many early paintings, the effectiveness of the narrative depends less on the artist's ability to evoke expression or a sense of reality than on the symbolic function of the image. The dark beast below the female figure is without doubt a dragon – a common symbol of evil and a direct representation of the Devil. Less certainty may be attached to the identity of the saint, who as well as the cross is also holding a short-handled instrument which may be an *aspergillum* – 'A brush with a short handle used by the priest in Catholic churches to sprinkle with holy water . . . those taking part in the ceremony of *asperges*. The aspergillum in art is particularly associated with the exorcising of evil spirits' (Hall 1974: 34). This would identify her as

Josef Kalleya, 1960s, *Portrait of Lucifer as the Prince of Light*

Martha, the sister of Mary, who subdued the Devil in the form of a dragon by sprinkling it with holy water. In the iconography of evil, the dragon is synonymous with the snake. In Christian texts both are used as interchangeable depictions of evil, and indeed both are signified by the Latin word *draco*.

The Snake

The spiral snake, which has been variously interpreted as a symbol of energy, fertility and the forces of nature, appears in prehistoric works of art in association with female figures. This snake's ancient symbolism, with no apparent connection to evil, seems to have roots in prehistoric Mediterranean cultures, eventually emerging as the goddess Athene/Minerva. In Graeco-Roman tradition the snake was associated with the qualities of Prudence and Logic (Hall, 1974: 209). Only much later does the snake take on the symbolism of evil, especially in connection with female imagery

(Dijkstra, 1986: 305), and most importantly to illustrate conflict and moral threat. The poisonous snake symbolised the pagan, anti-Christian element, and has appeared as a symbol of evil in much Judeo-Christian iconology.

The 'Miracic of St Paul' is a popular account of how the Maltese islanders were converted to Christianity the moment the ship-wrecked Saint threw off a viper, which had leapt from a fire and fastened on to his hand (Acts 28/3: 6). The fifteenth century *Retable of St Paul* in Mdina Cathedral, in Spanish International Gothic style (Buhagiar 1988: 15) is comparable to later Baroque examples, and particularly the images surrounding the nationalis-tic cult of St Paul in the nominal church in Valletta. The snake's spiral form in the imaginery of the altarpiece by Mattia Perez D'Aleccio is embodied in Melchiorre Gafa's titular statue, and most literally, coiled around the silver patina of the relic of St Paul's right hand: powerful symbols of Christianity over paganism, good over evil.

The Power of the Madonna over the Devil

In the iconography of Marian cults imported into Malta from Italy, a more specific representation of the Devil shows a serpent or demonic human figure being overcome by the positive powers of the Madonna. Of particular importance are the Madonna *del Soccorso*, or the *Succursus* Madonna, the Immaculate Conception, and the Madonna *della Lume* or *Tad-Dawl* – 'of Light' (V. Borg 1983: 87–102). While the first two date from the early sixteenth century, the latter is early eighteenth century. The cults were sufficiently popular to influence the dedication of various chapels and churches throughout Malta, and to become the subject matter of side-altars and other religious paintings in other churches.

In all cases the Madonna is depicted as a salvatrix of souls in danger and a superior force to the Devil. The rituals of veneration that grew up around these images include special prayers, feast cel-ebrations and the cult of the *ex-voto*, particularly through the phe-nomenon of *tabella* or small painting. This form of thanksgiving for a grace received was developed first in Naples and then moved to other southern Mediterranean towns, especially those with a strong tradition of Marian devotion. The *tabella* in Malta was a highly developed form of folk-art, each example containing an *ikon* of the saint whose intercession was sought for a grace. In most cases this was the Madonna, and here, the *ikon* was a version of the main altarpiece of the church, chapel, or side-altar where the cult was observed. As the artists who produced the *tabelle* were usually amateurs, the results were often in a well-intentioned but naïve style which replicated the image of the Madonna created by trained artists. Yet this very clumsiness increased its intensity as a holy *ikon*, providing a strong bridge between the common person and the mystery of faith by increasing its accessibility – a necessary step in the Church's campaign to unify the faithful during the Counter-Reformation. Much religious art, reproduced for a wide *public* audience, allowed the vernacular artist - with scant technical training yet a specialist in the field – to emphasise aspects of the iconography which were of particular dramatic interest. Features which were violent or ugly were exaggerated to draw attention to a narrative or symbolic meaning, essential to the ritual containing the image. In its varied forms and levels of artistic skill this is one of the recognisable features of late Baroque art, and one which may have indicated unconscious motives provoked by deeper fears.

In the iconography of the Immaculate Conception, the Devil is clearly overcome – crushed underfoot by the Madonna. In the late sixteenth century the growing popularity of this title, which has a tradition dating back to the fifth century, replaced the Marian cult of the *Succursus*, which was imported from Italy and showed the Madonna saving a child from the Devil. A surviving example, the *Triptych of the Madonna del Soccorso*, attributed to Salvo d'Antonio from Messina (1493–1526), is kept at the Cathedral Museum, Mdina (Buhagiar 1988: 28). As in the traditional iconography from Lucca, whence the late fifteenth century legend originated (V. Borg 1983: 88), the Madonna holds a stick in her right hand to beat off the Devil who appears in a dark archway and frightens a piteously naked child whom she enfolds protectively in her skirts. Two grotesque figures, one a soul in purgatory and the other a primitive, semi-bestial creature, are engulfed in the flames from which the Devil rises.

The representation of the creatures of darkness as somewhere between beast and human has a strong visual connection to the demons of Bir Miftuh. The contrast to the more humanistic treatment of the Devil in the Immaculate Conception, which by the seventeenth century had replaced the *Succursus* in churches and chapels throughout Malta, runs parallel to the general development of the human figure in European art during the High

Renaissance and early Baroque period. However, in the work of local artists with little outside contact, this gave way again to a more fanciful or beast-like representation towards the end of the seventeenth century.

The Immaculate Conception is the subject of titular and altar paintings and statues in a number of churches around the island, as well as in wall niches in town streets. An indulgence is granted to whoever recites a number of Hail Mary's under the image. In his study of the diffusion of the Marian devotions of the *Succursus* and the Immaculate Conception, V. Borg has specified which churches, chapels and altars throughout Malta are dedicated to these devotions, with 'a transitional development from the *Succursus* devotion to that of the Immaculate Conception' (1983: 88–89). An example by Mattia Preti (1613–99) at the Sarria Church, built in 1678 *in ex voto* for survival from the plague of a few years previously, is the main altarpiece of the Immaculate Conception showing the figure of the Madonna on a crescent moon with the Devil underfoot (V. Borg 1983: 259). Under him can be seen victims of the plague in death-throes. It is a composition that harks back to Preti's *bozzetti* for the Plague of Naples in 1656. Another painting of the Immaculate Conception, traditionally ascribed to Carlo Gimach (b. 1651), also shows the Madonna trampling the Devil depicted as a snake under the crescent moon. It perfectly corresponds with Paglia's interpretation (1990: 43):

> Mary trampling the serpent underfoot recalls pagan images in which serpent and goddess are one . . . the medieval Madonna, a direct descendent of Isis . . . has lost her roots in nature, because it is pagan nature that Christianity rose to oppose.

A further example by Giuseppe D'Arena (b. 1643) stylistically bridges the elegance of Preti and the decorative and rhythmic late Neapolitan Baroque. However, the apparition of the Devil within the horned moon, a symbol which appears in an apocalyptic vision of the Madonna in the Book of Revelations,[2] is considered to be a 'a touch of naïve realism' and 'to jar with the overall sophistication of the work' (Cutajar 1983: 52). As part of the iconography of the Immaculate Conception, however, it is consistent with other interpretations, by either trained artists or amateurs. In this context, at least, the 'vernacular' and 'high' art coincide.

In the popular religious art of the eighteenth century, a phenomenon occurred which was short-lived but pervasive – the votive cult of the *Madonna Tad-Dawl* – Our Lady of Light. The dream-vision of a Jesuit priest in Sicily in the first decades was transcribed into a composite *ikon* which had reached Malta by 1737 (V. Borg, 1983: 171). The Madonna is snatching a young boy away from the threatening figure of the Devil on her left, while the child Jesus, carried on her other arm, is offered a tray full of flaming hearts by an angel to her right. This image appears in the titular paintings of the altars of this dedication in churches throughout Malta. In some depictions, the image of the Devil has grown to a larger proportion and is threatening the boy that the Madonna is saving. The Madonna is seen here as an active *protectrix* rather than as a passive receiver of divine will, and the paintings show the Devil as a threat, the child representing an endangered soul in the same symbolic paradigm as the Madonna *del Soccorso*. The element of fear is produced in this vernacular image through the grotesque proportion of the Devil's monstrous head, with a huge mouth about to engulf the victim. A fear of being eaten may connect to other images of the Devil, particularly in medieval art (see also van Velzen and van Wetering, Geschiere, chapters one and two of this volume).

Baroque painting, intended for viewing by a public audience, had greater resemblance to the fantastic imagery of the medieval period than to the classically influenced, humanistic art of the Italian Renaissance which preceded it. It has greatly influenced the fervent veneration of images by the Maltese, and the symbolic significance attached to them. The almost caricatured depiction of the Devil is one of the features of D'Arena's work which made it popular among the clergy, conforming precisely to the dictates of the Council of Trent, which stated that religious painting should serve a representational purpose (Blunt, 1978: 110). In their didactic Counter-Reformation crusade, some seventeenth-century paintings paradoxically refer to pre-Christian art, even though the battle was on against all references to paganism. What was united had become divided into poles of opposing forces, but the totality of Baroque iconography served to fuse them into one complete image. Nowhere has this been so true as in vernacular art, where high art has been adapted to popular culture. This is typified in the composite *ikon* of the *Madonna Tad-Dawl*, which functioned as both narrative and holy image. In nineteenth-century art, the Madonna was no longer a powerful symbol of active good saving weak souls but a passive figure of docile piety, far removed from the persona of the *donna forte*, a European cultural phenomenon which had influenced the depiction of heroic female characters two hundred years before (Garrard, 1989: 171–72).

Fight the Heavenly Fight: St Michael the Archangel

Another example of iconography which has been vernacularised into widespread popularity shows the theatrics of the fight between Lucifer and the Archangel Michael:

> An angel with the key of Hell and a chain seized the dragon, 'that serpent of old', chained him, and threw him into a pit for a thousand years (Revelations vs 20)

A theme taken up by medieval artists, it was resurrected in Classical *contrapposto* by Raffaello Sanzio in 1518. Raffaello's painting was a break-away from the static iconography of Renaissance artists to whom the Archangel St Michael was a popular icon, and dramatically developed in the high Baroque idiom by Guido Reni (1575–1642) at the Church of the Capuchins in Rome. An engraving by De Rossi – *De Rubeis* – dated 1636 is the first of a series after this painting which would have been causal in spreading this image as an archetype throughout Europe. Reni himself made copies of the original (Pepper 1984: 272), which other artists also copied and exported to other countries. The image gradually entered the language of the vernacular Counter-Reformation iconography, open to unlimited adaptation to fit specific requirements. Mattia Preti's Maltese version of Reni's painting appears in the Co-Cathedral of the Order of St John, Valletta, dated between 1670 and 1680[3] The interpretation emphasises the humanity of the Devil, without resorting to caricature. The image keeps re-appearing countless times; on side-altars in churches, in reproductions on popular *santini*, and most sensationally as a sculpture in a wall-niche in Valletta. St Michael, in tight-fitting cuirass, stands triumphantly over the body of Lucifer who gestures upward with his right hand and scowls. The Baroque dynamics of Reni's painting are here interpreted in three dimensions, in the serpentine, centrifugal movement of the forms. A cartouche below the statue grants an indulgence of forty days to whoever recites a *Pater, Ave,* and *Gloria* to St Michael.

The popular legend, immediately refuted by Reni himself, that the face of the Devil was a thinly-disguised portrait of the enemy of his patron's family, lends itself to an interesting interpretation of this theme – and one very suitable to the Post-Reformist Church in Malta. Vernacular art at its most popular shows the Devil in the form of Martin Luther the Reformer, struck down by St Gaetano – or Cajetan – as a statue carved out of wood and decorated with gypsum and paint. This was borne in procession every year from the parish Church of St Gaetano, Hamrun, during the feast of this Saint, until it was damaged in a street-fight in 1991. The exact relationship between the Archangel and the Devil is so closely echoed that without a doubt there is a parallel motive in the iconography, and is suggested in the title which is *l-Eresija*, or *The Heresy*. It may be noted that no image of the Devil, either with the Archangel Michael or any denomination of the Madonna appears anywhere in the Hamrun Church, though there is a particularly gruesome *Ecce Homo* – a three-quarters statue of the mocked Christ wearing the crimson cape and crown of thorns of martyrdom with blood pouring from the eyes and mouth, in realistically painted plaster in a conventional form found in many churches. The sensationalism of folk art, of which this is an example, is repeatedly well expressed in the depiction of the Devil or evil in a grotesque form. The Devil's threat is in the direct quality of his ugliness rather than the subtlety of expression seen in works of art by the great humanists.

Since the late eighteenth century, small 'domestic' polychrome sculptured versions of Reni's image have been imported from Sicily and Southern Italy carved in alabaster, and copies locally made in wood. A model, in alabaster originally polychromed, shows St Michael and Lucifer in combat, on a detachable base of six writhing demonic souls in flames, similar to other similar alabaster statuettes in Malta. Painted versions by local naïve artists have also been privately commissioned and acquired (Vella personal communication). So far, the powerful and positive image of the Archangel Michael in victorious combat with Satan has been frequently copied in the most numerous versions, though each bears a direct visual link to Reni's original picture.

Tendencies in nineteenth-century painting bore less towards the theatrical symbolism of the Baroque and more in the direction of the Nazzarener movement which based itself on an interpretation of spirituality through realism. This did not mean that the symbolic image of St Michael was no longer sought for specific altars in the side-chapels of churches, only that it ceased to be re-interpreted by artists as a different version of the struggle, but regarded as an image which was as immediately recognisable as a Crucifixion and as readily copied. In Valletta, the niche of the statue of St Michael is aptly near the Market, and both the cult and Confraternity of St Michael, the patron of traders, grew in popularity in the nineteenth century, as the bourgeoisie blossomed. In the first few years of the twentieth century, a copy of a version of Reni's painting was made in marble mosaic for the altar of the Chapel of the Confraternity of St Michael in the Parish Church of St Paul's Shipwreck, Valletta. Here, rather than hideous, the Devil is suave and saturnine, a 'cool customer'. The Confraternity, patronised by the Guild of retailers, butchers, fishmongers and grocers, preferred to substitute their seventeenth-century painting with an unoriginal piece of fine craftsmanship in its eagerness to show its wealth, deciding that the permanence and value of the mosaic was a good replacement for paint on canvas.

'The Devil of the Brush'

Such was the epithet given to Giuseppe Cali` (1846–1930) by fellow Maltese artist Ignazio Carlo Cortis. Cali` was active throughout his life in the development of a number of religious themes for churches as well as private commissions (Fiorentino and Grasso 1991: 38–43). Cali` studied in Naples, where his parents had originated – the loose and confident brushwork of his style contrasts with the more rigid classicism of the Roman school which most Maltese artists of the period preferred, and is a sure reflection of this choice of academy. Apart from this he managed to infuse a narrative melodrama into his paintings, showing an ability to express a certain darkness and pathos which offset the heroic and ecstatic qualities – undoubtedly gaining him the popularity of a wide selection of patrons. In his interpretation of St Michael for the altarpiece of the Sacred Heart of Jesus Parish Church, Fontana, Gozo, the Saint stands proud over the vanquished Devil, portrayed as a dragon, in a stance which gives a romantic treatment to a medieval iconography – a static pose different to Reni's dynamic Baroque spiral and its many versions. The Devil's tail here is inscribed with the name of Cali`'s 'enemy', Mgr Paolo Pullicino, a powerful figure in the local Church who patronised a rival artist. In 1906, on the Devil's tail of another altarpiece, Cali` adds the names of Notary Zammit and Dr Muscat, signalling other adversaries of the artist (Fiorentino and Grasso 1991: 39). That an artist should relate the names of his opponents in life to the image of the Devil in a painting surely indicates a projection of personal enmity into religious vision. Yet despite introducing a new and instantly popular language of human expression into religious themes, Cali` did not find original ways in which to treat the iconography of evil. In his allegorical version of the Church's struggle with heresy, *St. Joseph as the Universal Church*, the composition includes a viper next to a book on the ground – yet another reference to the snake as a symbol of evil.

The Good Death and the Bad Death

The threat implied by the Devil waiting for the judged souls to fall into his grasp – by implication, the souls of the shopkeepers who cheated or gave short measure – grows to important proportions in the nineteenth century. The Catholic Church, sensing greater secularisation resulting from an increasing economic freedom, developed a strong popular culture which relied on readily available images for the communication of its ideas. These images may have originated from the Baroque paintings of artists with a Humanist background, but they were repeated and sold in quantity to private collectors – images of saints, crucifixions, Madonnas, and a peculiar parable called *il mewt it-tajba u il mewt il-hazina* – The Good Death and the Bad Death. This directly referred to the type of 'fire and brimstone' sermon that was preached from the pulpit with dramatic verve throughout the nineteenth century until the advent of the microphone in the late 1960s. Parishioners were warned of the terrors that awaited them if they did not strictly follow the commandments. The frightening image created out of the words of the preacher was clearly depicted in the image presented in the pair of pictures which appeared with increasing popularity in people's homes, usually in their bedrooms to remind them of their mortal fate before going to sleep. Basically, the *Good Death* showed a departing soul being serenely received into heaven by angels after a pious life, and the *Bad Death*, more dramatically being dragged off unwillingly by devils, leaving behind all the causes of his damnation.

In a similarly detailed but untrained hand as may be found in the naïve *ex-voto tabelle*, a small painting datable to the mid-nineteenth century illustrates the allegory of the *Bad Death*. The dying man on his luxurious bed – in the accompanying *Good Death* the mattress is made out of straw – is asked to make his final choice between the Cross his priest shows him in the Last Rites, or the casket of gold coins by his bed. A cord, tied to the sword of Damocles balanced over his temple, is about to be cut by Death. St Michael looks on in resignation, as the dying man turns towards his money. His heart is depicted resting on the coins, pointed out by one of the seven demons with pitchforks that surround him. One holds the scroll '*sette peccati mortali, che domandano vendetta, inanzi la giustizia di Dio*' – 'seven mortal sins, which demand retribution, institute the justice of God'. Another holds a portrait of his mistress in a gilded frame, eyes askance. On the left we see the Devil with cloven hooves in the wig and gown of a notary – an ironic comment about the profession – with the open book of deeds, stating '*350,000 denaro del Povero, rubbato, restituite il sangue del Povero o altrimente' al inferno*' – '350,000 denaro stolen from the poor, return their life's blood, or else to Hell'. Nearby, the frivolities of a life ill-spent lie wasted – a lute with music, a mask signifying both deceit and the theatre, a sword, and a set of cards. Above, Christ throws a thunderbolt, in the iconography of the Zeus-like *Cristo fulminante*. His Cross of Redemption is held by an unidentified figure, as 'Hope' in a green dress bows her head in humility. The lack of subtlety and the direct symbolism refer distantly to the medieval *Danse Macabre*, reminding God's creatures that Death awaits them all. The personification of Death and the frailty of Man is a recurrent theme in the iconography of fear in the Catholic Church where the rationality of Humanism has been less of an influence.

This iconography of evil is not only present in the public place of worship, but also in the private sanctum of the home. The nineteenth century was marked by an increase in the production of holy images, as demonstrated by the amount of oleograph reproductions available for sale, as well as the individually commissioned *santini,* or holy pictures, from artists who worked by copying readily available models. Until the early 1960's, printed images, nicely framed and hung near a night-light, would terrify and fascinate children sleeping in their parents' room, with their simplistic views of hell. More specifically for them, another *santino* was created, known as *The Guardian Angel.* It showed a boy on the edge of a cliff, reaching over to pick a rose from a bush below, while a devil behind pushed him. Meanwhile, a winged angel hovering above and dressed appropriately, kept a watchful eye on him and prevented him from falling. Such images were commonly available from shops which sold holy pictures, statuettes, and cards. This privatisation of art had wider consequences for the depiction of evil, which are discussed below.

Salome the Temptress

One of the great anti-heroines of Judaeo-Christian culture and a grand subject for both literary and visual images was Salome. She has a particular place in Malta's own religious-historical culture because of her crucial role in the Biblical story of the martyrdom of

St John the Baptist. The Knights of St John ruled Malta in effective theocracy from 1530 to 1798, and, as the Sovereign Military Order of Malta, still have a presence on the islands. A seventeenth-century depiction by Mattia Preti (1613–99) in the Co-Cathedral of St John, formerly the Knights' conventual church, shows Salome's dance, with which she 'won' the head of the Baptist. Painted in a grand manner with overtones of Veronese, and undertones of dark realism and drama, Salome's dance is more courtly than pagan, and she is dressed gracefully in contemporary seventeenth century costume, conforming to post-Tridentine requirements of decency in religious art. The Devil leans precariously over the roof above the action – a subtle interpretation as he gestures silence, almost superfluous to the tension held at the front of the tableau. Here, evil is depicted as discreetly apart from the human characters in the story, but himself possessing great humanity. Indeed, the Devil appears almost more human than the figure of the vanquished Turk that prominently sits above the main Cathedral door. This figure is more directly related to a recognisable visual iconography of evil than the Devil himself – a contorted horizontal figure in the same position as Reni's Lucifer in the struggle with St Michael.

Images of evil have not always confined themselves to religious art. The examination of art with a strong religious motivation reveals different interpretations strongly connected to the nineteenth century. The personal motivation for making these images, independent of Church patronage, makes the images worth analysing as projections of the artists. There was a strong fashion in European art of the late nineteenth century which showed images of women as a soul-threatening force rather than a symbol of fertility and abundance (Dijkstra 1986: 377). The depiction of the 'wicked woman' in art represented *bad* in the active principle, and the concept of evil as glamour was born. Rather than the traditional depiction of a figure with horns and a tail, evil became personified in women. Anton Spagnol depicted Salome in the persona of a demonic temptress (1993) and with more emphasis on fantasy than evil, Salvu Mallia visualised Salome as a TV siren with pneumatic breasts and Barbie-doll proportions, surely an ironic comment on cultural influences through the media (1994). Maltese conservatism, in which female glamour is considered evil, sporadically surfaces in the local press, as letters from members of the Church and its vocal supporters severely criticise topless sunbathing and provocative clothes as an immoral threat to family decency. In late 1995, Italian variety shows were lambasted as an influence on the growing rate of schoolgirl pregnancies. Such tensions, logically clarified, are bound to be reflected in images of evil, whether ironically or unintentionally (see also Mitchell, chapter three of this volume).

Noel Galea-Bason's Work

A more subtle statement was made in 1988 by Noel Galea Bason in a horned image in a bronze cast bas-relief *Giullare per un dio – Playing jester to a god*. A jester's head, with a belled cap symbolising horns, is juxtaposed on to a hermaphrodite's body, suggesting the erotic power of the Devil as a force combining both male and female elements. Through different periods the image of the hermaphrodite has been created as a powerful fusion of the sexes – the name *Hermaphroditus* has been used since Pliny's time for the androgen born of the union between Hermes and Aphrodite which had its roots in the Far East but was appropriated and developed in an idealised form in Greek art (Duca, 1961: 38). Notably, a gently suggestive feminine cast is given not only to the features of the face but also the body, apart from the penis, of the *Sleeping Hermaphrodite* (3rd century BC) and the Hellenistic bronze *Hermaphrodite*, both at the Louvre (Paris). In contrast, Noel Galea Bason's work basically represents a male figure and face – which has features similar to the artist's own – but with strongly delineated female breasts, giving the image a powerful, sexually ambiguous, *active* content, as though there are some darkly ludic forces at play. This is also suggested by the jester's crown and typical jester's pose – ironically obsequious and approaching a posture of *arlecchino* in the *Commedia dell'Arte* – with every intention to create confusion, but not without humour.

The reference to the more demonic (uncontrolled) energy of creative forces brings to mind the *duende* of Spanish mythology. This is a demonic sprite, a nature-spirit, which makes mischief, usually of a sexual nature, among humans, but is also an indication of a deeper and darker spirit of creation within the human psyche, as described by John Berger (1965: 38) quoting Lorca:

> These dark sounds are the mystery, the roots thrusting into the fertile loam known to all of us, ignored by all of us, but from which we get real art.

Berger describes the *duende* as 'a kind of undiabolic demon' yet one whose presence, either in life or in art, is bound to have tragic consequences. For all its playfulness, Galea Bason's image is the one which most closely approaches the fatal side of sexuality in contemporary art, without resorting to either cliché or pathos – the formal aspect of the work has a certain classicism about it which makes it deceptively harmonious and therefore easy to look at, and be 'taken in' by, which is surely the artist's intention. The title plays on the Faustian notion that some exchange of power is due. In more ways than one it approaches Mannerist *seicento* art which was made with the privacy of the collector in mind, as well as his cultured knowledge of antique mythology. Indeed, Galea Bason's work is occasionally bought in secret by *male* collectors who keep it hidden, showing it only to other male friends, because of its explicitly erotic content emphasising uncontrollable female power. This could be said to reflect the element of mystery and fear associated with female sexuality, still pervasive in contemporary Maltese society.

The Image of Devil in the Work of Psychiatric Patients

Quite apart from such self-conscious symbolism of sexuality and power, a poignant depiction of the Devil comes from mentally disturbed patients during art therapy. In 1989 Joe Busuttil organised an exhibition of the work produced over a fifteen-year period at Malta's Mount Carmel Hospital, where he conducted sessions in the Therapy Unit. Quoting André Malraux's description of the violence and darkness of the psychiatric patient's work because of the fear and confusion inspiring him, he describes art therapy as a way of 'exorcising demons' (Busuttil 1990: 501). The Devil, or image of evil, sometimes appears in the work of schizophrenics. Delusions, illusions, and hallucinations give rise to feelings of religious guilt which they express verbally in terms of the battle between Good and Evil – sometimes, but less often, these feelings are projected visually, either in clay through sessions in ceramics, or in drawings or paintings. The art of the mentally disturbed was considered a valuable source of unconscious imagery by European artists at the beginning of the century working in the Expressionist movement or connected to it. Later, the Surrealists and the Art Brut movement also drew on the themes of the mentally ill.

Examples of the work produced at Mount Carmel include an expressive ceramic sculpture by an ex-heroin addict. *The Demon of*

Compulsion stands in a corner between two right-angled mirrors, reflecting the equally divided face of the onlooker. Clay is a particularly good medium through which to express feeling, as unconscious impulses might not be adequately visualised by linear means, through lack of skill. Images produced in therapy rely more on symbolism than on representational ability – a simple picture by a schizophrenic patient includes a crucifixion with the Devil on the left-hand side and an angel on the right, as though the patient identified himself with the sufferings of Christ, whose face is obscured. The other drawing by this patient shows the Devil in control, seated on a throne, while four other demons holding pronged spears face him, one bowing. The codes are recognisable but ideational, unlike the skull and syringe produced by another patient, which clearly expressed the threat of Death in connection with drugs, though the Devil's power to tempt was not suggested.

The humanisation of the Devil – or Evil – in Maltese art recalls Dostoevsky (1927: 299):

> If the devil doesn't exist, but man has created him, he has created him in his own image and likeness.

A certain power and individuality is given to the Devil, in contrast to the popular symbol of the snake, which may represent evil, but goes no further in emotive terms. For both artist and viewer, the more sophisticated and 'human' the depiction, the more subtle and close to home it is. That said, the depiction of conflict with evil or the Devil is a rare feature of contemporary 'sacred' or 'religious' art. Rather, it is in the secular search for spirituality that the standard iconography of snake, woman and Devil appear. In the work of one particular artist, the image of the Devil has a more complex origin, having its roots in his own spiritual search reflected in his writings and through the memories of those who knew him closely.

Josef Kalleya – a Spiritual Journey

The Devil is one of the characters populating the stage of Josef Kalleya's rich spiritual life, one which has been described as a journey of questions leading to an almost subversive individualism in his experience as an artist and poet (E. V. Borg 1998). His death in October 1998, at the age of one hundred years, led to the immediate organisation of two events to commemorate and celebrate his life and work, which is now recognised as a breakthrough in the Expressionist idiom in Malta (Vella, 1998), although it is detached from any parallel movement elsewhere. He is regarded as a wholly indigenous phenomenon, a fact reflected in the service of commemoration which was a wholly *Maltese* event. No attempt was made to explain or advertise it to outsiders. Yet, his life-long closeness to Italian culture gives a clue to the origin of his meta-physical searching, his identification with Dante as the traveller who meets the Devil in his journey to God. His poem, *L'uccisione della Bestia* – The killing of the Beast – was read during the event. As we meet his Black Prince,[4] the brilliant muse of art, who seeks re-union with a Divine Eden of primordial innocence, we may understand Kalleya's argument that as an artist, his hope of salva-tion should be extreme humility. Pride would cast him out, and simply emphasise the transience of art. In his meditations on redemption, he conceived the Devil as a prodigal son who sought reconciliation and will eventually return.

Kalleya 'carved what he wrote: Satan kisses Christ through Judas's lips in the Garden of Gethsemane' (Attard 1998: 14–15). His method of working was to scratch and carve a language of ideograms, lines and symbols, onto brittle or unstable surfaces which seemed purposely to challenge any classical idea of formal-ity or permanence. Though Kalleya studied in Rome in the 1930s, his rejection of classicism and movement away from current Italian artistic strata indicated his development towards the most striking example of Maltese regionalism – and his engagement with the Devil is the strongest proof of the individualism that prevails among Maltese artists as 'loners' in a very small and conservative society. Here, images of the Devil exist on a note which, though conscious of the dominant religious teaching, is bonded to the artist's personal pre-occupations – which Kalleya was more than willing to share with his confidantes (Attard personal communica-tion), and which provides a key to decode some of the marks in his work which may at first glance be purely formal.

His fluidity as a draughtsman combined with expressive ability are seen in his drawings of the Devil. In *Portrait of Lucifer as the Prince of Light* (1960s), the face of an elegant young man is drawn incisively in pastels on a background of brown paper covered in lines which initially appear to be scrawls, but on closer examina-tion reveal a structure hinting at his hieroglyphic symbolism. A more unlikely interpretation of the Devil is not to be found anywhere in local art, as Lucifer's subtlety of expression – calm yet haughty – is a clear depiction of the abstract notion of Pride. A different, more dynamic energy runs through his more primitively drawn *Lucifer* (1977) in red and black slashes of chalk, in profile, like flames in the wind. The iconology is curiously linked to that of his sculpture *Christo Lacrimante* (1938), and *Dante* (before 1976) as we can perceive the vertical jagged lines on his face as tears – in Lucifer's case, expressing regret for his sin of pride. This is a mature and compassionate development of his earlier interpretation – Kalleya's beautiful but cold youth, calculated to attract but strike fear simultaneously. It does not oppose the notion that 'the European idea of an Anti-Christ presents a serene and beatific face masking hideous malevolence' (Parkin 1985: 18). Though unconventional, Kalleya concurs with tradition, and as a moralist, issues a warning through his art.

Conclusions

Maltese images of evil are in constant relationship to a changing society, and images of the Devil imported through the Church have been copied from existing material, combining a traditional basis with direct links to developments in European artistic movements. References to the Devil also appear in indigenous folk art, although not in great profusion. No images of evil or the Devil were revealed in a search of documents regarding Devil-worship and witchcraft accusations in seventeenth-century Malta (Cassar 1993: 316–34).

In contrast to other European societies where peasant art has revealed demonic images which are intentionally decorative and amusing, the Devil in Maltese folk art is unambiguous. Evil, however depicted, represents a threat – a danger which one may avoid either through the intercession of the Madonna, or through leading a good life as prescribed. Here we have examined and emphasised the difference between public art in the sixteenth to eighteenth centuries, and the private patronage of art mostly produced for homes in the nineteenth and twentieth century. Included within the latter category are the *ex-voto tabelle*, incorporating a personal element relating to the donor's experience, but nevertheless produced for churches. Whilst the former might be described as doctrinal in its emphasis and orientation, the latter present more of an opportunity for deviation from the official. For example, a late eighteenth-century *ex-voto tabella* at one church dedicated to the

Madonna shows a swarm of demons issuing from the mouth of a girl after being exorcised (Buhagiar, 1983: 73). The representation demonstrates an artistic license taking it beyond the actual rite of exorcism. As a participant in rites of exorcism explained to me, 'the image of evil and the experience of confronting its reality and overcoming it through exorcism are two different things'. This suggests that the proliferation of images, invented in the manner of previously made archetypes, emerge as non-standard formulations of evil, that are nevertheless recognised by us as realistic forms which we are sensitive to and afraid of.

Examples of eighteenth-century vernacular art show a fear of being eaten, or of the Devil invading cultural and intellectual life – as in the San Gaetano statue. In both cases the emphasis is on the struggle between good and evil, which strongly reflects the Baroque culture imposed by the Church, best exemplified in the image of St Michael Archangel and Satan. In the nineteenth and the first part of the twentieth century images of the Devil and of evil in art were a continuation of previous ideas, but with a strong emphasis towards a particular purpose – that is, to educate an audience by warning them of the dangers that might befall them, underlining the responsibility of their choices. Many of these reminders – for example *The Good Death and the Bad Death* – now began appearing in the private homes of people, or continuing a specific iconography – for example the serpent in St Paul, or Satan in St Michael. Nineteenth-century art also reflected a duality of intention between art produced for outsiders – travellers, tourists or British colonial functionaries who bought views of the harbour or idealised country scenes (Sant Cassia 1993: 357) – and art produced for insiders. This was part of the continuing Baroque tradition — it is here that images of the Devil are to be found. The Baroque produces art as an offer of gifts to the divine:

> the desperation expressed in art forms corresponds to the more generous giving of gifts, to a stronger appeal, to an increasingly impatient magical invocation to draw the divine down into everyday life . . . to magnify and increase the gift presented to God, so as to entice Him into the labyrinth of human exchanges ... at the time when capitalism was forcing Europe into the modern age. (Duvignaud 1967: 84)

This focus on exchange is most directly manifest in the *ex-voto*, where folk traditions of giving in exchange for security are materialised in the production of art. Likewise, images of the Devil, like scenes of martyrdom, are prompted by the duality of appeasement and fear – elements intrinsic to a Baroque society and representation.

In the later part of the twentieth century, the demonisation occurs in a private context, made either for a particular audience, or ultimately as an expression of the artists' own experience. Art produced independently of religious patronage reflects the individual concerns of the artists. By its very nature, this is likely to contain an intended element of conscious self-irony or even moralising – unless it is the therapeutic exorcism of fears which are internalised. If we are seeking original statements about evil it is among these works that we are likely to find examples, though even Noel Galea Bason makes his choice from a given stock of images in a consciously subversive manner, while other artists, like Spagnol, do this in a way which is consonant with the teachings of the Catholic Church. It is in the art of Josef Kalleya that we find an iconography which is at the same time coded as a message to those who can 'read' it. As a humanist, he depicts Satan not as a grotesque caricature but as one who has a chance of redemption through divine mercy, like all others. In one strange drawing, his inclusion of the Devil in a cryptic exhortation to whoever studies his work is not directly through an image but through the words which accompany four biro sketches of the poet-philosophers:

> A few thoughts . . . he stood closest to the Creator – he lost his beauty – he rode his unruly horse over the world. Origene, Dante, Papini, Milton and other great thinkers plumbed the depths of this terrible mystery . . . *Study him*. (Kalleya 1998)

Notes

1. Datings for both the Bir Miftuh frescos and the icon of St Margaret and the Dragon were provided by Dominic Cutajar, Curator of the Museum of Fine Arts, Malta.
2. 'a woman robed with the sun, beneath her feet the moon, and on her head a crown of twelve stars' (John, 12: 1–6).
3. Dated by Dominic Cutajar.
4. A reference to Iris Murdoch's *The Black Prince*, 1973, London: Chatto.

References

Attard, C., 1998, 'Wishes Ever So Great', in *Kommemorazzjoni Josef Kalleya M.O.M. 1898–1998*. Malta: Ministry of Education.

Bautier Bresc, G., 1976, 'The Paintings at Hal-Millieri', in A. Luttrell, ed., *Hal-Millieri: A Maltese Casale, its Churches and Paintings*. Malta: Midsea.

Berger, J., 1965, *Success and Failure of Picasso*. Harmondsworth: Penguin.

Blunt, A., 1978, *Artistic theory in Italy 1450–1600*. Oxford: Oxford University Press.

Boissevain, J., 1965, *Saints and Fireworks: Religion and Politics in Rural Malta*. London: Athlone.

Borg, E. V., 1998, 'Creative and Active at 100 Years', *Malta This Month*, May: 26–30.

Borg, V., 1983, *Marian Devotions in the Island of St Paul*. Malta: Lux Press.

Bradford, E., 1974, *The Shield and the Sword: the Knights of Malta*. London: Fontana.

Buhagiar, M., 1988, *The Iconography of the Maltese Islands 1400–1900*. Malta: Progress Press.

Busuttil, J., 1990, 'An Art Therapy Exhibition: a Retrospective View', *British Journal of Occupational Therapy*: 501–03.

Cassar, C., 1993, 'Witchcraft Beliefs and Social Control in Seventeenth-Century Malta', *Journal of Mediterranean Studies* 3, no. 2: 316–34.

Cutajar, D., 1983, *Marian Art during the 17th and 18th Centuries*. Malta: Friends of the Cathedral Museum.

Dijkstra, B., 1986, *Idols of Perversity*. Oxford: Oxford University Press.

Dostoevsky, F., 1927, *The Brothers Karamazov*. London: J. M. Dent and Sons.

Duca, L., 1961, *De Erotica: A History of Eroticism*. Paris: Jean Jacques Pauvert.

Duvignaud, J., 1972 [1967], trans. T. Wilson, *The Sociology of Art*. London: Paladin.

Fiorentino, E. and Grasso, L.A., 1991, *Giuseppe Cali`*. Malta: Said International.

Garrard, M. D., 1989, *Artemisia Gentileschi*. Princeton NJ: Princeton University Press.

Hall, J., 1974, *Dictionary of Symbols and Subjects in Art*. London: John Murray.

Kalleya, J., 1998 [1973] trans. from Maltese, 'Origene, Dante, Papini, Milton, dated 25th January 1973, Friday 3am and inscribed "to my dearest biographer E.V. Borg with greatest admiration"' in *Kommemorazzjoni Josef Kalleya M.O.M. 1898–1998*. Malta: Ministry of Education: 3.

Mitchell, J. P., 1996, *Gender, Politics and Ritual in the Construction of Social Identities: the Case of San Pawl, Valletta, Malta*. Edinburgh, Unpublished PhD thesis.

Paglia, C., 1990, *Sexual Personae: art and decadence from Nefertiti to Emily Dickinson*. London: Yale University Press.

Parkin, D., 1985, 'Introduction', in D. Parkin, ed, *The Anthropology of Evil*. Oxford: Basil Blackwell: 1–25.

Pepper, S. D., 1984, *Guido Reni: A Complete Guide to His Works with an Introductory Text*. Oxford: Oxford University Press.

Sant Cassia, 1993, 'The Discovery of Malta: Nature, Culture and Ethnicity in Nineteenth Century Painting', *Journal of Mediterranean Studies* 3, no. 2: 357–77.

Stanford, P., 1996, *The Devil: A Biography*, London, Henry Holt.

Vella, D., 1998, 'Salvation', in *Kommemorazzjoni Josef Kalleya M.O.M. 1898–1998*. Malta: Ministry of Education: 3.

Conclusions: The Political Economy behind the Powers of Good and Evil

Paul Clough[1]

University of Malta

To comment on the great variety of ideas and images of good and evil analyzed by our authors, risks doing injustice to their insights into specific regions of the world.

The volume includes articles as diverse as Jojada Varrips' provocative essay on the place of video nasties in the Dutch social order (chapter seven of this volume) and Hildi Mitchell's exploration of the ormon cosmology of good and evil (chapter six).

This essay simply tries to distill some patterns from the daunting complexity. But it does so in a particular way. I am primarily concerned with the connections between the religious imagination and power, as a political, economic and intellectual construct. I will argue that five themes emerge from reflecting on the rich material in this volume concerning the forms of both religious imaginings and the social organization of 'force'.

First, most of the contributors discuss communities or societies which have often been defined as Peripheries in relation to a global Centre, or as 'pre-modern' undergoing the throes of 'modernity'. The contributors study the development of social beliefs and relationships in response to impulses emanating from the industrial, scientific heartland of northern Europe and North America. The fact that most of these societies were colonies of Western empire and are moving with each passing year into the problems of a post-colonial world, gives added interest to these accounts. Even Hildi Mitchell's chapter on Anglo-American Mormons can be construed as a fascinating account of a conceptual and actional 'periphery' in the centre of the United States.

Secondly, the articles invite us to address the question: to what extent are Peripheries mentally and conceptually dependent on, or subordinate to, the value-and-thought systems of the Centre? For example, Meyer argues that Pentecostalist Christianity in Ghana is a movement in which people are trying to come to terms with the commodities emanating from the West, and a value system which stresses the moral right of the individual to seek self-gratification. In contrast, Geschiere's analysis of changing witchcraft in Cameroon paints a picture of the interplay between Western and African systems of belief, power, production and exchange.

Inversions of Power – Gaps in Power

A third main theme to emerge is power. Van Velzen and van Wetering show that historical moments when people visualize the invasion of dangerous supernatural beings, can be aligned with inversions of power between young and old, female and male, in a world 'gone awry'. In societies very differently situated in time and space, accusations of witchcraft or demonic possession intensify when communities feel their marginality in relation to an economic growth pole in world trade. This trauma reverses the ordinary scheme of power: women accuse men (Suriname), children accuse adults who are then condemned to execution (Sweden), young girls accuse rich male merchants (New England). Geschiere's discussion of the complex discourses of occult power in Cameroon reveals that the supernatural is imagined as both invisible and highly physical. Among the Bakweri, young men accused old men of witchcraft, believing them to constitute a magical barrier to enrichment during the banana boom. Elsewhere, a complex discourse concerning the occult envisages sorcery as inflicted on the rich, but at the same time, the wealthy are associated with the invisible power to protect themselves against sorcerers. In the savanna, chieftaincy represents a conceptual pole around which people see the power to contain occult forces. But they also see a change in the balance of economic and political power: a new business and political elite is using the occult in order to become rich. In the Mediterranean island of Malta, Jon

Mitchell analyzes the conditions which have led people to construe the invasive power of drugs, commodities and hedonism as being supernatural in origin. Also in Malta, Theuma's account describes how Catholic Charismatics are seeking through the power of the Holy Spirit a more direct order over society undergoing rapid change, than that provided by traditional Church rituals and beliefs. In America, Hildi Mitchell's analysis of Mormons demonstrates not only that they believe church leaders to be in direct contact with God; they also see personal problems as the result of Satanic affliction, to be remedied by the invocation of God's power in the lay priesthood.

Geschiere's study of witchcraft beliefs in various societies of Cameroon introduces the fascinating idea that people are conscious of a 'power imbalance' arising from the colonial political economy – even of a 'gap' between the international existence of power and its absence from local society. Local consciousness of various kinds of 'power imbalance' or 'power gap' partly explains the proliferation of discourses about unseen powers controlling social life. Through all of the societies which he explores, there is an awareness of powerlessness in the growing sense of a vacuum in communities, into which evil spirits step. In the savanna, where chiefs exercised a central spiritual authority in the past, the 'dangerous powers of the new rich' signify a decline in the stable local control of occult power. In the forest, communities imported a fetish to control evil spirits, only to find after a period of years that the keepers of the fetish had become corrupted. Along the coast, the longstanding association between chiefs, entrepreneurs and witch-doctors has been replaced by a growing fear that sorcery is out of control, because it attaches to anyone involved in the market economy. People complain that elders no longer control the occult. Boy healers have emerged amid popular alarm at the multiplication of evil spirits. The belief that international power is involved in this local decline is conveyed in the story that European sorcerers and phantoms were undermining the stability of local obligations. Mount Kupé was even described as a relay station in the traffic of local victims to Europe!

It is interesting to compare these fears of the Other with the very different beliefs of the *sapeurs* in Congo-Brazzaville (Friedman 1990: 324). When workers return from France, they pour their energies into the imitation of Western lifestyles, because the *accumulation* of Otherness signifies power (ibid. 324). Cameroonian anxieties also contrast with the Cargo Cults which rose up in the

Melanesian Pacific in the wake of colonial conquest and the attraction of Western commodities. These movements believed that a cornucopia of Western material goods would shower down by supernatural means. Accepting the doctrines of the cult, and often following its visionary leader, people rejected established cultural patterns and hoped for a Millennium of Western prosperity (Burridge 1969, Worsley 1968).

Anxieties about unseen powers often refer to a power which is distant or overwhelming. During the seventeenth century in the remote areas of rural Sweden, witchcraft accusations visualized the Devil as flashily dressed in the manner of a merchant or manager at the giant copper mine of Falun, an international engine of growth in the Swedish economy. Today, among the Ndyuka of Suriname, the problem is that when a person acquires a demon in order to exercise control over others, he cannot control its explosive multiplication (van Velsen and van Wetering, chapter one of this volume). In Cameroon, a great change has occurred in occult discourse. It has replaced witches who eat their victims with witches who sell the souls of their victims to invisible plantations where they labour to make witches rich. This new discourse originated in Duala, the first and major point of contact with European trade, and people directly link the idea of selling a person to the old slave trade (Geschiere, chapter two of this volume). There have been similar changes in occult discourse among the Ewe of Ghana. Fears of jealous witches who consume their more wealthy kin are changing to anxieties that the witch spirtually sacrifices a family member for quick money gain. Moreover, the narratives concerning *Mami Water* spirits, circulating along the African coast, locate the power to acquire Western commodities *outside* the society – at the bottom of the ocean, among White or Indian spirits (Meyer, chapter four of this volume). In Malta, the rising desire for goods and pleasures, sometimes associated with Satan, is seen to be foreign in origin (Jon Mitchell, chapter three of this volume).

In another study, Ralph Austen also posits an association between magic, wealth, danger, death, and external power. For him, it is striking that several West and Central African cosmologies link witchcraft with the deployment of victims in a nocturnal or distant 'second universe' echoing the Atlantic slave trade. Witchcraft is part of a discourse linking the acquisition of wealth and power to a more powerful outside world (Austen 1993: 89, 91–92).

The Persistence of Non-capitalist Logics in a World Power System

The intermingling of historical residues and present perceptions in the religious imagination leads me from the issue of power to a fourth theme – violence. Palpably, these are beliefs and images of a horribly destructive power. We are drawn to ask what kind of international economy is implied in these narratives of good and evil. We need to consider the forcible submission involved in the development of world markets. Among the disenfranchised of different races in the upper reaches of the Amazon Basin, Taussig clearly anchors the fears which draw them to the therapy of sorcerers, in a European regime of conquest, forced labour, poverty and violence (Taussig 1987). In this regard, Albert Bergesen's contribution to *Global Culture* (1990) supplies a sharp critique of the 'world system' theory of Emmanuel Wallerstein. Wallerstein traced the development of a capitalist world economy to the emergence of unequal exchange between 'core' states and 'peripheral' areas. Bergesen, however, argues that the exertion of military and political power *preceded* unequal exchange (see also Marx, *Capital*, vol. 1, part 8). In contrast to Wallerstein's emphasis on commodity chains between production points (Wallerstein 1983: 30), Bergesen focuses on *conquest* as the original fact. Violence has been at the heart of all social formations constructed out of the Centre-Periphery relationship. In Wallerstein's model, Core and Periphery emerge from exchange. In contrast, Bergesen argues that the world division of labour is inherently both a power and a production relation: 84 per cent of the world's surface was subject to Western colonial control until the twentieth century, forced to produce specified products. While accepting the existence of societal modes of production, he stresses that there are also relations of production on a world scale, precisely because peripheral social formations are still owned or controlled by a 'class' of states that have common political and economic relations with the rest of the world (Bergesen 1990: 70–75).

Bergesen's outline of a 'single global property relation and mode of production' is subject to the well-known criticisms directed at Andre Gunder Frank's earlier theory of a uniform global hierarchy, in which surplus is appropriated and moved upward from 'satellites' to 'metropoles', nationally and internationally. Such a perspective does not give sufficient attention to the complex variety of distinctive relations of production. These are profoundly different from the production relations of capitalist industrial society. Moreover, they generate powerful social strata which are partly responsible for the reproduction of global inequalities (see, for example, Foster-Carter 1987: 210–43). Nevertheless, Bergesen achieves his main goal – to place power 'at the heart of the analysis' (Bergesen 1990: 80).

The nature of global economy is directly relevant to our understanding of occult discourse. Jean and John Comaroff criticize modernization theory, and more generally, theories of 'modernity' for assuming a unidirectional course of history, in which non-Western peoples move towards the individualist, materialist mentality of the West (Comaroff and Comaroff 1993: xii). While admitting that global transformative processes are real, they take issue with analyses of their symbolical effects. They argue that African ritual, and by extension, witchcraft play a 'significant role in the articulation of local and global orders of production and exchange' (Comaroff and Comaroff 1993: xiii, xxiv). Yet their insistence on the multi-vocality of plural world cultures implies both *an acceptance and a denial* of Westernizing trends. We need a clearer distinction between the local and global orders of production and exchange.

I distinguish between global economy and capitalist economy. A very long-term process of incorporation has subdued large parts of the world as producers of primary products for, and consumers of commodities from, the Western industrial capitalist economy. But that has *not* led, usually, to the local establishment of capitalist relations of production. Capitalist economy involves the historical dispossession of peasants in agrarian society, the creation of a disciplined workforce, its control by bureaucratic management, and the regulation of production by the logic of *capitalist* accumulation. Capitalist accumulation is a process whereby surplus value is appropriated from hired labourers in factory and on farm, realized as money profit by employers in commodity exchange, and then re-invested in the expanded reproduction of the capital-wage labour relationship, or the increased technical productivity of existing workers (Marx, *Capital*, vol. I, chapters 23 and 24). But in the Peripheries of the global economy, sometimes peasant, sometimes tribal, and often petty-commodity relations of production continue to prevail. The continuing importance of kinship and clientage in the production process means that complex forms of accumulation are developing through the world market. These involve the intermingling of household, client and capitalist forms of accumulation, which depend upon while at the same time constraining each other. (For West Africa, see Clough and Williams 1987, Clough 1995, and Clough 1999.) *The global economy is a commodity market structured by political and military power. The capitalist economy is only one pole of that market.* Inside the global market, we should distinguish much more sharply than hitherto between capitalist and other kinds of economic, political or prestige accumulation.

Surely, the very mystery of commodities and labour markets so vividly portrayed in the magical and religious movements of this volume, is a sign that capitalist production relations have not become entrenched in these societies. The local efforts to control the acquisition of capitalist commodities by magical means reveal a failure to understand the workings of capitalist production, or resistance to its workings (see Austen 1993: 105). Even on Malta, in the immediate geographical periphery of the capitalist economy, the mental linkage of materialism with Satan (Jon Mitchell, chapter three of this volume) occurs where large-scale enterprises are only beginning to undermine small-scale businesses centred on the kin. In South America, Taussig has shown that the continuing strength of the occult among workers in capitalist enterprises signifies *both* their resistance to an economic form which reduces labour to a commodity, and their continuing involvement in peasant economies (see Taussig 1980). Again, the Cargo Cults in the Pacific, earlier in the twentieth century, involved an anxious local search for a new economic order, but without acceptance of a complex division of labour or of money as a measure of personal value (Burridge 1969: 46).

While unseen powers may flourish in the non-capitalist or semi-capitalist societies of the global market, *some* forms of supernaturalist discourse are clearly compatible with capitalist relations of production. In her analysis of Mormons in Utah, Hildi Mitchell shows that capitalist economy does not inevitably destroy a strong distinction between good and evil in people's minds (Hildi Mitchell, chapter six of this volume). Indeed, the Mormons' understanding of these terms involves a belief in the direct intervention of good and evil spirits. The worldly actions of Mormons inside the capitalist economy reproduce a moral economy which in some respects is strikingly different from that of the rest of American society. Their theological continuum from God through spirits to humans, all having bodies of a more-or-less purified nature, places 'corporeality' at the center of 'goodness'. Thus, the Mormon belief in Divine intervention is hugely empowering in a capitalist economic world.

Comparing this belief with the fearful spiritual discourses of non-capitalist areas, a basic difference is the confidence in human ability to channel the supernatural toward a beneficial increase in worldly goods and earthly happiness. Societies where most production is subsistence, peasant or petty-commodity, reveal ambivalence toward the world of striving – a strange combination of attraction and revulsion (van Velsen and van Wetering; Geschiere; Jon Mitchell and Meyer, this volume). The logic of these discourses is consistent with the conceptual framework of societies where production and consumption are still orientated to kinship and its moral obligations. The world of earthly power and wealth is associated with community destruction. Austen may be correct in distinguishing between the witchcraft discourse of Africa, where the capacity for biological and economic reproduction is assumed to be scarce, and that of early modern Europe, where it was assumed to be abundant (Austen 1993: 104–05). Among the Mormons of North America, physical multiplication and material enrichment are possible and desirable. Thus, across a range of societies, the logic of occult discourse is consistent with the workings of the local economy.

The Persistent Power of the Local

Nevertheless, logical consistency between economic perceptions and religious beliefs tells us little about the directions of cause and effect. A fifth theme to emerge from this volume is the action of local individuals 'with strength' who carve out human domains of religious influence (Taussig 1987: 447–67). Considering the growth of the Mormon religion, we are drawn to the lay preachers and pastors, Evangelists, healers, organizers of fetishes to counter evil spirits, and Charismatic leaders (see the chapters by van Velzen and van Wetering, Meyer, Theuma, and Hildi Mitchell, this volume). Individuals create religious discourse. In doing so, they appeal to specific social groups and types of personality. Where they succeed, they draw people to themselves, and by altering the balance of religious belief, alter the total pattern of social influence. The elaboration of religious discourse and the activity of persuasion can be seen as political process. How local leaders carve out domains of influence or force over others is a theme which relates dynamically with the previous themes of Centre versus Periphery, conceptual subordination or independence, and the alignment of supernatural with economic power. It helps us to explain why beliefs in supernatural causation, and in the supernaturally invasive quality of moral attributes, continue to hold their own. At the least, such beliefs mold into local patterns a Western conceptual system based on material causation and the autonomy of individual selves.

Reflection on these themes leads me to one conclusion: 'globalization' contributes to rather than diminishes the diversity of social beliefs. Here, I have in mind not only globalization as the very long-term historical movement whereby a group of Western states subdued the rest of the world and created a world market. I refer as well to Max Weber's argument that the circulation of money and the division of labour lead to the onset of an individualist, profit-maximizing rationality and thereby to the 'dis-enchantment' of the world (Weber, *General Economic History*). In contrast, the world remains a strangely eclectic, enchanted place (Comaroff and Comaroff 1993: xi–xiv). We therefore need to consider in what ways the technical possibilities of global trade and communication empower conceptual and relational diversity (Miller 1995: 21–23, 48–54).

My second conclusion links with Michael Taussig's *Shamanism, Colonialism and The Wild Man* (1987). I offer it speculatively, as a possible conceptual framework for rendering more meaningful the connections between occult discourse and the global variations in political economy. In van Velzen's and van Wetering's Suriname, Geschiere's Cameroon, and Meyer's Ghana, we see a widespread, grass-roots tendency continually to transform old supernatural entities or spawn new ones. For me the most striking feature of Taussig's book is also a radical proliferation of images at the base of Colombian society. He describes a whole series of lowland and highland shamans, and new spirit media of popular folk saints in a syncretistic Christian-Indian tradition, to whom anxious men and women appeal when beset with the fear of envy (Taussig 1987: 139–63). He records the interaction between the fabulous images and dreams of the very poor, and the saints and Virgin of the Catholic Church. Powerful cards can be purchased at marketplaces, which combine black, mestizo, and Indian divinities. The popular stories surrounding the miraculous power of Nina Maria (both a numinous Woman of the Rainforest and a god-like Mother) show uncontrolled variety. They give free rein to individual imaginations concerning ancient times and a distant 'past' (ibid. 165–70, 183–84, 188–208). Taussig argues that this 'strength of improvisation' shows 'active human agency . . . mediated by the shaman and the patient in the *jointness* of image-making' (ibid. 467 [my italics]).

Of course, Taussig seeks to demonstrate that this imaginative proliferation is controlled. Poor Indians and blacks are situating and evaluating their pre-colonial past. They are trying to handle the psychic disturbance arising from their consciousness of deep class and racial polarities in South America. Popular forms of magic express a 'gathering point' for class and racial antagonisms (ibid. 188–208, 447–67). These arguments locate the invention of supernatural powers in a violent, post-Conquest political economy. But surely, we can argue simultaneously that the sheer *alterability* of meanings in religious and magical discourse shows widespread consciousness of society as being in a state of flux. Social fluidity empowers the religious imagination.

Discipline of the Church-State and Discipline of Thought

Could it be that 'Church' dampens down this radical proliferation of spiritual entities? I have in mind the idea of Church as an ecclesiastical power which disciplines minds. In his late reflections on power, Foucault proposed that we can analyze three social forms whereby individuals are turned into 'subjects': forms of domination (ethnic, social and religious); forms of economic exploitation; and forms which instill a specific kind of subjectivity and so construct the individual's sense of Self. These forms are best understood by examining the struggles against them. 'Power' implies resistance (Foucault 1983: 210–13). Foucault argued that Christianity was the only religion which had organized itself as 'Church' – an institution which has developed the techniques of 'pastoral power'. Thereby, the pastor explores individual minds and directs their consciences. Though ecclesiastical institutions have lost vitality since the eighteenth century, pastoral power has spread out into the social body through techniques of individualization exercised by a wide range of institutions concerned with family, medicine, psychiatry, education and labour relations (ibid. 214–15). At the same time, the spectrum of techniques for the direction of individual conduct has become increasingly centralized in the state. Thus, the state is the 'modern matrix of individualization' (ibid. 215, 224).

With regard to our case studies, my first point would be that in areas outside Europe, the Christian Church does not exercise 'pastoral power' uncontested. Priests and pastors are often of a different race and language from the people, who see the Church as being linked to relations of domination and economic exploitation (Taussig 1987). The production of self-knowledge is influenced but not defined by the European church (Meyer, chapter four of this volume). Here, note Foucault's stress on *resistance* to various relations of power. We can contrast European and non-European areas. In Europe, Protestant resistance to Catholic ecclesiastical power historically incorporated at the same time as it superceded earlier beliefs and techniques. For example, Calvin's church was profoundly, ruthlessly, pastoral (Johnson 1976: 286–89). But in South America and Africa, the churches imposed on local populations were too divided from them by language and race, and the memory of conquest, to govern the process of individualization. In this respect, I would argue that the Ghanaian Pentacostalists explored by Meyer in this volume are not 'Church'. Their pastors and preachers do not govern souls as did the churches of European history. Therefore, where Church as pastoral power is weakly developed, there is no stopping the proliferation of explanations of fortune and misfortune, good and evil.

A different point can also be made. Foucault discusses the European transition to 'state' from a medieval combination of pastoral power and political power, rivalrous yet linked (Foucault 1983: 215). However, he does not dwell on that combination. He is, rather, concerned to pinpoint the difference between medieval pastoral power in the Church and modern pastoral power in a host of institutions. But surely, it is the deep inter-penetration of religious and political power in the Middle Ages from which modern life springs. Then, the practices of political and religious power were highly interwoven. Thus, Foucault's insights concerning the continuities in pastoral power can be taken a step further. Where ecclesiastical and sovereign institutions are historically inter-related (as in medieval and early modern Europe), this creates preconditions for the rise of disciplined, obedient mass action, and therefore disciplined thought-operations in the unfolding genealogy of the human sciences. In this way, the 'pastoral power' of the European Church was transmuted into 'discursive strategies' whereby a range of new sciences and techniques operated on, and made uniform, individual bodies and minds. However, where the linkage between ecclesiastical and sovereign power is weakly developed or absent, there is no stopping the

proliferation of explanations for fortune and misfortune – by Surinamese boatmen, Cameroonian healers, or Ghanaian preachers.
In this sense, too, Meyer's Pentecostalists are not 'Church': we can
see that these 'anti-ecclesiastical' churches constantly metasta-
size.

In summary, the long-term, gradual, and successful translation
of ecclesiastical–sovereign power (Foucault) or industrial organization (Marx) into a unified 'conceptual apparatus', dampens
down the proliferation of supernatural entities. Where this process
is absent, or incomplete, conceptual 'peripheries' remain
unclaimed and untamed. But even where this process has achieved
a fair measure of success, it is still important to stress that the
widespread tendency of local religious leaders to carve out power
domains renders contested the hegemony of a centralizing conceptual apparatus (Theuma and Hildi Mitchell, chapters five and
six of this volume).

Between 'Centre' and 'Periphery': A Liminal Case

The case of Malta is intriguing. Although geographically peripheral
to Europe, ex-colonial, and full of ambivalence about integration
with Europe, the Maltese for centuries have been thoroughly
immersed in the rituals and dogmas of the Catholic Church (Jon
Mitchell, chapter three of this volume). The physical presence of
the Church, amplified by the small size of the island, seems almost
overwhelming. At least as important, 'pastoral' power has been
exercised through the confessional. Surely, the reader will say, the
Church in Malta is a prime example of 'pastoral power', and therefore the popularity and intensity of the Catholic Charismatic movement (Theuma, chapter five of this volume) remain unexplained.
Here, we need also to consider Borg's account in this volume
(chapter eight) of the unfolding Maltese iconography of evil. In
effect, Borg argues that the evidence shows no exceptional interest
in the Devil, no deviance in the imagination of religious art. Even
the continuing pre-occupation in Maltese art with a dynamic contest between good and evil falls squarely within the central tradition of the Catholic Church.

Nevertheless, historical evidence suggests that as recently as the
nineteenth century, pastoral power did not exert itself fully over the
illiterate and semi-literate masses. Charles Cassar's vivid portrayal
of popular mentality in Malta at the turn of the seventeenth

century, when the Tribunal of the Inquisition worked to standardize beliefs and practices among the agrarian population, reveals that the Church never really managed to control completely local and imported folk values. Archival evidence of the Inquisition indicates that the orthodox notion of Satan as all-evil and the cause of sin did not replace the idea of the Devil as the trickster of folklore, which remained strong even in the nineteenth century (Cassar 1996: 86–87). Rather than the eradication of a folk world-view, literate and oral cultures co-existed across that period. Most people approached religious symbolism dualistically, 'whether it offered the comforts of the sacramentals or that of witchcraft' (ibid. 88).

I have argued that the close linkage between state and ecclesiastical institutions is a historical pre-condition for the subsequent rise of a commonly accepted, materialistic world-view. In Malta, this process has been flawed. Ruled by the Order of St John from 1530 to 1798, it was the scene of a continual contest over jurisdiction between the Order, the Inquisition and the Bishop. Under British rule between 1800 and 1964, the gap between Church and state widened further. By 1960, the sense of the foreign nature of the state was such that for many Maltese, the local church was regarded as the repository of indigenous identity (Boissevain 1993: 134). Under the Labour government from 1971 to 1987, the contest between Church and state divided the population (Jon Mitchell, chapter three of this volume). Thus, I would argue that no hegemonic apparatus of thought and power ever fully imposed itself on Maltese society. Indeed, in his sociological overview of the literature on Malta, Edward Zammit argues that there were conflicting loyalties, institutions and norms. The normative structure which had developed by Independence was imposed on the population, and so lacked full legitimacy (Zammit 1984: 38–39).

Malta may well be a test case which allows us to analyze the connections between the general themes which I have outlined. It could be argued that the Maltese are 'liminal' between Central and Peripheral status. Radically denied power through centuries of foreign control, the Maltese are still developing a political culture, and so feel deeply anxious about who controls the State. Exposed, moreover, by the small size of most enterprises and the vagaries of a tourist economy, the classic conditions are present for a radical sense of 'power deficit' in people's lives. Studying the perceptions of work, power and class structure among Maltese dockyard workers, Zammit argues that in an internationally weak ex-colony, the condition of national powerlessness is reflected in people's perceptions of *individual* powerlessness (Zammit 1984: 31–38). Under these circumstances, I argue that local Charismatic groups can appeal to people's diverse anxieties, and invoke the ecstatic healing power of the Spirit. At the same time, the Charismatic movement remains mediated by the conceptual apparatus of the Universal Church. Thus, we see the Religious Imagination playing – in a limited way – upon shared consciousness of a power deficit.

Comparisons and Reflections

Essentially, then, this essay draws a distinction between 'tight' and 'loose' cosmologies of the unseen powers of good and evil. By the former, I mean views of man in the universe which reproduce themselves over time in a stable manner, and offer legitimation of the social order. As concerns the latter, I refer to loosely-related schemes of supernatural order, which offer free-floating and improvised explanations of fortune and misfortune. I have related the difference between these kinds of cosmology to two factors – the close or weak linkage in history between ecclesiastical and sovereign power, and the existence or absence of capitalist relations of production. Where there is a loose cosmology, it is sometimes because a hitherto tight cosmology has become unhinged when the West exerted violent force to develop an international market, fracturing the former union of temporal and spiritual authority, and so reducing the tight coherence of political and moral ideas (as among the societies of Cameroon, Geschiere, chapter two of this volume). And yet, no economic or political framework can fully explain a prevailing cosmology. There is a strange area of human freedom. In this space, prophets rise up unpredictably. They call their people to repentance, healing – and power. Political and intellectual hegemony will always meet resistance in this space.

The contributors to *The Anthropology of Evil*, edited by David Parkin (1985) provide insights which resonate with this story. Macfarlane's rich analysis of the *absence* of a language of 'evil' from the court and church documents of an English parish from at least the fourteenth century, leads him to argue that the early development of commodity circulation and production collapsed a distinction between good and 'radical' evil in the universal equivalences of money value (Macfarlane 1985: 57–76). For Macfarlane, the homogenizing force of early capitalism reduced the sense of both evil and the supernatural. Nevertheless, some of his remarks suggest a different interpretation. Apparently, the Church itself intervened actively to extirpate ideas of magic and the need for 'protections' against magic (ibid. 64). We must bear in mind that England developed pervasive ecclesiastical institutions and laws from at least the twelfth century, strongly supported by the monarchy.

Caplan's analysis of Pentecostalists in South India makes for interesting comparisons with Theuma's account of Maltese Charismatics in this volume. He argues that industrialization and class differentiation led to social division between orthodox upper-class and Pentecostal lower-class Christians in Madras. But it is also clear that the Pentecostalist poor were reflecting a deep sense of a gap in social power, and the radical contingency of their lives, in their fears of *peey* demons (Caplan 1985: 110–27). Their incorporation of Hindu demons into a Christian cosmology leads us to reflect on the nature of Hinduism itself. Hinduism as a social and religious system historically enshrined profound inequality (Inden 1985: 162–63). At the same time, I would add that it was intrinsically pluralistic, incorporating new spiritual entities. It lacked a central power structure.

In Japan, Brian Moeran's discussion of adventure stories on television illustrates how the Confucian concern with social harmony and individual self-control still pervades Japanese social organization. Moeran comments that Confucianism is an 'ethico-political system' which has shaped Japanese society for 1,500 years. Its moral doctrine is primarily concerned with the ordering of human relations within a state (Moeran 1985: 94, 95). He summarizes the evolving differences in Japanese thought during the Tokugawa period, when the shogun-state unified the society. The major philosophical differences revolved around the extent to which human spontaneity could be allowed to affect the hierarchy of social relations. This question remains at the heart of Japanese debates concerning tradition and modernity (ibid. 96, 97). Thus, it appears that a tightly controlled moral universe developed together with an hierarchical, centralized political system (for Confucianism, see also Weber 1978: 453, 464, 476). The inter-penetration of religious and political power was taken to a limit where religious ideas were almost reduced to a social ethic.

But it is Overing's analysis of the myths of Piaroa Indians in the Amazon Basin which resonates most strongly with the themes of this volume. The Piaroa are a people without government, except for the guidance provided by 'wizards'. Their over-

riding value is self-control and moderation in actions toward others. Her account of Piaroa myths of origin, and of the educative
role of the 'wizards', shows a religious imagination which is not
profligate but tightly coherent (Overing 1985: 244–78). As a self-
contained society directly dependent on nature, the Piaroa can
hardly be defined as 'peripheral'. She presents a unified society
without a sense of an internal or external 'power gap'. Ideas of
good and evil reflect prevailing definitions of social responsibility
and irresponsibility. The Religious Imagination appears largely
devoted to explaining the need for individual self-control in
Piaroa society. Strangely enough, in the least hierarchical society
surveyed in Parkin's volume, there are strong analogies with the
structure that my argument has outlined. Where a unified conceptual apparatus is internalized by most people, and there is little sense of a 'power deficit', the religious imagination does not
proliferate entities.

In reflecting on the chapters in *Powers of Good and Evil*, and
searching elsewhere for analogies, my argument can only point to
tendencies in a complex variety of social beliefs and relationships.
Where consciousness of a power gap between Centre and Periphery exists, the *local*, feverishly pre-occupied with its religious
imaginings and its efforts to exert influence over others, always
acts as a counter-claim on human minds against centralizing
groups and elites. And globalization itself increases the conceptual
possibilities through mass communications. Under these conditions, the conceptual and procedural techniques of the Western
intellectual explanatory apparatus become more rather than less
problematic.

I end with an apocalypse. Will the Centre's purported hegemony over peripheral images and beliefs collapse nervously on
itself? Will the circulation of ideas and images of good and evil in
a global economy heighten awareness in the capitalist heartland of
conceptual diversity, and lead to a decline in intellectual and moral
self-confidence? Even the President, Mr Reagan, needed his sooth-
sayer. And his crystal ball. This may be frightening to Western
minds – but in the South and East of the global economy, not so.
Our authors have been confronting, not just the clash of cultures,
but also of histories – even of geographies. If accepted doctrines in
the Centre become displaced, religious creativity will continue –
anchored in locality, influenced by habitat.

I recall Taussig's friend, the shaman Santiago, swishing his net-
tle wand as he moved among his patients in the rain-forest,

chortling over the pride of the White and the rich (Taussig 1987).
Santiago's reflections are more than resistance to capitalist thought
and force. They are an under-rhythm. As if the forest, however
damaged, and the plains, however dry, themselves give birth.

> *The piers are pummeled by the waves;*
> *In a lonely field the rain*
> *Lashes an abandoned train;*
> *Outlaws fill the mountain caves.*
>
> *Fantastic grow the evening gowns;*
> *Agents of the Fisc pursue*
> *Absconding tax-defaulters through*
> *The sewers of provincial towns . . .*
>
> *Cerebretonic Cato may*
> *Extoll the Ancient Disciplines,*
> *But the muscle-bound Marines*
> *Mutiny for food and pay.*
>
> *Caesar's double-bed is warm*
> *As an unimportant clerk*
> *Writes I DO NOT LIKE MY WORK*
> *On a pink official form.*
>
> *Unendowed with wealth or pity,*
> *Little birds with scarlet legs,*
> *Sitting on their speckled eggs,*
> *Eye each flu-infected city.*
>
> *Altogether elsewhere, vast*
> *Herds of reindeer move across*
> *Miles and miles of golden moss,*
> *Silently and very fast.*

(W. H. Auden, *The Fall of Rome*)

Notes

1. I am very grateful for comments on the earlier drafts by Jeremy Boissevain, Jon
   Mitchell, Cris Shore and David Zammit. I am deeply indebted to Gavin Williams
   for many discussions about the nature of rural economy in Africa. I have bene-
   fitted much from reading Ralph Austen's 'The Moral Economy of Witchcraft'
   (1993) and Michael Taussig's *Shamanism, Colonialism and the Wild Man*
   (1987). I thank Professor Helga Reimann and the staff and student members of
   her Sociology seminar at the University of Augsburg for their helpful criticisms
   of the penultimate draft of this paper. I owe a special debt to Sybil O'Reilly
   Mizzi, former head of the Anthropology Programme at the University of Malta,
   for encouraging me to initiate this book with Jon Mitchell.

References

Austen, R., 1993, 'The Moral Economy of Witchcraft: An Essay in Comparative History', in Comaroff, J. and Comaroff, J., eds, *Modernity and its Malcontents*. Chicago: Chicago University Press: 89–110.

Bergesen, A., 1990, 'Turning World-System Theory on its Head', in Featherstone, M., ed., *Global Culture: Nationalism, Globalization and Modernity.* London: Sage: 67–82.

Boissevain, J., 1993 [1965], *Saints and Fireworks: Religion and Politics in Rural Malta*. Malta: Progress Press.

Burridge, K., 1969, *New Heaven, New Earth: A Study of Millenarian Activities*. Oxford: Basil Blackwell.

Caplan, L., 1985, 'The Popular Culture of Evil in Urban South India', in Parkin, D., ed. *The Anthropology of Evil*. Oxford: Basil Blackwell: 110–27.

Cassar, C., 1996, *Witchcraft, Sorcery and the Inquisition*. Malta: Mireva Publications.

Clough, P., 1995, *The Economy and Culture of the Talakawa of Marmara* [Nigeria]. D.Phil. diss., Oxford University.

Clough, P., 1999, 'The Relevance of Religion and Culture to Commercial Accumulation: Fieldwork on Muslim Hausa Exchange and Agricultural Trade in Northern Nigeria', in Harriss-White, B., ed., *Agricultural Markets From Theory to Practice*. London: Macmillan: 305–22.

Clough, P. and Williams, G., 1987, 'Decoding Berg: The World Bank in Rural Northern Nigeria', in Watts, M., ed., *State, Oil, and Agriculture in Nigeria*. Berkeley, Institute of International Studies: University of California.

Comaroff, J. and Comaroff, J., eds, 1993, *Modernity and its Malcontents*. Chicago: Chicago University Press: 168–201.

Friedman, J., 1990, 'Being in the World: Globalization and Localization', in Featherstone, M., ed., *Global Culture: Nationalism, Globalization and Modernity.* London: Sage: 311–28.

Foster-Carter, A., 1978, 'Can We Articulate 'Articulation'?', in Clammer, J., ed., *The New Economic Anthropology*. London: Macmillan.

Foucault, M., 1982, 'The Subject and Power', in Dreyfus, H. And Rabinow, P., eds, *Beyond Structuralism and Hermeneutics*. Chicago: University of Chicago Press: 208–26.

Inden, R., 1985, 'Hindu Evil as Unconquered Lower Self', in Parkin, D., ed. *The Anthropology of Evil*. Oxford: Basil Blackwell: 142–64.

Johnson, P., 1976, *A History of Christianity*. London: Penguin Books.

Macfarlane, A., 1985, 'The Root of All Evil', in Parkin, D., ed., *The Anthropology of Evil*. Oxford: Basil Blackwell: 57–76.

Marx, K., 1954, *Capital* vol 1. London: Lawrence and Wishart.

Miller, D. ed., 1995, *Acknowledging Consumption*. London: Routledge.

Moeran, B., 1985, 'Confucian Confusion: The Good, the Bad and the Noodle Western', in Parkin, D., ed., *The Anthropology of Evil*. Oxford: Basil Blackwell: 92–109.

Overing, J., 1985, 'There Is No End of Evil: The Guilty Innocents and Their Fallible God', in Parkin, D., ed., *The Anthropology of Evil*. Oxford: Basil Blackwell: 244–78.

Parkin, D., ed., 1985, *The Anthropology of Evil*. Oxford: Basil Blackwell.

Taussig, M., 1980, *The Devil and Commodity Fetishism in South America*. Chapel Hill: University of North Carolina.

Taussig, M., 1987, *Shamanism, Colonialism, and the Wild Man: A Study in Terror and Healing*. Chicago: University of Chicago Press.

Wallerstein, I., 1983, *Historical Capitalism*. London: Verso.

Weber, M., 1978, *Economy and Society* vol. 1. Eds. Guenther Roth and Claus Wittich, Berkeley: University of California Press.

Weber, M., 1981, *General Economic History*. New Brunswick: Transaction Books.

Worsley, P., 1968, *The Trumpet Shall Sound: A Study of 'Cargo' Cults in Melanesia*. New York: Schocken Books, Inc.

Zammit, E. L., 1984, *A Colonial Inheritance: Maltese Perceptions of Work, Power and Class Structure with Reference to the Labour Movement*. Malta: Malta University Press.

Index